© 2016 by Emanuel Hyde III

All Rights Reserved. No part of this book may be reproduced or transmitted without written permission by the owner.

Table of Contents

Red Lodge Plantation Introduction 1

Major John Archer 2

William Segar Archer 6

Grub Hill Church 11

Gov. William B. Giles 15

Overview of Slavery 17

Tabb Connection 19

Freedom, Churches, School, and Community 26

Brown Family 47

Banks Family 150

Bates Family 164

Miles / Baugh / Perkins Family 168

Gary Family 169

Archer Family 179

Harris Family 193

Johnson Family 194

Venable Family 205

Thrower / Scott Family 206

Fisher Family 207

Jasper Family 208

Hines Family 223

Gary/ Jackson Family 227

Tyler Family 228

Hicks Family 235

Lewis Family 237

Bannister Family 243

Dixon 244

Table of Contents (Continued)

Banks/Mondrey 247

Emma Wilson 249

Acknowledgements 252

Research Resources 253

If there is any person of the families that are not listed in this book. Please let me know and they will be added in at a later time.

Deuteronomy 32:7 Remember the days of old; Consider the generations long passed. Ask your father and he will tell you, your elders and they will explain to you.

FORWARD: For as long as I can remember, the community of Red Lodge has always been a part of my life. As a child I was told the oral history of my family and many stories of the families who lived in Red Lodge, such as the Banks, Smith, Hyde, Jones, Perkins, Hicks, Ruffin, Harris and Tyler families. In the late 1980s or early 1990s the road leading to Red Lodge were named Archers Creek Ln and Red Lodge Ct. I was told that Red Lodge was a part of a plantation but, little did I know, I am a descendant of the people who were enslaved and lived free on this plantation. While researching other family lines, Doris Banks Booker instructed me to go the Library of Va. She told me I would be surprise at all I would discover. During this time, I began helping Carolyn Hyde Carroll who has been researching the Hyde Family history. I assisted Carolyn in lookups which lead to the discovery of my great- great grandmother's (Jenny Hyde Jones) parents, Preston Jones and Nancy Brown. Since that time, I have connected with many people, held countless interviews and with the help of DNA analysis, I have connected with family across the world. Through the research of wills, land deeds, census records and other official documents I have since then connected the dots of who the slaves of Red Lodge were, who their descendants are and the many family connections that connect us all as one. As you will see, this is more than a Family book, this is a journey in time to understand the hidden secrets of slavery and to enlighten future generations of an African American People who was forced to give up their own identity, name, and honor but, did not lose hope. They went from being owned to becoming land owners and many of their descendants are college graduates, preachers, teachers, historians and etc. This book could not be completed without the many people who shared their stories with me, some who are now deceased. Thankfully, Garland Ervin, a Texas native and descendant, along with Darlene Lewis Robinson, Heather Hyde Johnson, Howard Hyde Jr., and Christopher Harris DNA played a major role in helping me understand our connections and trace the brown family back to the 1700s. In the words of Darlene Lewis Robinson "It's a Brown Thing" Darlene and Carolyn, and Mrs. Evelyn Harris efforts to this book have been a blessing. Many of the slave descendants are connected with the Brown Family. There were so many slaves of the plantation; many were sold to other plantations and others died before the ending of slavery, leaving no trace of descendants. However, in this book are the names of those who have been identified and many of their descendants who have been traced. It all reflects on all of my documentations and experience during this 2 years of research.

I've always felt "If you don't know where U come from, how can you appreciate where u r going." I pray this book gives a better appreciation and understanding of African American History and will be considered as another effort to preserve the Legacy of Red Lodge. To all the descendants of this book, this is our story, let us never forget the names of the ancestors listed in this book. They paved a road to freedom from their suffering. May we always cherish each other.

Emanuel Hyde III (Author)

Red lodge Plantation

The Unfinished mansion owned by Senator William S. Archer on the Red Lodge Plantation

Photo courtesy: Old Homes and Buildings of Amelia County written by: Mrs. Mary Armstrong

Major John Archer

(September 30, 1746-March 3, 1812)

John Archer was born September 30, 1726 to Col. William and Elizabeth Royall Archer in Norfolk VA. After becoming an adult, John moved to Amelia County, Virginia where he purchased 1,147 acres' plantation that he named Red Lodge Plantation. It has been documented that John was married three times. However, it is confirmed that John Archer married Elizabeth Eggleston the daughter of Joseph Eggleston. From this union 5 children were born; Captain James B. Archer; William Archer (1789-1855); Elizabeth Archer; Martha J. Archer (1803-1882); Ann Marie Archer (1805-1880); In the summer of 1781 John Archer was attending the session of the Legislature in Charlottesville, VA although he was not a member. During this time, it was outbreak of War at Shadwell, the birthplace of Thomas Jefferson, in the battle with the Tarleton and Dragoons. John also served as an aide to Gen. Lawson and was severely wounded by a sword in the battle of Tarleton at Shadwell (President Thomas Jefferson birthplace). With the aid of Dr. George Gilmer and his wife, John made a full recovery and returned to his estate Red Lodge.

John Archer was a major in the Revolutionary War, and served as an aide to General Wayne at the battle of Stony Point where he acquitted himself. Pictured is a portrait of the battle of Stony Point. In 1793 John served as Justice of Amelia.

Major John Archer had many slaves and so did his children, the surnames of some of the slaves were; Brown, Johnson, Woodson, Smith, Hobson, Prim and Kelly families.

During the Ante- Bellum period, the administrator of the estate was the widow of John Archer. Women in those days did not have a voice in society. After Major Archers death in 1812, his wife, Elizabeth Archer sued her son, William S. Archer, the administrator of Major Archer's estate. The Senator contested the will and decided to file a Chancery Suit. It was a dispute over slaves that were sold to: John Lane, John Robertson, and George Walker, after his death. Records of the Chancery Suit indicates that the slaves were sold after Archers death. Elizabeth was fighting for her dower (a widows share for life). Also, listed as slave-owners were John Robertson, and Joseph T. Eggleston

November Court 1812

Inventory and appraisement of the estate of [illegible]

Negroes

Name	Value	Name	Value
Cate	333	Rachel	150
Sarah	125	Pompey	400
Ben	150	Cyrus	50
Hamilton	425	Patty	300
Jenny	400	Alexander	500
York	500		
Moses	300	Jean	300
Billy	300	Lucinda	300
Sally	200	Nancy	150
Jack	375	Harry	50
Milly	250	Mourning	300
Lucy	250	Jenny	250
Saul	150	Peter	400
[illeg]	110	Frank	500
Jerry	100	[illeg]	200
Amy	100	[illeg]	150
Libby	250	Jack L.	350
Sarah	175	Jenny	250
George	150	Lucy	300
Jesse	150	Esther	300
[illeg]	110	Lucy	300
Hannah	75	Peggy	250
Nancy	500	[illeg]	225
Phebe	250	Nancy	175
[illeg]	250	Billy	100
[illeg]	300	Phebe	75
Dinah	320	Dinah	300
Michael	175	Stock &c	
Just Kitty	150	one Bay Horse	
Bob	120	one bay mare	45
Lyer		1 do	55
Bilcah	75	1 do	40
Jack Penn	220	1 do	35
Betty	150	1 Sorrel do	50
Jesse	220	1 black do	35
Fanny	300	1 Mule	30
Hannah	250	1 Cart and harness	10
Daphney	200	1 Sorrel mare and colt	50
Plenty	150	2 Small Colts	20
[illeg]	300	4 yoke of oxen	175
Bessy	200	1 Cart Colr	10
Amos	170	Stock of Cattle [illeg]	250
Effy	150	36 fattening hogs at $4	144
[illeg]	110	48 Sheep	95
Lucy	75	18 Geese	8.50
Jesse	65	1 Riding Carriage	300
Jenny	320	1 Old Gig — without wheels	6
Selina	200		
Cooper	100		

During the Ante- Bellum period the administrator of the estate was John Archer widow. Women in those days did not have a voice in society. After Major Archers death in 1812, his wife, Elizabeth Archer sued her son, William S. Archer, the administrator of Major Archer's estate. The Senator contested the will, and decided to file a Chancery Suit. It was a dispute over slaves that were sold to: John Lane, John Robertson, and George Walker, after his death. Records of the Chancery Suit indicates that the slaves were sold after Archers death. Elizabeth was fighting for her dower (a widow's share for life). Also, listed as slave owners were John Robertson, and Joseph T. Eggleston.

To the worshipfull court of Amelia county in Chancery sitting

Humbly complaining sheweth unto your worships your oratrix Elizabeth Archer that some time in the beginning of the present year John Archer of this county departed this life seized and possessed of considerable estate real and personal; That he having died intestate ~~letters of~~ administration on the estate of the said Archer has been granted to a certain William S. Archer in this worshipfull court; That your oratrix is the widow of the said Archer and as such has title to one full third part of his real property and of every description
Thus his effects which she has accordingly demanded of the said William S. Archer should be sett out and assigned, as so in right and equity ought to be done But so it is That the said William S. Archer has hitherto declined to comply with this just demand of your oratrix, alledging a defect of competency in himself or the apprehension of hazard ~~from~~ in doing and the necessity of incurring a longer ~~res~~ ~~igating~~ without the intervention and assistance of a tender consideration sanction of this worshipfull court whereof and forasmuch as your oratrix is without remedy in the premises only by the

William Seger Archer

(March 5, 1789- March 8, 1855)

William Seger Archer was born March 5, 1789 in Amelia County, Virginia at the Red Lodge Plantation. He was a member of Grub Hill Episcopal Church Raleigh Parish in Amelia County, Virginia.

William Archer attended William and Mary College, where he studied law and after graduation, he served as a lawyer in Amelia and Powhatan Counties.

Indeed, Archer served in politics, as did many of his family members including his uncle; Joseph Eggleston, his second cousin once removed, Thomas Jefferson, and countless others of the Archer, Coke, Eggleston, Royall, and Kennon families. William served in the Virginia House of Delegates in 1812 and 1819. He was elected to the United States House of Representatives serving from District 3 (March 4, 1812- March 4, 1835); William served in the United States.

William Archer served on the United States House of Represenatives from the 17th district January 3, 1820- March 4, 1823. William served as a chairman of the Foreign Affairs Committee and was an advocate to the Annexation Texas. William Archer, was elected as a Whig in the United States in 1840 serving in office 1841-1847. While in the Senate, he stood out for being outspoken in the debates of the Mexican War and was frequently consulted by President Polk. He also served on the committee of Naval Affairs.

After the death of his father John Archer in 1812, he became full owner of the Red Lodge Plantation which he dubbed, "The Lodge." William S. Archer never married but, he lived with his three sisters at the Lodge. From 1812 until 1855 William had made countless transactions of slaves with many prominent slave owners throughout the United States. It is documented that Archer had some slave purchases in Caswell, and Person, NC, Mississippi, and many other counties in Virginia. Archer also bought and sold slaves from relatives, friends,and neighbors including cousins, Robert Archer, and Joseph Archer in Powhatan County, Virginia. In 1824, William cousin Richard Thompson Archer (a physician) who was born in Amelia Virginia, moved to Claiborne, Mississippi and in a short time became one of the largest slaveholders in Mississippi. Richard's plantation was called Anchuca. After close financial and slavery business connections with Richard T. Archer, Senator Archer purchased land in Holmes County, Mississippi, a distance, but not too far from the Tchula and Attala counties; and built the Killona Plantation in 1835. In 1845 the Killona plantation was renamed Archula and because of the changes of boundary lines and the founding of new counties, Archula became part of Sunshine County, Mississippi. According to the book, the Emergence of the Cotton King in the Old Southwest Mississippi, Archer took 80 slaves with him where they worked the lands, breeded livestock and sadly but truthfully became breeders themselves. In 1843, a number of 52 hogs were killed from the Killona Plantation which produced 7,837 pounds of pork. According to the 1850 United States Census, Archer owned 103 slaves in his Killona plantation. During this time, livestock was very profitable in Mississippi. With the help of overseers and patrolmen, Archer kept Killona in operation even while returning to the Lodge which was 979 miles away .

After the illness and death of his neighbor in Amelia, VA, Govenor William B. Giles, Senator Archer served as a board member of the new found Amelia Academy Training School that was started at the late Govenor's plantation Wigwam. William also served as a board member at William and Mary College.

With the fame and fortune of the time, William S Archer decided to add some new additions to the family home. After retiring from the public eye, Archer had a great desire to make The Lodge one of the greatest plantations in Virginia.

The Big House on The Lodge estate was situated on a hill overlooking his approximate 1,893 acre plantation. According to an article writtten by Kate S. Berkely, Acher's sisters would be often seen in their carriage driven by black horses and the driver slave Tilman who sat in a high seat; Shutters screened the windows from the glare of the sunlight and inside lay constructed stepswhich unfolded and reached to the ground. William also had his own carraige, he was also an orator and avid reader who owned 2,500 books in his personal library.

William S. Archer's plans to finish his home were halted on Wednesday morning March 28, 1855 at 7:30 am when he died suddenly at the age of 66 years old. Tributes, letters and sympathy was expressed in just about every newspaper in the United States. Old oral history suggest that the slaves buried him which is believed to be correct. He is buried along in the family cemetery that is near where the Big House once stood.

After his death, existing debts mounted up against new ones made prior to his death. John B. Harvie and Thomas Tabb were in charge of the estate for the sisters. An inventory account of all of his assets were taken and filed in the Amelia County Courthouse. According to the 1860 United States Census, in 1860 Martha and her sister Ann Archer owned 110 slaves. His Washington stage coach decayed while stored away and years later, a major portion of the home was destroyed by fire. The remaining fragments of the house was later sold to Williamsburg for restoration and by the late 1880s his three sisters were all buried at the cemetery near the Big house at The Lodge.

Death of William S. Archer.

We received the painful intelligence, last evening, of the death of the Hon. William S. Archer. He died suddenly at his residence in Amelia County, yesterday morning, about 7 o'clock—having retired the previous evening in his usual health. This melancholy announcement will be received throughout the State and country with emotions of deep regret and sorrow. For no purer, no loftier, no braver man ever lived than WILLIAM S. ARCHER. He has filled many high and responsible public positions, and uniformly acquitted himself in all with honor to himself and benefit to his country. He has served in the Legislature of his own State, has been a Representative in Congress, and a Senator of the United States. He was a man of fine talents and high character—amiable, frank, chivalrous, and true. In short, he was a gentleman in the true sense of the word—a true Virginia gentleman, which is a nobler title at last than monarch ever enjoyed. Only within the last twelve months have we had the pleasure of his personal acquaintance; but there are few men whose noble qualities and manly bearing ever impressed us so favorably. We sincerely lament the death of such a man. In the hearts of his friends and his State—a State he loved with all the affection of the father for his child—his memory will long, long be cherished.

Here is a rare photo found of Senator William S. Archer that was taken not long before his death.

BY virtue of a Deed of Trust executed to me by Sherley Eggleston, of the county of Amelia, for the purpose of securing a debt therein recited to be due to William Archer of Powhatan, will be sold for cash, at Amelia court-house, on Saturday, the 11th of January, two negroes, called Katy and Isbell, the property of the said Eggleston.

W. S. ARCHER.

Dec. 21.

William Archer will in Mississippi 1855

Copy of Will of Wm S Archer

I William S Archer of the County of Amelia and State of Virginia make my last will as follows. I give my estate, of every description to my three Sisters and appoint as my Executors Thomas G Tabb and John D Harvie for this State and Stephen Farrar Doct. James Towns and S E Leigh for the State of Mississippi in which I have a large property. I hope that the three last named gentlemen who reside in the State of Mississippi or any one or more of them will consent to undertake the trust for the friendly sentiments which I think they entertain for me. I desire that my executors who may act be held to no security and request my Sisters to make them in addition to their legal compensation which will be large such further liberal compensation as the circumstances and condition of the property when their administration is settled up will justify. Witness my hand this 15th day of July 1854 the Body and Signature being entirely in my writing

W S Archer

Virginia

In Amelia County Court 26th April 1855. This paper purporting to be the Last Will and Testament of William S Archer deceased was this day offered for Probate and there being no subscribing witnesses to the same William L Booker and Samuel S Weisiger were sworn and severally deposed that they are well aquainted with the Testors hand writing and verily believe the said writing and the name therto subscribed to be wholly written by the Testator own hand. Whereupon the said writing is ordered to be recorded as the true Last Will and Testament of the said William S Archer Deceased and on motion of Thomas G Tabb and John D Harvie Executors named in the said Will, who made oath as the Law requires and entered into and acknowledged a bond in the penalty of fifty thousand dollars (without security the Testator by his will desiring that none should be required) conditioned according to Law. Certificate is granted the said Executors for obtaining a probat thereof in due form.

State of Virginia
County of Amelia } SS I Edward H Coleman Clerk of the County Court of Amelia County in the State of Virginia do hereby certify that the foregoing is a true transcript from the records of said Court.

In Testimony whereof I hereunto set my hand and affix the Seal of the said Court at the Courthouse the 7th day of May in the year 1855 and in the 79th year of the Commonwealth

Edward H Coleman Clerk

Copy of Will of Wm S Archer

State of Virginia
County of Amelia } SS

I Lewis E Harvie Presiding Justice of the Peace for the County of Amelia in the State of Virginia do hereby certify that Edward H Coleman who hath given the preceeding certificate is Clerk of the said County Court of Amelia in the State of Virginia and that his said attestation is in due form. Given under my hand this 9th day of May in the year 1855.

Lewis E Harvie P J P

Jackson Miss June 4th /55

To the Judge of the Probate
Courts of Holmes & Sunflower
Counties of the State of Miss

Dear Sir Having been appointed of the last Will & Testament of the Hon W S Archer formerly of Amelia County Va in union with Dr Towns & Mr Saml E Leigh one of his Extrs for the State of Miss & believing that the interest of the legatees will be best subserved by the actions of the two last named Exrs Viz Mess Towns & Leigh I hereby declare to you that I cannot & do decline to act as Extr of the said W S Archer decd and it is my desire that the gentlemen above named may qualify as his Exrs given under my hand the 4th day of June 1855

Stephen C Farrar

Grub Hill Church

Over 160 years the brick church that sits on the side of route 609, Grub Hill Church Road, has stood the test of time. The church was formed in 1754; the original wooden structure was built and the Rev. John Brunskill was the first rector of the church. Parishioners include The Archer, Tabb, Bannister, Hardaway, Booker, Meade, Eggleston and Giles families. All of these families were all genetically connected to one another and they all lived near or around the church. Rev. Brunskill was a loyalist and against the Revolution. He once proclaimed from his pulpit that anyone who participated in the Revolution was taking part in rebellion. The parishioners threatened him and walked out and caused the end of Rev. Brunskill's tenure at the Church. The members sought out other leaders and several rectors were installed. Years later, a new structure was needed and a brick structure was built; and on June 4, 1852 Bishop William Meade consecrated the new building naming Grub Hill, St. John Episcopal Church. At the time, the church was used from the front entrance of the building in front of the road. After the rerouting of Rt. 609, then called Archers Road, the entrance of the church was used from the rear. Rev. Parke Berkley served as rector for many years. Today, the church and the cemetery, which tombstones dates as far back to the 1700s, has been well preserved with time. Many of Amelia's prominent families are buried there. Among the member's name that are buried there are the Hardaway, Archer, Hemmings, Coke families, Berkley and many others. The church is now a Virginia Landmark.

After the death of Senator Archer, a monument was erected in his honor at his gravesite; 151 years after his death, the base of the monument erected in his honor still stands; the steeple of the stone is broken into two pieces and is situated on the ground over the top of stones. Being that the graveyard was abandoned many years ago, it still shows a glimpse of the past. On March 22, 2016 I am thankful that I had the opportunity to see the graves first hand. Some of the stones were very hard to read but thankfully a member of Find A Grave.com took pictures in 2008. At that time the stones were much easier to read.

Inscriptions on stones: Senator Archer Stone (on one side)

To mark their affection and devoted affection veneration and Love. These humble inscriptures and inadequate tribute to his worth is from the hand of one who knew and loved him from his cradle to his grave. The kindness of his disposition the generoand his high and refined sense of and his high and refined sense of moral right endeared him to his friends. His highly cultivated literary taste his high mind well stored with ornamental and useful knowledge. His calm and profound judgement and his noble chivalry of character placed him in the council of the nation in the proud rank of the distinguished men of his time. He lived and died without fear and without reproach.

Sen. Archers stone (other side)

This Monument is erected to the loving memory of William S. Archer, by his affectionate sisters, to whom he stood almost throughout their lives, in the double relation of father and brother; he was born March 5, 1789 and died March 28, 1855

Gov. William Branch Giles

While researching the Lodge plantation, I thought about the name of the district in which the former plantation, which is presently the Red Lodge community, and surrounding areas is part of the Giles District. I began to research the former Governor of Virginia William Branch Giles. While visiting his plantation, The Wigwam, I noticed what's left of an old structure, which was known as Giles Mill; and later known as Jones Mill which had a flour Mill. The Mill, and former property was in close proximity to the former Lodge Plantation. Over the past year through DNA evidence of a pool of participants, we were able to trace the Brown, Giles and several other families. I have also researched the Governor's documents thoroughly including his will, Autobiographies, Newspaper articles and was able to trace to slave owners who bought land, and slaves from the Wigwam after his death. One of those who owned a portion of land after Giles' death was Mr. Samuel Jones, the nephew of Gov. Giles who inherited some of the property and the Mill, which was called Jones Mill. Some of the slaves' owners who purchased the land and slaves were John B. Harvie of the fighting Creek Plantation in Powhatan, VA, brother of Lewis E. Harvie; families that were in his plantation that I was able to identify were The Finney, Smith family of Mattoax, VA., Brown, and Jackson family just to name a few. Benjamin Finney, of Powhatan, who owned a slave named John was said to be a descendant of an African King. This slave, John Finney, is the ancestor of The Finney Family of Powhatan, VA. Also on the Wigwam plantation was Major Smith who was sold to the Harrison family and lived in Mattoax, VA. He was the father of Samson Smith, grandfather of Samuel Smith. Deacon Gustavus Jones was also a part of the Harrison Oaks plantation. Gustavus is the ancestor of Margaret Hill and is believed to be related to my ancestor Preston Jones

Many of the Governor William Branch Giles (August 12, 1762 – December 4, 1830) owner of the neighboring planation the Wigwam was born (at the Wigwam plantation. His parents were William Branch and Ann Branch. His father was a plantation owner who was originally from Henrico, VA but moved to Amelia VA acquiring a lot of land which he turned into The Wigwam plantation and a member of Grub Hill Church.

William Branch Giles studied at William and Mary College and at the College of New Jersey now known as Princeton. He studied law under the Professor of Law, George Wythe. He became a lawyer in Petersburg, VA and worked there (1784 – 1789). He married and was elected to the First Congress and served from (1790 until 1798). He served in the Senate (1804 – 1815) and also served two terms in the U.S House of Representatives from Virginia's 9th district (1790 -1798) and (1801 -1803). He served in the

Virginia House of Delegates (1816 – 1817) and (1826 – 1827). He was elected Governor of VA March 4, 1827 and served three one year terms until March 24, 1830.

According to his will, Governor Giles owned over 1000 acres of land and had many slaves. He was noted for his intellect and educated mind. He was a Republic Alley of Thomas Jefferson and was his friend. According to Will Book 208 Amelia Va., he had a lot of land. His home: "The Wigwam" which is now a Virginia Historic Landmark, was first built in 1790 and is located in the Brackett's Bend area. It is situated on private property and after the death of Governor Giles, Professor William Henry Harrison owned the property and had the first Amelia Academy on the plantation which patrons were: William S Archer, John Cocke and Edmund Ruffin. Many of my DNA matches have ties to the Wigwam.

The Old Giles Mill

William Archer Slave list 1855

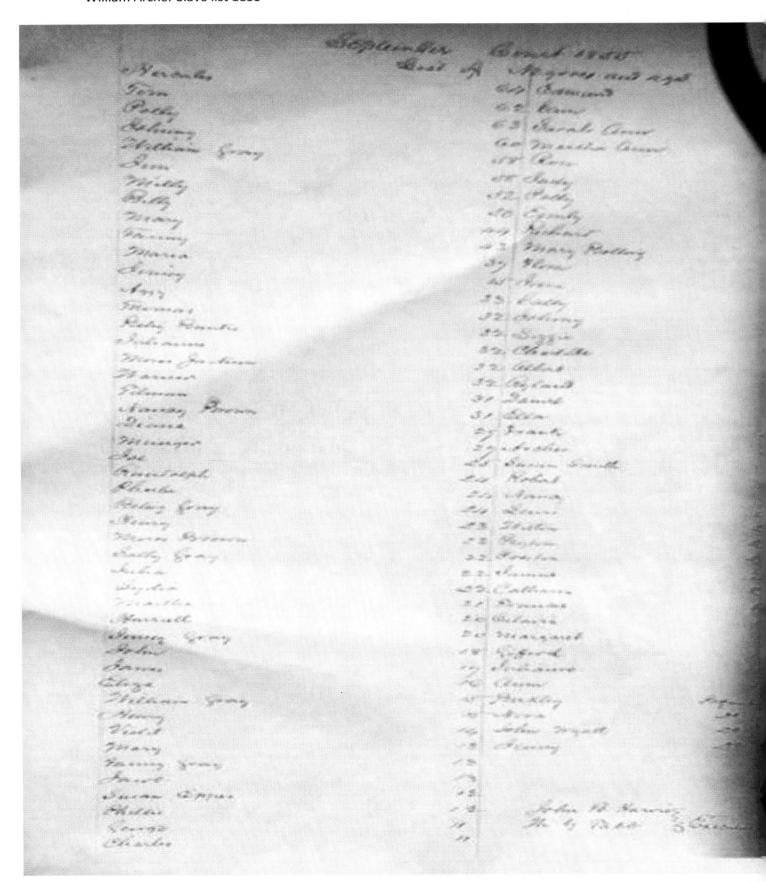

Overview of Slavery History

In 1790 Amelia and Nottoway counties had the highest slave population in Virginia. Amelia consisted of 11,300 slaves, and 106 free blacks which was un-parallel to any other county in the state of Virginia. By 1860 the slave population had decreased to 7,655. After carefully listening to oral history, and examining other documents including Archer's will, and inventory account, it's obvious to know that life for the slave on Red Lodge or any other plantation was unjust. Red Lodge consisted of house slaves who served as cooks, nurses, and maids. Also, it consisted of Garden workers and Field hands who worked the fields sun up to sun down; along with skilled workers who were carpenters, farmers, wood workers, shoe makers, and blacksmiths. By day, there were hundreds of blacks who worked the fields ploughing, planting and harvesting oats, corn, wheat and tobacco. The cattle, oxen, pigs, geese, sheep, mules, and horses all had to be fed. Ripened fruit was picked from the fruit trees and placed in the fruit baskets; Wagons, and ox carts were used to load crops. All plantations had smoke houses, ice houses, spring houses, dairy houses, kitchens, store houses, barns, cattle, pig pens, an overseer house, and meeting house for church services. To my knowledge there are no existing slave dwellings at Red Lodge; however, from my research of other plantations, it can be documented that most slave dwell houses were no more than one to two room shacks. Many of the dwelling houses did not have floors, however some did. The cabins had fireplaces that were used regularly to cook. In all plantations there were slave Overseers who were in charge of managing that slaves completed each task. His main task was to keep order in the plantation. Overseers distributed weekly food allowances; They had to oversee all activity while slaves worked to make sure all livestock was fed. Overseers were predominantly white but there have been many black overseers as well. Overseers in most plantations were cruel to slaves carrying out commands from the owner of the land. In the majority (but not all) plantations' slaves, during slavery's shameful era, were tied to trees and whipped, beaten, maimed, or killed by being hung or in some other malicious way.

Most large plantations during the Ante-Bellum period had slave drivers. It was a trusted positon in the eyes of a plantation owner; slaves were selected to direct the daily work of the slaves especially in a big plantation such as Red Lodge. In most of all the plantations, slaves were accustomed to corn shucking festivities; neighboring slave plantations would shuck corn, tell stories, playing instruments that were made by themselves; singing and dancing would be allowed. A meal would be prepared and liquor and apple cider would be served as a payment for their labor as if there was a choice. Although not listed in the will, threshing machines were popular during the time for corn stalks. In many cases slaves were hired out to work in other plantations. In and near all plantations there were Patrolmen slaves, also called paddy rollers, who were posted to monitor slaves who walked to other plantations and to catch

runaways. In most cases, captured runaways experienced gruesome punishment that could also prove fatal. The disciplinarian actions that took place in the Lodge is still unknown. However, what is known is that 88 of his slaves walked from Amelia County to the Killona plantation in Holmes County, Mississippi. Oral history and other documents indicate that some walked back when Archer returned home. The Appomattox river, which is in close proximity to Archer's home site, was once utilized frequently for various reasons other than for water supply; the river also serves as a form of transportation. Traffic was so frequent that it is said that tolls collectors were set up in Mattoax, not far from the plantation. There were so many slaves that lived and died on the plantation and many were sold to neighboring plantations in the county as well as across the county. Throughout the South, slave owners would breed slaves; arrange marriages that were not truly legal according to the laws of the land. There were slaves that would often be hired out in some cases, to fulfill a debt. The slaves would work in various places and even factories. If the owner died and had a will, all slaves would return to be given to whoever the plantation owner purposed them to be given to. Also, slave owners would rape, or in few cases fall in love with their slaves. In the 1800s there was a major rise of the mulatto population. In 1807 The slave trade Act was enforced; it was an Act for the abolition of the slave trade, which abolished the Atlantic Slave Trade which imported slaves from Africa to the United States. With the passing of the law slave owners used many black slaves as breeders. In many cases slave owners would pick the breeders and didn't care at all about the family relationships of black people. Some of the slave women had children beginning in their early teens until they no longer could conceive. Many slave women died during childbirth. Breeding was a way for plantation owners to maintain or gain more financial gain and to produce more field hands.

The majority of slave owners would sell slaves, dividing husbands from wives and children from their parents. All rights of humanity were taken away for the black slave and learning how to read and write was forbidden by law. The only hope the slave had was their faith, and in most cases their songs. Freedom Songs were not only a beacon of hope but each lyric had a message of instructions that could be used for plans to escape. Songs like, "Jimmie Crack Corn", "Wade in the Water", "John the Revelator", "Deep River"; "Steal Away"; "Go Down Moses"; "Farewell, Farewell" or a song that has resurfaced in recent years in the movie, '12 Years a Slave' "Roll Jordan Roll", written by Charles Wexley. There were other songs of an everlasting hope, that could be heard in the fields in chorus and response. There was no piano or drums in the rhythm, yet sound would arise from the depths of their soul. Songs like, "I Want to Be Ready to Walk in Jerusalem Just Like John" spoke of a promise of everlasting hope. For all that they went through, being chained and treated no greater than property just like the cattle and the horses, they lived a reality of no hope, but the songs they would sing encouraged their soul; and a built a hope and desire for freedom. For some, the only taste of freedom they received was through eternal life.

The Tabb Connection

One of the fields that was once a part of the Forest Plantation

The Tabb Family of Amelia and Chesterfield Counties, Virginia were closely connected to all the names mainly through inter- marriages. The Tabb Family was once one of the greatest landowners during and even before the Ante Bellum Period.

Col. Thomas Tabb (1719 – 1769) was in Gloucester, VA and in 1748 he later moved to Amelia, Virginia which was formerly known as Prince George County. Thomas became one of the richest merchants and slave traders in VA and a member of the firm, "Rubold, Walker and Tabb". This firm handled tobacco, imported slaves, and built and chartered ships. It was headquartered in England. He married Elizabeth Mayo in 1719 and had one child, Elizabeth Tabb. After Elizabeth died, Thomas later married Rebecca Booker in 1736 and had two children Tabb and Mary Marshall Tabb. He was the owner of the Clay Hill Plantation which was also called Obslow, and Haw branch properties.

John Tabb was reared in Amelia, VA but stayed for a time in England where he was educated. He later returned to Amelia, VA, was elected to the House of Burgess in 1761, and was a member of the militia; Tabb also served on the Virginia Committee of Safety. John was twice married; his first wife was Marianna and he later married Frances Peyton Cook Tabb. John acquired approx. 18,792 acres of land; the majority was in Amelia, VA and Chesterfield County, VA owning eight plantation tracts, Clay Hill, Grub Hill, Haw Branch, Obslow, Northern Tract, Chesterfield Tract, The Forest, and Winterwomac. The Forest which was located near the Lodge was once called a worker's tract. At one point, John owned over 257 slaves; there were many slaves sold throughout the neighborhoods and to other plantations.

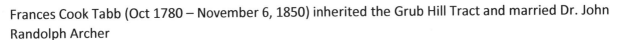

Children of John Tabb

Martha Tabb Giles (February 2, 1776 - 1808) married Gov. William B. Giles

Frances Cook Tabb (Oct 1780 – November 6, 1850) inherited the Grub Hill Tract and married Dr. John Randolph Archer

Mary Polly Tabb (1781) married Dr. Bathurst Randolph of Amelia, VA

Thomas Tabb (1780 – 1823) inherited the Chesterfield tract of land. He married his cousin Mary Tabb Bolling and they had one son Thomas Bolling Tabb.

John Yelverton Tabb (1782) inherited the Forest Plantation; married Mary Cary (Polly) Peachy. Two children: Harriet Peyton Tabb (1807 – 1834) and Thomas Yelverton Tabb (1809 – 1877) married her cousin Marianna Elizabeth Betrand Archer John Randolph Archer and Frances Cook Tabb. They had four children; Harriet Tabb (1809 – 1877), William Barksdale Tabb, John Banister Tabb

Seginora Peyton Tabb (1787 – July 31, 1864) inherited the Clay Hill Plantation and married Theodorick Bland Banister. They had several children one named: Monroe Banister

Harriet Tabb (1791) inherited the Northern Tract

Marianna Tabb died in 1856 William Jones Barksdale. She inherited the Haw Branch Plantation

William B Tabb   Father John Tabb

Below is the Historic Monument in honor of Father Tabb that is located on Rt. 609 near the former Forest plantation.

12	Am.t B.t forward		$1500	$10,390	
1	Negro Man Scipio		$50		
1	" Woman Rhoda & Child				
1	" " Edward		$350		
1	" Woman Aggy		$300		
1	" Boy George		$250		
1	" " Sucy				
1	" " Catharine		$250		
1	" Man Ross		$150		
1	" Woman Becky		$25		
1	" Man Jordan		$400		
1	" " Randolph		$400		
1	" Girl Betsy		$150		
1	" Man Jim		$450		
1	" Woman Amy & Child				
1	" " Amy		$400		
1	" Girl Lizzy		$130		
1	" Boy James		$125		
1	" Girl Kate		$100		
1	" Boy Thomas		$100		
1	" Woman Aary		$25		
32			$5175		
	To Lott N.o 4 To pay Lott N.o 3		$20	$5195	
	Am.t Carried forward			$15,585	

	Am.t B.t forward				$15,585
	Lott N.o 4 drawn by Thomas Tabb heirs				
1	Negro Man Parker old &				
1	" Woman Lucy old		$125		
1	" Man Anthony		$600		
1	" Woman Milley				
1	" Child Sally				
1	" Boy John		$350		
1	" Man Jim		$450		
1	" Woman Polly & Child				
1	" " Mary		$350		
1	" Man Levi		$75		
1	" Woman Sarah		$25		
1	" Man Munroe		$400		
1	" Boy Freeland		$375		
1	" " Berkly		$150		
1	" Girl Betsy		$100		
1	" Man Simon		$800		
1	" Woman Eve & Child				
1	" " Wyatt		$450		
1	" Man Davy		$300		
1	" Woman Patience & Child				
1	" " Mary		$500		
21				$5250	
	To Lott N.o 4 To pay Lott N.o 3	$20			$5195
	To pay Lott N.o 5	$35		$35	
					$20,780

Slaves owned by William J. Barksdale; slaves identified: Thacker Archer, Randolph Archer, and Anthony Archer

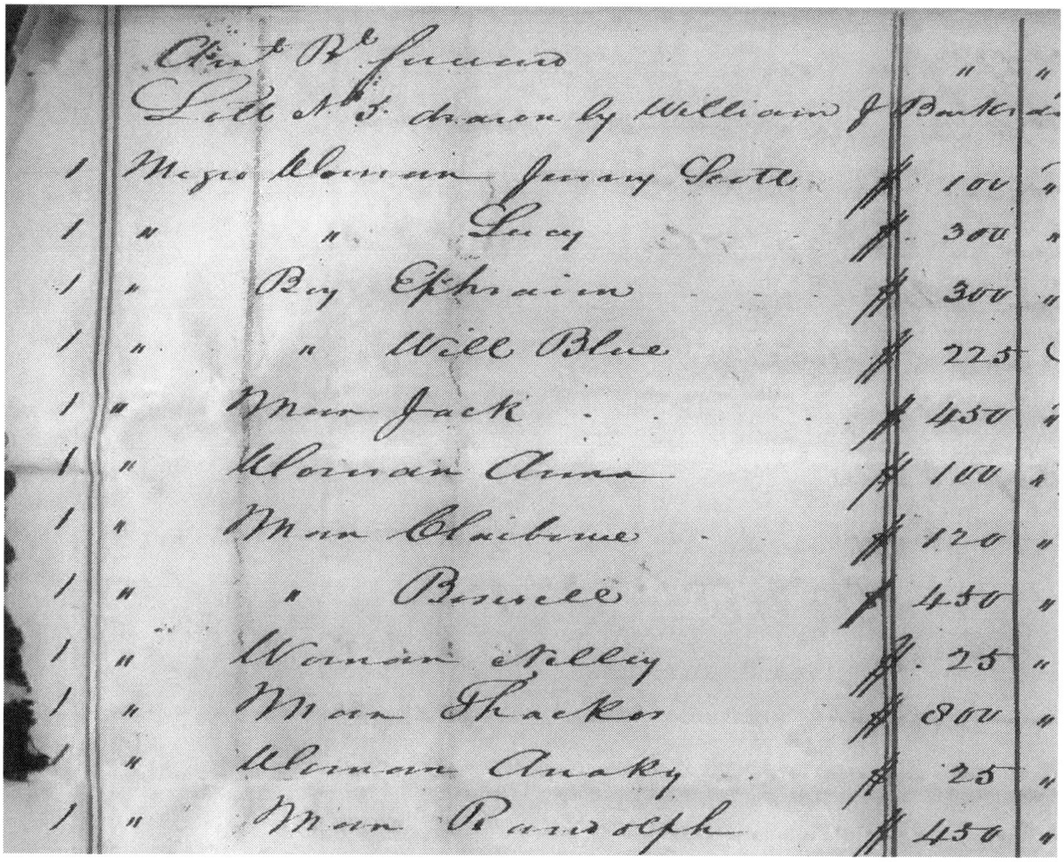

Amt Bt forward

Lott No. 5 drawn by William J Barksdale

1	Negro Woman	Jenny Scott	$100	
1	" "	Lucy	$300	
1	" Boy	Ephraim	$300	
1	" "	Will Blue	$225	
1	" Man	Jack	$450	
1	" Woman	Anna	$100	
1	" Man	Claiborne	$120	
1	" "	Bennett	$450	
1	" Woman	Nelly	$25	
1	" Man	Thacker	$800	
1	" Woman	Anaky	$25	
1	" Man	Randolph	$450	
"	" "	Bennett	$150	
"	Woman	Judy & Child } Billy	$350	
"	Boy	John	$150	
"	"	Rowland	$100	
"	Man	Anthony	$450	
				$4995

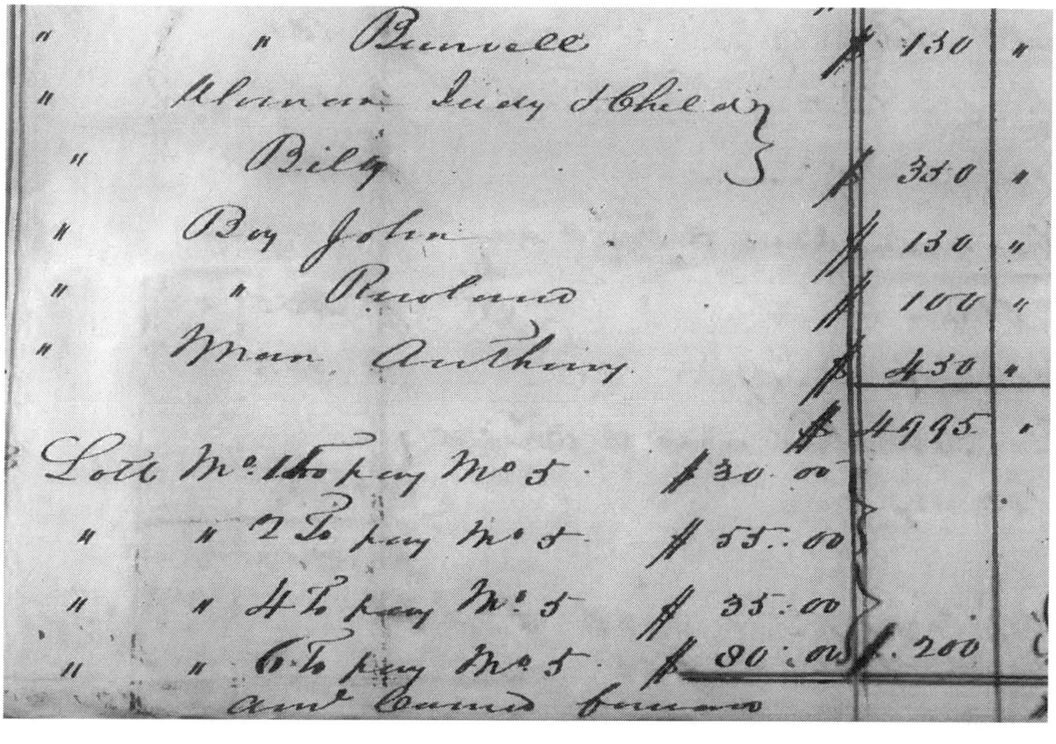

Lott No. 1 to pay No. 5 . $30.00
" " 2 To pay No. 5 $55.00
" " 4 To pay No. 5 $35.00
" " 6 To pay No. 5 $80.00 $200

Amt Carried forward

Lot 6 owned by John Randolph Archer; slaves identified: The Jaspers

		Amt. Bt. forward		$25.975
		Lott No. 6 drawn by John R. Archer & wife		
1		Negro Man Mack &		
1	"	Woman Plato	$100	
1	"	Man Mack	$450	
1	"	Boy John	$400	
1	"	Girl Peggy	$250	
1	"	Boy Charly } Peggy's		
1	"	Boy Henry } Children	$225	
1	"	Woman Rose & Child		
1	"	William	$175	
1	"	Man Scipio	$450	
1	"	Boy Ranch	$300	
1	"	Girl Rosa	$200	
1	"	Boy Bustro	$225	
1	"	Woman Caroline & Child		
1	"	Warner	$200	
1	"	Girl Phoebe	$225	
1	"	Man Tom Jasper	$50	
1	"	Woman Phoebe Jasper	$200	
1	"	Man Warner	$800	
1	"	Woman Peg	$300	
1	"	Boy John	$275	
1	"	Girl Susan	$250	
22		Amt Carried forward	$5075	$25.975

The slave family identified The Lewis family

Division of 149 Negroes (6 of whom are invalids) belonging to the estate of the late Mrs. Mary Randolph dec'd

Lott No. 1. drawn by Martha P. Giles heir

1	Negro Woman Old Fanny		$50	
1	" Man Nathan		450	
1	" Woman Nancy		250	
1	" Man Grandison		600	
1	" Woman Betsey & Child			
1	" Smith		350	
1	" Woman Catharine		300	
1	" " Donna		300	
1	" Boy Charles		300	
1	" Girl Betsey	$225	225	
1	" " Helen			
1	" " Becky			
1	" Boy Bathurst			
1	" Girl Harriett		550	
1	" Woman Hannah & Child			
1	" Lily		300	
1	" Boy Grandison		150	
1	" " Peyton		100	
1	" Man Ovid		500	
1	" " Wilson		350	
20	Am't Carried forward		$4775	

25

From Chains to Freedom

Deuteronomy 32:7 Remember the days of old; Consider the generations long passed. Ask your father and he will tell you, your elders and they will explain to you.

AMELIA COUNTY (VA.) FREE NEGRO AND SLAVE RECORDS, 1781-1866, N.D.
1160443_0011_0004
Library of Virginia
Index To [A list of Free Negroes 1855]

Some of the names are from the families of this book.

William Anderson	59	farmer
Frank Anderson	51	farmer
Alfred Anderson	49	farmer
William Anderson Jr	26	farmer
Nathaniel Anderson	28	smith
Alfred Anderson Jr	23	farmer
Richard Anderson	25	farmer
Henry Anderson	23	farmer
Larnett Anderson	18	farmer
Peter Anderson	16	farmer
James P Anderson	21	farmer
George H Anderson	12	farmer
Davy Brumskill	49	ditcher
Paschal Brumskill	32	ditcher
Peter Brumskill	34	ditcher
Albert Brumskill	30	ditcher
Henry Deshazer	55	groom
Edmund Deshazer	34	carpenter
Edmund Delany	47	stone mason
James Delany	21	ditcher
William Delany	20	smith
Samuel Dunnavant	32	unknown
Joe Finney	51	carpenter
Edward Finney	60	carpenter
Grief Finney	39	unknown
Field Finney	28	unknown
John Farley	36	rock mason
John Fletcher	26	boatman
Phill Fletcher	21	boatman
William Green	58	carpenter
Peter Gray	61	farmer
William Gray	26	black smith
Harrison Gray	24	black smith
George Gray	16	farmer
Dick Hamm	65	ditcher

Name	Age	Occupation
Sam Hamm	35	ditcher
Harry Hundley	42	black smith
Lebo Harriss	59	shoe maker
Allen Holland	34	farmer
Madison Holland	22	farmer
Jordan Hendrick	58	farmer
Bob Hill	28	ditcher
Henry Hill	44	ditcher
Pleasant Hill	32	ditcher
George Hill	30	farmer
William Hill	22	farmer
Henry Harrison	30	farmer
Nathaniel Harrison	28	farmer
Emit Harrison	23	farmer
Robert Harrison	21	farmer
John Harrison	18	farmer
Robert Johns	34	shoe maker
Riley Lipscomb	31	farmer
John Morris	34	unknown
John Pleasants	44	farmer
Hal Perkinson	39	carpenter
George Perkinson	41	carpenter
George Pride	33	unknown
Jim Richeson	42	stone mason
Henry Richeson	28	farmer
Branch Rummells	26	farmer
James Scott	33	farmer
Alfred Scott	26	farmer
William Smith	18	farmer
Stephen Walden	35	groom
Walker Jackson	53	farmer

AMELIA COUNTY (VA.) FREE NEGRO AND SLAVE RECORDS, 1781-1866, N.D.
1160443_0011_0004
Library of Virginia

Securing Our Pathway On the Road to Freedom

Finding our Liberty

Liberty Baptist Church aka: Brick Church formerly Mt. Tabor Baptist Church

Liberty Baptist Church was first formed when a group of former slaves was seeking a building for a church. In 1880 Deacons and Trustees Daniel Jones, Gus Jones, and David Scott found out that they could purchase an abandoned church and the property it was situated on. The church was formerly called, "Mt. Tabor"; one of the many churches in Virginia during the Ante Bellum period. While in operation, it served as the house of worship for several families that lived near or on Genito Road. Some of the members who worshipped at Mt. Tabor were Rev. John Steger Hardaway, Edmund Harrison, Nathaniel Harrison and the Featherston family, just to name a few. All of the names mentioned were well known plantation owners during that era. One of the last pastors of Mt. Tabor was Rev. L. W. Moore. With the shackles of slavery broken the group of black freedmen purchased old Mt. Tabor and named it "Liberty Baptist Church" in honor of their freedom. The first pastor of Liberty was the Rev. Preston Smith. Since that time other Pastors have lead this great congregation: Rev. Scott, Rev. Isaiah Henry Hines, Rev. Isaiah Wilkinson, Rev. Sadler, Rev. Manning, Rev. Neal Jackson, Rev. Robinson, and Rev. Kevin Jones. For 136 years, Liberty has stood the test of time and many of its founding officials; and members were once slaves of the Lodge, Oaks, and several other plantations in the area. The leadership has been strong and steadfast. The deacons of the old church who served in the years past: Henry Hill, Matt Tyler, Richard Dick Hardaway, Davis Brown, Wilson Tyler, Peter Johnson, Peter Clements, Robert Hyde, Joe Banks, Richard Watson, Walter Jones, Ned Ruffin, Preston Jones, David Smith, John Lewis, Joseph Bannister, Archer Jones, Roger Hicks, Arthur Hicks, Emmett Robinson and Freddie Smith. There were many who served in later years and some who are presently serving in the church. In early years there was a bell outside of the church that members would ring for funerals. Thomas Brown once said that during his childhood most blacks were extremely poor; he could vividly remember the men white washing the walls of the church with lime and water, during the summer, because they couldn't afford paint. Sarah Louise Banks remembers, when she was young, walking to the church for Sunday school; and on third Sundays they would stay for worship service. She recalled the people singing and shouting and having a good time in the Lord. Also, Sarah Louise Banks remembers church meetings would start at twelve and sometimes would not end until four. In those days, each neighboring church had worship services once a month. Liberty Baptist Church services were held on third Sundays; Pleasant Grove Baptist Church services were on the second Sundays, and Flower Hill Baptist Church service was held on the fourth Sundays. This pattern allowed other neighboring churches to fellowship with one another. I was told from the elderly that remembered the old time church that there was nothing like hearing Lottie Hyde Person playing and singing; There is a fountain filled with Power in the blood or Blood drawn from Immanuel veins or years later seeing Mr. Ossie Ford shouting down the aisle while singing a hymn. Another voice who years later I had the opportunity to hear was Mrs. Alberta Hickman of Pleasant Grove who would often sing the old hymn, we are Climbing Jacob's Ladder, Soldier of the Cross. Her voice rocked the church. During Homecoming service, which is annually held on the 3rd Sunday of August, the church would be filled to capacity; food would be served outside that was prepared at the homes of its members. Back in the day, if you attended a revival you may hear the great voice of a lady named Basin Betty. She was known throughout Virginia and could sing with a deep bass voice that would rock the house. She was often accompanied by pianist Ola Mae Melvin. Betty had her own group called the, "Heavenly Lights Gospel Singers" who traveled with her. From all the reports given, when Basin Betty would visit Liberty she would sing acappella. With the little they had, the men and women of Liberty Baptist Church served God; and because of their labor and sacrifice, Liberty remains the strong pillar it has been for many years.

.

Liberty Baptist Church Aka: Brick Church

Present day   Liberty Baptist Church

An event at Liberty: Lillian H. Hicks and Rosa Jones Hicks

Rev. George Wyatt Manning

(April 24, 1906 - February 3, 2000)

Out of all the great past and present pastors who shepherd the flock of Liberty Baptist Church, there is one who's name would shine as bright as the stars above in the hearts and minds of all of his members, and colleagues.

Rev. George W. Manning was born in Brunswick County, VA on April 24, 1906 and was a part of a great family lineage in that county. His father George died at sea. His mother was Hannah Manning. His grandparents were Wyatt Manning who was a farmer and Sarah Williams Manning. After moving to Richmond, VA around 1925 he attended Baker Street School, night classes at Armstrong High School, and Virginia Union University School of Theology. He was married to Willie Drumgole and lived on 2716 Fendall Avenue in Richmond, VA. For many years, he worked as an oil tank installer and a cement finisher however, that did not in any way keep him from being an effective leader; he was there for all of his churches. Rev. Manning was known as a circuit preacher, preaching, singing, and baptizing many converts in branches and ponds which in those days would symbolize the River Jordan. In 1931, Second Antioch Baptist Church in Powhatan, Virginia was seeking a pastor. According to my cousins, Celestine Gray and the late Floyd Bates, my great – grandmother Rosa Woodfin Goode was responsible for Rev. Manning being chosen to pastor the Second Antioch Baptist Church in Powhatan, VA. He was a fire and brimstone preacher that carried an anointing that grips the ear and hearts of all who heard him. The following year he was called to pastor Liberty Baptist Church; he also was the pastor of Mt. Sinai Baptist Church, Little Zion Baptist Church. He remained faithful, there is no price or time limit that can equal or total the times he went to see the sick, counseled his church members and many others, encouraged someone, preached his fiery sermon or sang one of his shouting metered hymns. He would often sing songs like, "He that Believeth", "Drinking of the Wine", and "I Shall Not Be Moved" just to name a few. During a time when preachers did not get a salary and the church members could not afford to pay him they would share what little they had as their appreciation. Deacon Joe Banks, and many others would remember Reverend Manning when they would kill their hogs. Deacon Emmett Robinson who was a great gardener, would plant Rev. Manning his own garden; and when they could raise or give money, the congregation would do just that. When recollecting on Rev. Manning, Mrs. Della Montague said that he was a great leader, he would never ask you to do something that he would not do himself. He lived on 2716 Fendall Avenue in Richmond, VA. For many Rev. Manning was their spiritual leader from the cradle to the grave. He was a counselor and one of the most revered men in Virginia. In addition to being pastor of four churches, he was also the moderator of the United Protective Association of Amelia, Nottoway, and Prince Edward Counties. Also, he was moderator of the James River Baptist Association of Powhatan, Cumberland, and Goochland. It is unknown how many weddings Reverend Manning officiated, how many people he baptized, or how many funerals he eulogized but, one thing is for sure, Reverend Manning cared about all mankind and was concerned for their soul. Reverend Manning was a mentor to many including Dr. James Taylor and Bishop Lawrence Taylor. A few recalled when Rev. Manning had to Eulogize a church member after the committal was done at the cemetery; Rev. Manning would stand at the cemetery until the

grave was covered. Others recalled at other occasions Rev. Manning making sure the guest preachers would have enough to eat. He was very unselfish and giving. In later years, Rev. Manning became pastor emeritus of Liberty Baptist Church. In February 2000, many traveled to Powhatan County, VA to pay tribute or silently salute the man who touched the lives of so many people. Leaving behind a Legacy that "He that believeth in the Father and Son, haveth everlasting life."

Rev. Manning baptizing candidate at 2nd Antioch Baptist Church   Rev. and Mrs. Manning

Liberty Baptist Church Baptism

For many years, the Liberty Baptist Church used a pond on the church property that is adjacent to a branch. Hundreds of people have been baptized in the pond. Deacon Emmett Robinson once told me he was baptized in that pond by Rev. Sadler. While interviewing about 20 present and former church members about their memories of being baptized at Liberty, many remembered the old baptizing pond. Mrs. Evelyn Harris one of the eldest active members of the church remembers she was 12 years old when Rev. Manning baptized her. Sarah Banks remembers being baptized as a young girl. She recalled standing on Rev. Manning feet while waiting to be dipped in the pond. Mrs. Mary Jasper remembers Rev. Manning singing from the Church "I shall not be moved, like a tree planted by the water, I shall not be moved." Viola Harris Booker remembers walking around the church while singing. Other songs were sung as well such as "Take Me to The Water", "Marching to Zion" and others. Many entered the pond which symbolized the watery grave and a rising from the pond which symbolized becoming a new creature. It was a public symbol of what God has done when they were converted. It's an unforgettable experience and Rev. Manning, with his boots on, dipped countless in the pond.

In later years, a temporary baptism hole was beside the present day church, which many of the children of those who were baptized in the pond were baptized in; the watery pond. It is aid, my uncle Pleasant and several others were baptized in the temporary baptism hole. Later, the present day pool which is in the new church was built, and Rev. Manning and other pastors who succeeded him, including Liberty's present Pastor Rev. Jones, has baptized converts in the pool.

Below left is a picture identified as a baptism at Liberty Baptist Church pond. Rev. Isiah Wilkinson baptizing an unknown candidate in 1912.

Reverend Manning baptizing a candidate; year unknown. Bottom Left and right present day The old baptizing pond has dried enormously over time. Pictured right is (me) E.A. Hyde III kneeling in front of the pond.

 The Reverend, James Taylor, is a man of God who started his Christian journey at an early age and is still found faithful as a Pastor, Author, Leader, Visionary, and a man of wisdom to all that encounter him. Dr. Taylor was reared in Powhatan, VA and is a member of Second Antioch Baptist Church where he began his Christian journey under the leadership of Rev. Manning. He served in the United States Army on active duty in 1982; he was licensed to preach the gospel in March 1982. He was ordained and served as assistant pastor of Liberty Baptist Church from 1984 - 1981. He has served as pastor of the Race Street Baptist Church of Farmville, Virginia since 1992.

Dr. Taylor has earned an Associate Degree from J. Sargeant Reynolds Community College and a Bachelor's Degree from Virginia Commonwealth University. Dr. Taylor is also a graduate of the Samuel DeWitt Proctor School of Theology, Virginia Union University, Richmond, Virginia, with a Master of Divinity Degree. He received the Doctorate of Ministry Degree from United Theological Seminary in Dayton Ohio in May 2006. Dr. Taylor is a published author and his book entitled "Equipping Laity for Servant Leadership" is available online at Amazon.com and on his website: JHTaylorMinistries.org.

Dr. Taylor is married to the lovely Olivdean Silver Taylor of Enfield, North Carolina. They are proud parents of four children and six grandchildren.

Dr. Taylor is retired from Alcoa/Reynolds Metals Company where he served as Director of Corporate Security and Equal Opportunity Affairs. He most recently retired as Professor and Program Chairman of the Criminal Justice Department at Southside Virginia Community College, Christanna campus. He is President of J. H. Taylor Ministries, Inc., a (501 (c) (3) Non-Profit Organization whose mission is to train church leaders for effective ministry, to empower "Young Minds" to impact today's society; and to touch lives through meeting needs in the community holistically.

Dr. Taylor served honorably in the United States Army on active duty from 1966 to 1969, serving two overseas tours. He retired from the Army Reserves in 1990 as a Command Sergeant Major (Infantry). In March 2016 I had the opportunity to ask Dr. Taylor if there was one word he could give to describe Rev. Manning; his response was "He was a man of wisdom." Dr. Taylor shared many stories with me about Rev. Manning and his character as he was able to reflect on the many years he learned from his mentor. He shared how caring Rev. Manning was and spoke highly of his integrity. I was thankful for those moments to hear, and learned so much of Rev. Manning; of a man who followed in his footsteps and now stands on the shoulder of a forerunner for Christ. Whenever Dr. Taylor visits Liberty he is sure to remind us of the memory of Rev. Manning through some of the shout metered hymns Rev. Manning loved so well.

Brick Church School

According to Mrs. Kathleen Hadfield's book, Historical Notes of Amelia County, Virginia, the first African American schools were started by Mrs. Samantha Jane Neil, a Presbyterian under an oak tree. Mrs. Neil taught the young and the old; and some churches were organized under her influence. Hadfield mentioned that Allen Memorial Presbyterian Church also known as Allen Mission, was the first of many churches that a school derived out of. Mrs. Neal also had two assistant teachers; Mrs. Nuna Booker, who was trained by Mr. Hatfield. As the years progressed, just about all of the black churches had schools.

It's not certain when Liberty Baptist's first school was founded, however, the Brick Church School house's first location was behind the Liberty Baptist Church. Mrs. Nolie often talked about the old school which her and many others attended. Most students during the early 1900s-1930s went only to the third grade; some went to sixth grade. Education was limited for African Americans during those times and many were forced to quit school to work the fields and help their families. In the 1930s a new two room school house was built by local carpenters, Royal Hyde and William Henry Green. Some of the teachers who taught at the school were Alice Lewis, Mrs. Bettie Harris who taught grades 1,2,3, and 4; and Mrs. Lucy Tyler who taught 5th, 6th, and 7th grades. Other teachers who taught at Brick Church school were Mrs. Geraldine Barley Scott, Mrs. Martin, Mrs. McGhee, Mrs. Blaylock, and Mrs. Stanley; substitutes were Mrs. Susan C. Smith and Mr. Kemp Barley.

In the winter months, Deacon Emmett Robinson and McKinley (Jake) Jasper would get to the school early in the morning to get the fire started. Freddie Jasper would cut the grass at the school during the spring and summer. Also, there were other people of the neighborhood who helped in whatever capacity they could.

From this school, many attended Russell Grove High School and some were privileged to further their education and graduate from College. This school house today is not in the best condition, however, it still stands today as a reminder of where African Americans came from and it is a symbol of how segregation used to be. We have come a mighty long way!

BRICK CHURCH SCHOOL

Picture of Brick Church School in 1941. Only one has been identified: Elizabeth Robinson Walls

(photo courtesy of Kathleen Hadfield)

Red Lodge Community

Tyler's Store

In just about every interview I have done many mentioned Tyler Store. Hearing these stories and reflecting back on stories I have heard as a child, The Red Lodge Neighborhood was a community in itself. The community had stores, funeral home and even a baseball and later softball team. Mr. Matt Tyler was one of the first store owners and had his own funeral home dubbed "Tyler's Funeral Home." Mrs. Ethel Morris remembers Mr. Emmett Robinson Sr. worked at the store which was located behind Mr. Tyler house. Mr. Tyler sold everything you need. In earlier years Mrs. Nora Jones also had a store in the community. Years later, Frank Tyler who worked as a foreman on Wood farm built his home, and opened a store and funeral home on Genito Rd. Mrs. Eloise Banks and others such as Van Rison and William Pappy Hyde were employed at the store. It is said during the 1950s and 60s you could get 2 cookies for a penny. There were paths in the field that many people would walk to get to the store. Emanuel Hyde Jr. and his brother Pappy, Big boy and Allen Harris and others often worked the Frank Tyler farm. Frank Tyler store also was a place where families would hang out. Baseball games and other events like the annual Easter egg hunts was held. The store holds a lot of memories for the people who grew up in Amelia and surrounding counties. It served as a store, a place for events, dances, and directly behind the building was where the baseball field.

Pictured Upper right: Deanna Banks and Elizabeth Robinson Walls on the Red Lodge which was made in 1932 before that time there was only a wagon road in Red Lodge.

Red Lodge Hunting Club

There were many men from the neighborhood that was part of the Red Lodge Hunting Club. Archer Jones Jr, Freddie Smith Sr., Isaiah Smith, Mike Banks Jr, Junius Smith, and others. They would have meetings and host parties and other events.

Baseball at Red Lodge

Charlie Banks was the first person who made a ball diamond and started a baseball team in Red Lodge during the 1940s later John Banks and Leslie Banks. Frank Tyler also had a team Amelia Cubs and his diamond was behind the store. One of the many team mates was, Reuben Broadnax. Many people came from various cities and counties to the baseball games.

Mr. White who lived in Chesterfield, VA drove a bus that was filled with meats, ice cream and other food items. He was said to have been a very nice man and would allow people to receive their food on credit to their account until they could pay for the merchandise. J.T Jones was the Iceman who would deliver large blocks of ice to residents in the Lodge and elsewhere.

Back in the 1950s and 60's there were a lot of children in Red Lodge. They worked hard in the fields, cutting wood and performing other daily task like feeding the pigs, and cows and the other livestock. However, they also enjoyed growing up in Red Lodge. Connie Banks, Reginald Dale Hyde and others recalled to me, that when they were young, they would roll tires down the road or get long sticks and pretend to ride horses. In those days, many would put together their own bicycles and basketball rims would be posted on the trees. It should be mentioned that there were so many children in Red Lodge that there wasn't much grass in most of the yards. Most of the youth would hang out in a park like setting at Pleasant and Anna Hyde house. Joseph Ruffin remembered when he was young playing with the kids at the park. He also recalled the many times he would ride bikes to Powhatan and throughout Amelia along with Alvin "Duck" Ruffin, and Elder Emanuel "June" Hyde Jr. Some remember for fun going up in Buster Tyler fruit trees taking what that can or the games at Tyler's or at the ball diamond across from Mr. Booty Banks. The youth of Red Lodge also enjoyed purchasing candy from Mrs. Alberta Banks who sold candy from home. It wasn't like the present time when kids are gamers, but back then kids were outside most of the time. If their parents had company, they could not sit around and take in what was said children were simply children. Red Lodge was a community in itself and one book could never define this community and all of its great history. During the late 1960's and early 70s Harold Jones started a female softball team with his assistants: Jeffrey Booker and Solomon Banks they named the team, The Red Lodge Pacers. In a conversation with former team mates Connie Banks, Karen Banks Carter, and Daphne Jasper Holman I learned this Softball team was a force to be reckon with. The Red Lodge Pacers were proven undefeated numerous times. They traveled to Richmond, Powhatan and surrounding counties making names for themselves everywhere they went. Some of the Alumni of this team: Brenda Jasper Scott, Debbie Henderson Clarke, Anita Jasper Royal, Jackie Henderson Gray, Rosetta Broadnax, Andrea Banks, Sherry Banks, Brenda Trent Smith, Daphne Jasper Holman, Vanessa Jasper Booker, Karen Banks Carter Rozena Jones Jackson, Gail Banks, Gloria Lewis Nelms, Charlene Lewis Yates, Diane Moseley, Shirdene Banks Harris, Wanda Banks Spurlock and others.

Pleasant Grove Baptist Church

The Pleasant Grove Baptist Church was first formed when the missionaries came from the north to teach the freed slaves. The first meeting places was at the homes of participants. A log building was built, and it was used as a school during the week and church on Sundays. The first pastor of the church was Rev. Henry Taylor. The first deacons were; George Brown, Ned Gibson, Warner Jasper, Ned Gibson, Sidney Robinson and Joe Robinson. There were many families that were founding members: The Brown, Robinson, Gibson, Jones, Thompson, Banks, Epps, Goodman, Archer, Gray, and Miles families. In 1933 William Henry Green, assisted by Royal Hyde built a brick church structure (It is said that the bricks were built around the old structure this evidence is still being confirmed.) One of the first pastors was Rev. Henry Taylor. Pleasant Grove Baptist Church still stands today in the pleasant Grove Community of Amelia, VA.

Pleasant Grove Baptist Church in the 1930's

Flower Hill Baptist Church

This church has stood the test of time and is still standing tall. The early pastors of the church were Rev. Preston Smith, Rev. William Thomas and Rev. S.P. Randall, who served for many years. Later, Rev. Horace Montague became pastor in 1956 and served as a great shepherd of the flock. Rev. Horace Montague loved to sing gospel songs as well; his favorite was, "God Built the Shelter". He served his church faithfully, baptizing, marrying and eulogizing many. His legacy and memory will never be forgotten. Flower Hill's early members were the Woodson, Epps, Ruffin, Jeter, Jackson, Gilliam, Brown, Seay, Harris, Rison and many other families. In the field, on the church property, are many headstones of the people buried there. Mrs. Annie G. Mondrey, recalled that her grandfather Edmund Gilliam, made many of the older tombstones that are in the cemetery.

Rev. Horace Montague, who served the Flower Hill Baptist church for many years, also served as Pastor of Reed Rock Baptist Church in Amelia, VA. He was a devoted husband of Mrs. Montague. Reverend Montague was a faithful leader and a chosen man of God. He could preach and sing. One of the most noted songs he used to sing was, "God Built the Shelter" with an echoing chorus response. Keith Evans, who was baptized at Center Union Baptist Church, remembers as a child singing with Rev. Montague a song called, "I Wanna Go Where the Thunder Don't Roll". The late Mrs. Lillian Montague, his wife, told me of another song that he used to sing entitled "Sure Love talking about the Lamb of God." There are many memories of this leader who is still highly respected and remembered to this day. Still today, if you visit Flower Hill Baptist Church's homecoming or revival I'm sure you'll hear, "God built the shelter for me to live under, for me to live under; God built the shelter, for me to live under, and he built it on Calvary!" Rev. Montague used to shout down the aisle while telling the story through song, lyric by lyric while having the young and the old on their feet. There have been several pastors who have served since the 1990s.

Former Pastors of Flower Hill Baptist Church

Rev. Samuel Randall

(April 4, 1870 – April 11, 1955)

Rev. Horace Montague   and   First Lady Lillian Montague

The Families of the Plantations
And the Descendants

The Brown Family

It is still unclear what African tribe my Brown family originates from however, the earliest finding of the Brown family in the United States according to the confirmation of DNA matches was in Brown's Gap and Brown's Cove which is located in Albemarle, VA. Benjamin Brown an Englishman originally from Sussex, England migrated to the United States and settled in Hanover, VA. He moved westward and later owned over 6,000 acres of land in the in the 1700s.

The DNA analysis suggest during the lifetime of Peter Jefferson who also lived in present day Chesterfield County, Virginia. Peter Jefferson owned land in Henrico, Albemarle, Goochland, Powhatan and Amelia County in the 1700s. He later resided at the Shadwell Plantation in Albemarle County, Virginia. As we all know it took slave labor to build and operate plantations which in effect ran the counties as a whole. Peter Jefferson was the father of President Thomas Jefferson. At the time Field Jefferson, the brother of Peter Jefferson who was a known slave owner lived in Amelia, VA. It is documented that Peter Jefferson patent 744 acres on Deep Creek in Amelia, VA to Laurence Brown on April 20, 1735. Gov. William Branch Giles who had a close friendship with the Jefferson family and William S. Archer also had many business dealings with Peter, Thomas, and Field Jefferson. A family of Brown's were sold to them and to some other plantation owners. It is understood that slave breeding was enforced, and The Brown family were sold with the Jefferson, Woodson, Banks, Epps, Monroe, Branch, Johnson, Smith, Giles, and Granger families. Some of the slaves were sold to the Cabell family of Nelson and Buckingham County, VA, Cumberland, VA and to other plantations across the United States. DNA matches confirms my research.

After these findings, I asked selected DNA cousins to work together with me to find confirmations. Each participant showed fact their DNA matches were all descending from Peter Jefferson and the Jefferson family. There are two who match the Hemings family who is related to the wife of Thomas Jefferson. It was during this time I found out that many of the same Heming family descendants are buried in Amelia, VA.

It is believed that Davy Brown (1799 – 1879) son of Hal and Sally Brown was the earliest Brown descendant I was able to find in the red Lodge Plantation and community. It is believed that he is the father of many of the Brown descendants whose slave ancestors were slaves on the Red Lodge Plantation.

On a cold day in February 2016 my God-sister Lakisha Johnson who is also a great researcher in her own right asked me to ride with her to see Thomas Jefferson's Monticello. Once we arrived and she parked the car in the parking lot, we quickly took the tour guide bus ride up the mountain to Monticello. Arriving on the top mountain a few minutes before the tour was to start I remember looking at the view and knowing that in that same county and area hundreds of years before my slave ancestors once stood. I've always been an open minded type of guy that views life from a historical perspective however, I was not ready to hear the story of the lives of the slaves of Monticello. While during the tour of President Thomas Jefferson, home the tour guide did a great job on telling the truth about President Jefferson and the slave life for the slaves "Way up on a Hill." I remember during the process of the tour, the guide asked the group of us did we have any questions. Before I could say anything, Lakisha pointed to me and said "he does." So I asked the lady about the Brown family. She told me that some of the Brown slaves was related to Sallie Hemings the slave that had several of Thomas Jefferson children. Jefferson like most plantation owners had many slaves during his lifetime and so did his father. I can also remember the guide telling us that there was no water on the mountain so the slaves had to carry buckets of water from the creeks and rivers on the flat land to the top of the mountain where the plantation house stood. After trying to process all of what she said, she then directed us to Mulberry Row where Replicas of slave cabins were erected in the same location where the former cabins once stood. There were several pictures of slaves such as Isaac Granger Jefferson and many others who carried the last names of the former Amelia slaves. After the tour I spoke with the guide and told her there was evidence of a connection with my family in Amelia and the Brown slaves there. She took down my info in her office and seemed amazed that I could tell her my family tree without paper. She later pointed the direction of Thomas Jefferson grave and a group of us walked to the fenced in Jefferson cemetery. After catching the bus back down the hill at 5pm. The tour guide who was closing out her shift for that day told Lakisha and I that she would show us where the slave cemetery was sadly enough it was discovered some years ago while the parking lot was being constructed. A fence was erected with a sign right over from the parking

lot for the mass grave. However, I have the feeling that there are more graves in that area and perhaps some of the slaves are buried under the parking lot. This is the reality of how useless a dead black slave was to its slave owner. The next day after my visit, my cousin Helen Hyde Phillips told me that her sister Bonita Hyde Redd met a lady named Vivian Brown who originated from Albemarle, VA. Vivian's family lived right behind Monticello and after I talk to Bonita she sent me a picture and I was yet again amazed at the family resemblance. Without a doubt our family is connected to Thomas Jefferson's family the lines of Amelia, VA possibly are through Peter Jefferson and Field Jefferson. Some of the slave family surnames of Monticello that are also in Amelia, VA are: Granger, Monroe, Jefferson, Brown, Trotter, Hughes, Martin, Lee, Dean, Wayles, Woodson, Smith, Scott families

Pictured left: Vivian Brown

As stated in the forward after finding out the name of my third- great grandmother and with the help of over eight DNA matches, talking over my findings with several other family researchers and some professional historians, along with oral histories all led me to confirm the findings of my ancestor's siblings and their descendants. Examining the land deed and other documentation of my third great - parents Preston jones and Nancy Brown land (which is still in our family today) led me to examine the Browns. According to all of my findings and problem-solving it is believed her parents were Davy and Chloe (Chlora) Brown. Her siblings were Moses Brown, Julia Ann Brown Epps, Russell Brown (1829), George Brown, John Brown, and Richard Brown. With the advancement of DNA, it is confirmed Davy's brother named Ben Brown and his descendant Darlene Lewis Robinson aided me along with others with this verification. During slavery years, black families were huge, to have more than ten children were normal at that time. Some slave mothers had up to twenty children so it is believed that Nancy had more siblings possibly across the United States.

Nancy Brown

(1824-abt.1865)

Nancy Brown is the ancestor of the Jones and Hyde descendants of Red Lodge was born in 1824. She is believed to be the daughter of Davy and Chloe Brown. There is little known on Nancy's Life, but what is known is she was married to a Preacher Preston Jones born around 1823 and died between 1900-1904. Preston was the son of Daniel Jones and M Jones who lived to be over 100 years old. As quoted in the 1932 interview, Preston and Nancy's son Rev. Royal Jones stated that his parents were field workers. In the words of one of their sons Rev. Royal Jones his parents were "tillers of the soil". Preston and Nancy were freed before the ending of slavery. Nancy died around 1865 after the birth of her youngest child. She was buried on her land. The couple was given 50 acres of land by word of mouth by Sen. Archer and later Tabb (administrator of the estate). After Nancy's death in 1870 Preston and youngest son Royal lived in the house together. On January 30, 1874, Rev. Preston Jones married Emily Robertson daughter of Joseph and Molly Robertson on December 30, 1874. Emily died in and Preston died in the early 1900s and was buried in the family cemetery on the hill.

Children of Preston Jones and Nancy Brown Jones

Elizabeth "Lizzie" Jones Steger (1852)

Daniel Jones Sr. (1851)

Preston Jones Jr. (1853)

Jennie Jones Hyde (1855)

Royal Jones (1860)

Millie Jones Thompson (1865)

As a child I was always inquisitive about my family history, I remember once while at the home place of my cousin the late Archer Jones. My Dad told me that his grandmother grave was up on the hill in the woods. After pointing to the direction of the hill, he recalled going back there when he was young with his father to get lighter wood. My grandfather showed him where his grandmother Fannie Kyle Hyde was buried. He remembered there were several sinks there but he did not know who was buried there. In 2014 in a conversation with Carolyn she recalled her father Howard showing her the grave as well. On August 3, 2014 I stopped by my cousin Kirk Jones home (Kirk is the grandson of Archer jones) I recalled the story to him and he told me he never heard of graves back there but he was willing to walk with me back there the next evening after work. On August 4, 2014 I called aunt Carolyn from my cell and she used her memory to guide us through the woods. We reached the branch but felt dismayed about finding the cemetery. It was getting late so I suggested to Kirk that maybe we should wait until the leaves fall to search again. After calling it quits I told Carolyn I would call her back. I remember Kirk saying "Scoop back then they buried people by the riverside, you know like the song". Of course, we were not by a river but we were at a branch so I responded to him "we are close." I placed my hand on a tree and then I noticed the bark less tree was carved with the initial EJ (Emily Jones). We started looking for other trees with inscriptions on it and there was three of them. One had the initials NB with the carving of a bird by the letters I knew instantly NB was Nancy Brown. On the same tree was P. Jones OTC23 which possibly meant Oct 1823. And other letters and numbers some hard to make out. It was getting dark so We decided to return the next day to mark the bottom of the trees and chalk the markings to see it more visibly. We found some unmarked graves out there and amazingly by standing in the woods you can see the impressions of the wagon trail that lead to the graveyard.

On February 29, 2016 I revisited the cemetery for the third time with my father who was unaware of the cemetery I found. He said that his grandmother was buried in an unmark grave across the branch up on the Hill but today it is impossible to find. Although her grave has been lost, the graves of my other ancestors that were found has been a blessing. As I looked at the branch that flowed freely with minnows, my Dad told me that if you walk further down the branch disappears. The water goes underground he then mention how much God has given mankind. He recalls during his childhood, fruit trees were plentiful on the family land and though no one was rich they knew how to survive. What amazed me the most was the recollections of stories my dad shared about the white sand at the branch. He said his father told him that my great – grandfather Royal used to take the sand from the branch and from the Appomattox River and mix it with rocks and lime to make mortar for the foundations of the houses he built. On the next page are pictures taken from Feb. 29, 2016 visit.

Creek on the family land

Daniel Jones Sr.

(1850)

Daniel Jones Sr. (1850) was born a slave on The Red Lodge Plantation. After Slavery, he worked at former plantations as well as on his own land. He married Jeanette Dickerson (Crump) and from this union, 5 children were born. Ann Jones (1870); Lizzie Jones (1872); Preston T. Jones (1873- 1964), Daniel John Jones (1877). There is no other information on the lives of his daughter Ann and Lizzie.

In 1880 Daniel became a founding member and one of the first Deacon of the Liberty Baptist Church.

After the death of Jeanette, Daniel later married Ella Hill Ford Jones on September 17, 1902 in Amelia VA. At the time Ella was a widowed mother who lived in the Mattoax community. After the marriage Daniel moved to Mattoax and worked for the Mason Family. After 1910, Daniel disappeared from the United States Census. It is believed that he died between 1912-1920.

Children of Daniel Jones

Preston Thaddeus Jones

1873-1964

Preston Jones was born December 15, 1873. He attended Brick Church school and received fourth grade education. He was a farmer and on April 10, 1901 he married Nora Jasper (1878-1981) the daughter of Cary Jasper and Lydia Bannister. From this union five children were born. After the death of Nora sister Isabelle, he also helped raised his wife nieces and nephew. He was a member of Liberty Baptist Church where he served as a Deacon and a church clerk for many years. He is remembered for taking church meetings very seriously. No one left the meeting until Deacon Jones made his point clear. Preston, was a farmer and he had several fruit trees. His wife Nora was hardworking and it is said that she was the first store owner in Red Lodge that was also used as a dance hall called Slab Town Hall. In later years, Preston health began to fail and he later became an amputee. Nora took care of him until his death. Nora Jones lived to be 103 years old.

United States Registration Card signed by Lewis Harvie

Preston and Nora Children

Thaddeus Jones (1902-1915) died at the age of 13.

Norman Jones (November 29, 1909 - October 9, 1989) married Elizabeth Rison in Amelia, VA. He was employed at the saw mill. He was hardworking. Five children were born to the union of Norman and Elizabeth Jones. 1. James Thaddeus Jones (1936 - 1995) who served in the U.S Navy on November 3, 1955. He married Juanita Jones Nov. 16, 1963 in Richmond, VA. From this union two children were born. 2. Shirley Rebecca Jones Smith (1938 - 2002) lived in Washington, D.C for many years before returning to Amelia, VA. She had an adopted daughter and granddaughter; 3. Elnora Elizabeth Jones 4. John Jones 5. Harold Jones was born August 2, 1943. During his teenage years, Harold would walk a great distance to work on the Gerald farm. Harold is the husband of Barbara Trent Jones and has two daughters and grandchildren.

Lydia Jones Harris born (April 13, 1904 - December 20, 1961)

Paul Leroy Jones (1918 - 2004) also known as "Oakie" married Flossie Lottie Anderson on August 16, 1937. His favorite word in a sentence would be "John Brown" Leroy and Flossie had two sons, Paul Jones Jr. (1938-1989) he lived in Richmond, VA. and George Jones.

Daniel John Jones

(1877-1950)

Rev. Daniel Jones was born the second child born to Daniel and Jeanette Jones. He was a preacher and was an associate minister of Brick Church. He was a farm laborer for the Dennis family and worked for Mrs. Mason. Daniel was married four times, his first wife was Vinnie Wilson the daughter of Rev. Jeff Wilson and Margaret Goodman Wilson on Nov 28, 1900 in Amelia, VA. From this union four children were born and the couple resided on the Dennis farm near Liberty Baptist Church. According to family history Daniel and his family lived in a small dwelling house over a cellar. After the death of his wife Vinnie, Daniel married Julia Goode Martin daughter of Alfred Goode and Ellen Masters Goode on April 6, 1910. In 1910 Daniel returned to the lodge, later he married his third wife Flora Johnson (1891 - 1932) and from this union six children were born. On August 8, 1936 Daniel married his fourth wife Charity Powell (1882 - 1977). It was discovered by Carolyn Hyde Carroll that Charity was the daughter of Woodrow Simms and Rebecca Hyde Simms was the sister of Robert Hyde.

Daniel was also a lifelong worker of the land, although he worked on farms under contract, he also worked his own land, tended to his fruit trees garden, mules, cows, and pigs. Rev. Daniel Jones officiated many marriages during his tenure as a minister. Victoria R. Archer who married James Archer once recalled Rev. Jones officiating her wedding ceremony at his home. Rev. Jones died on August 29, 1950 and was buried at Liberty Baptist Church cemetery on Saturday September 2, 1950.

Pictured below: Royal Hyde and Rev. Daniel Jones (right) 1st cousins.

Children of Rev. Daniel Jones

Jeanette Jones Jefferson (January 18, 1902 - August 22, 1923) was the daughter of Rev. Jones and wife Vinnie Wilson. After the death of her mother, she was raised by her aunt Jennie Jones Hyde and her husband Robert Hyde. She was baptized and attended Liberty Baptist Church. She married Norman Jefferson Sr. and had a son; Norman Jefferson (February 22, 1922 – January 23, 2000) served in the United States Army and resided in Richmond, Va. He was married to Arabella Jefferson.

John Jones (1903-1956) was the son of Daniel and Vinnie Jones. He married later Susan Jones.

Charlie Jones (1906) was also the son of Daniel and Vinnie Jones. He worked for a furniture company and also at Chamberlayne Restaurant owned by his brother William Irving Jones.

Dorothy Maude Jones Hudgins (December 10, 1910 - November 29, 2001) daughter of Daniel and Flora Jones married Johnny Hudgins on December 7, 1946.

Archer Marshall Jones (October 18, 1917 - March 9, 1982) son of Daniel and Flora Jones married Alice Banks daughter of Warner and Bessie Banks on August 13, 1939 and lived on the family land in the Lodge. He was a hard worker and a devoted brother, father, and grandfather. He was a lifelong member of Liberty Baptist Church where he served as deacon. He was known for his faithfulness and prayers. Archer knew the importance of church and made sure that his children and other children in the neighborhood would go. Archer and Alice Banks Jones had 5 children.

1. Bessie Jones (1941 – 2014) she has 1 daughter and grandchildren. 2. Flora {Irene) Jones Banks married Harold Banks. Harold and Irene has 3 daughters, 1 deceased, Wanda Spratley and grandchildren 3. Clara Jones Squire who is the mother of 3 and has several grandchildren 4. Mary Alice Jones has a daughter and 5. Archer M. Jones Jr. was married to Rebecca has 3 children and grandchildren.

William Irving Jones (1919-1977) Son of Daniel and Flora was born June 20, 1919. He served in the U.S. Navy and married Queen Taylor and later Mary Hunter Booker on May 12, 1973 in Richmond, VA. He was the owner and operator of East End Oil Company which he started in 1956. William also started the Chamberlayne Restaurant in Richmond, Virginia. His daughter Patricia stated his business after visiting Philadelphia, Pennsylvania. William's was the first restaurant to have Philly hoagies in Richmond. He was a member of the Metropolitan Business League. William was a member of Trinity Baptist Church where he served as a deacon. He was the father of two daughters; Flora Ann Massey (deceased) and Patricia Jones Jackson.

Mary Edna Jones Drumgole daughter of Daniel and Flora was born in 1921. She married Irvin Robert Drumgole of Brunswick County, Virginia on September 4, 1941. After the death of her mother, Flora was raised by her great aunt Martha Brown in the Brick Church Area. Mary is the Matriarch of the Jones Family. She has been an asset to this project. Her wisdom, history and the time she made to tell me about the past has been a blessing. Mary had four children, Robert Drumgole, Edith Powell, Willie Mae, and Yvonne Delores Drumgole.

Flora Ann Jones (1924-1932) Known as Ann Jones

Daniel Edward Jones (January 10, 1926 – February 20, 1980) was known as Bubba married Martha Rison on March 29, 1952 in Powhatan County, Virginia. Daniel and Martha lived on Baker Street in Richmond, Virginia. Daniel and Martha had children and grandchildren

Deacon Archer Jones   Mary Jones Drumgole   Patricia Jones Scott

seated: Flora Irene Banks, Bessie Ann Jones, Archer Jones Jr. standing: Mary Jones and Clara J. Squire.

Wanda B. Spratley   Veronica Pat Jones   Mary Jones

William Irving Jones

Norman, Nora and Elizabeth

Mary Jones Drumgole

Elnora, Shirley, John and James Jones

Elder Rozena Jackson

Right: Norman Jefferson

Preston Jones

(1853)

He was born in the Lodge and after the death of his mother he lived with his first cousin Susan Epps Finney and her family which was found in the United States 1870 census. He married Jennie Lee of Powhatan County on March 14, 1877. In 1880 Preston and his family lived in Fairfield, Henrico, Virginia. Preston and Jennie lee had four children.

Children of Preston and Jennie Lee

Nannie Jones (1877)

Ida Belle Jones (1879 - February 24, 1940) lived in Richmond, Virginia

Preston Jones (February 1881 - June 4, 1926) married Nora Neal Rogers. The couple resided in Richmond Virginia.

Leila Jones (1898)

Elizabeth Jones Steger (1852) was born a slave in 1852 at the Lodge. After being freed Lizzie married Edward Steger (who is also spelled Stiger) on October 27, 1867. After her mother Nancy's death, Lizzie raised her youngest sister Millie Jones. By 1880 Edward, Lizzie and her family moved to Westmoreland County, Virginia.

Children of Edward and Lizzie Stiger

Archer Stiger (1872)

Thomas "Tom" Stiger (1874) married Bettie Johnson March 16, 1899 in Westmoreland, VA. He was a farmer for many years. Thomas and Bettie had four children; 1. Royal Stiger (December 25, 1902 - March 11, 1965) who married Laura Johnson. 2. Mary Stiger (1906) 3. Nannie Stiger (1908) 4. Rose Stiger Barnett (September 22, 1917 - October 27, 1998) who lived in Pennsylvania.

Edward Stiger (1877 - May 17, 1926) He married Alice Hackett March 1, 1896 -December 14, 1917 in Westmoreland, Virginia. From this union, one son was born. Edward was a member of Salem Baptist Church. He worked as a gardener for the Wetherill family in Cople, Westmoreland County, Virginia. He later married Mary Dorsey Ashton of Westmoreland, VA. Edward and Alice had one son Clarence Stiger (July 5, 1907 - October 1984) married Gertrude Crawley (May 30, 1907 - August 31, 1982). From this union two children were born 1. Fred Stiger (1923 - 1971) 2. Helen Stiger (1930)

Annie Stiger (July 10, 1878 - October 2, 1929) married George Thompson in Westmoreland. At the time of her death she lived in Philadelphia, Penn.

Below is the marriage Record of Edward Stiger and Lizzie Jones

Date of license	Names of Parties	Remarks
1868 Oct 27	Edw Stiger and Lizzie Jones	Girls father being present authed clerk to issue license

Jennie Jones Hyde

(1855-1931)

"She heard the bells ringing on the hill and the slaves start hollering they were free"

Jennie Jones was born in 1855 the fourth child of Preston and Nancy Brown Jones. Carolyn Carroll remembers her father Howard Hyde Sr. recalled Grandmas Jennie's account of the ending of slavery at the Lodge "she heard the bells ringing up on the hill and the slaves start hollering because they were free." From all research accounts and this oral history account, has led me to believe after the death of Sen. William Archer in 1855 her parents and siblings were freed. Jennie married Robert Hyde of Powhatan, VA on January 4, 1879 in Amelia, VA.

Robert Hyde (1850 – 1922) was the son of Cambell and Parky "Martha" Hyde. According to the research of Howard Hyde Jr. Cambell Hyde was a slave of Hyde Park in Nottoway, VA. While researching the Red Lodge Plantation, I found out that slave owner Martha Hyde Fowlkes and her slaves originated from Amelia, VA. By 1900, Parky lived with her son Robert and his wife Jennie in Red Lodge where she died in 1902.

As mention earlier in 1904, Jennie Jones and many other slave descendants of Red Lodge fought to keep the land in which they had inherited. She was one of the many who rallied together, attended court proceedings and won the chancery case. Oral history suggest that Jennie spearheaded the case. Deacon Emmett Robinson once told me that his grandmother Jennie was a great cook and was a very strong Christian woman. Like her siblings, she was also a founding member of Liberty Baptist Church where her husband Robert served as a deacon. Jennie proven to be a faithful member to the end. She helped raised not only her own children, Royal, Harrison, Willie (August 1895 – January 1896), Rosa, Lizzie and Lottie Hyde. She also had a hand in the upbringing of her grandchildren, and two of her nieces as well. Jennie Jones Hyde died January 20, 1931 at the age of 76 at her home in the Lodge. She was buried at Liberty Baptist Church in Amelia, Virginia.

Pictured above: Jennie Hyde, pictured at right Deacon Robert Hyde

CERTIFICATE OF DEATH
COMMONWEALTH OF VIRGINIA
Department of Health
Bureau of Vital Statistics

No. 123

1. PLACE OF DEATH
   COUNTY OF Amelia
   MAGISTERIAL DISTRICT OF Giles

   REGISTRATION DISTRICT No. 40 e   REGISTERED No. 2

2. FULL NAME: Jennie Hyde
   (A) RESIDENCE: Mattoax Va

PERSONAL AND STATISTICAL PARTICULARS

3. SEX: female
4. COLOR OR RACE: colored
5. SINGLE, MARRIED, WIDOWED, OR DIVORCED: widowed
5A. HUSBAND OF (OR) WIFE OF: Robert Hyde
6. DATE OF BIRTH: unknown
7. AGE: about 70 or older
8. TRADE, PROFESSION: Housework
9. INDUSTRY: for self
12. BIRTHPLACE: Amelia Co Va
13. FATHER NAME: Preston Jones
14. BIRTHPLACE: unknown
15. MOTHER MAIDEN NAME: Nancy Brown
16. BIRTHPLACE: Amelia Co Va
17. INFORMANT: Royal Hyde, Mattoax Va
18. BURIAL: Amelia Co Va   DATE: Jan 22, 1931
19. UNDERTAKER: John M Dennis, Mattoax Va
20. FILED: Jan 21, 1931   Otelia G Harris, Registrar

MEDICAL CERTIFICATE OF DEATH

21. DATE OF DEATH: Jan 20th 1931
22. I HEREBY CERTIFY: unattended

Principal cause of death: Had been sick two or three days with a cold.

104 a

(SIGNED) W O Rucker M.D.
(ADDRESS) Mattoax Va

This is Jennie Hyde death Certificate. (Her age was not correct)

Royal Hyde

(April 26, 1879 - December 17, 1951)

Royal was the eldest of the children born to Robert and Jennie Jones Hyde. He was named after his uncle Royal Jones. He married Fannie Lillian Kyle (1887 – March 29, 1917). At the time Fannie was living with Royal's uncle Rev. Royal Jones and his wife Mattie Lee Jones who was Fannie's mother sister. Mattie become Fannie and her siblings Mary, Royal and Esther legal guardian. Fannie was a Sunday school, organist, and noted singer. Her voice could be heard at the Second Baptist Church and many Baptist conventions throughout Akron, Ohio. The couple married on June 6, 1906 in District of Columbia. Royal was a skilled carpenter and farm hand. He built many homes along with Mr. William Henry Green and by himself. Some of the houses he built still stands today.

Royal and William Green built a Brick Church school which is located on Genito Rd. and Kennons lane in Amelia, VA. He also assisted William Green in the remodel of Pleasant Grove Baptist Church. After Fannie's death, Royal with the help of his sisters Lizzie and Lottie cared for his six children. Evelyn Harris remembered Royal as a quiet man, and hardworking. Edwin 'Ed' Wilson remembered his father Raymond Wilson recalling the times he would help Royal Hyde build homes. Raymond became a skillful carpenter because of Royal Hyde. Ed also recalled his father Raymond telling him that Royal Hyde would request three dollars a day for his work while other carpenters were getting paid one dollar. When it came to building houses, other than William H. Green, few could do it better. Mrs. Ethel S. Morris remembers Mr. Royal Hyde would visit her grandmother Nannie Smith who he dated for many years. They both had lost their spouses when they were still young and although they never remarried, they both shared a relationship until Nannie's death. His granddaughter Fannie, recalled a story of him walking with a cane she said he suffered from arthritis. Royal died on December 17, 1951. His funeral was held at Liberty Baptist Church where he was buried.

Pictured right: Fannie Kyle Hyde

Royal Hyde Draft card

REGISTRATION CARD—(Men born on or after April 28, 1877 and on or before February 16, 1897)

Serial Number: 299

1. Name: Royal Hyde

2. Place of Residence: Mattoax, Amelia, Va.

[THE PLACE OF RESIDENCE GIVEN ON THE LINE ABOVE WILL DETERMINE LOCAL BOARD JURISDICTION; LINE 2 OF REGISTRATION CERTIFICATE WILL BE IDENTICAL]

3. Mailing Address: Same

4. Telephone: —

5. Age in Years: 63

Date of Birth: April 26, 1879

6. Place of Birth: Amelia, Virginia

7. Name and Address of Person Who Will Always Know Your Address: Mrs Rosa Robinson, Mattoax, Va.

8. Employer's Name and Address: Self

9. Place of Employment or Business: Mattoax, Amelia, Va.

I AFFIRM THAT I HAVE VERIFIED ABOVE ANSWERS AND THAT THEY ARE TRUE.

(Registrant's signature) Royal Hyde

D. S. S. Form 1 (Revised 4-1-42) (over)

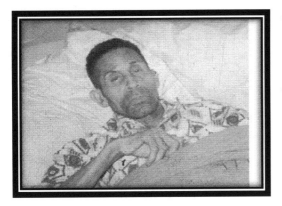

Children of Royal and Fannie

Pleasant Royal Hyde Sr. (1906 - 1972) grew up in the Red Lodge. He attended Brick Church School. After the death of his mom Pleasant and his brother Alvin moved to Akron, Ohio and lived with his great-uncle Royal Jones. After Pleasant, returned to Amelia, VA where he married Anna Blanche Mitchell (1973). Like all the people of Red Lodge, Pleasant was no stranger of hard work. He raised tobacco and wheat. He also had a garden with tomato, watermelon, cucumbers and other vegetables. Pleasant was like his father, a skillful carpenter and also worked for Sonny Anderson at the Saw Mill before an accident caused his health to decline. After his injury, Pleasant was converted. Although disabled he was baptized at Liberty Baptist Church. Pleasant was a man of few words but he was a great provider for his family. He was said to be very reliable and his word was his bond. Anna was a great mother and grandmother that raised her children with great values. Anna loved to laugh and was the type of person who would also speak her mind. Anna was also a disciplinarian, for an example: One night Ernestine "Teeny" and a cousin decided to sneak back in the house after being out late. They started to make their way into the house through the window but the cousin went in first. Anna started to beat her and the girl replied "It's Me! Aunt Anna" when Anna realized she wasn't whipping Teeny She replied 'Lord Jesus Aunt Rosa going to kill me." Laughter fills the air whenever that story is told.

Children of Pleasant and Anna Hyde: 1. William Royal Hyde (October 14, 1934 - June 8, 2007) married Mary Sumpter. William, owned a taxi service in Washington, DC. 2.Pleasant McKinley Hyde (1937 - 1974) 3. Fannie Hyde born in 1938 had one daughter, a granddaughter Shannon Henderson who is an author and other grandchildren. 4.Helen M. Hyde Phillips 5. Catherine Virginia Hyde married George Booker on March 26, 1960 has children, grandchildren and great- grandchildren. 6. Esther Lee Hyde Fleming has children and grandchildren, and great- grandchildren 7. Ernestine Hyde (November 7, 1948 – July 23, 2005) "Teeny" lived in Maryland. She had two sons. 8. Anna Hyde Epps "Tiny" has one son and grandchildren. 9. Sylvia Hyde Mitchell has two children and grandchildren. 10. Leon Haywood Hyde. 11. Lewis Hyde (1953 - 2016) was the twin of Celeste Hyde served in the Armed Forces. He was married to Apostle Verniecer Sims and served as a Pastor. He was the father of three children and a granddaughter. The couple lived in Arizona and later moved to Texas. 12. Celeste Elizabeth Hyde (October 29, 1954 – March 12, 1955). 13. Reginald Dale Hyde graduated from Amelia County High School in 1974. He has one daughter and grandsons. 14. Bonita C. Hyde Redd has two sons and a grandson.

Children of Pleasant and Anna Hyde

Ernestine Hyde

Fannie Baylor

Catherine H. Booker

Anna, Helen, Fannie, Bonita, Catherine and Sylvia

Ernestine Hyde

Faded pic: Pleasant McKinley Hyde

William Hyde

Esther Fleming and children

Alvin Hyde

Reginald Dale Hyde

Bonita, Lewis, Dale, Clyde, Emanuel Jr.

Helen H. Phillips

Mr. and Mrs. Juan Booker

Anna, Sylvia, and Catherine

Lewis Hyde

Eric Hyde, Tony Hyde, Rodney Booker and E.A. Hyde III   Mr. and Mrs. Rodney Booker

Regina Hyde   Children of Juan Booker   Lewis and Verniecer Hyde

Reginald and Howard

Latroy and Mervin

After the Home Going of Lewis Hyde, and his mother-in - law and sister in law, the family gathered together once again. In the midst of loss new family connections were made with Lewis wife and children. After the service family met back at the old home place of Robert and Jennie Hyde.

Karen, Fannie, Sylvia, Helen, Lewis, Anna, Carolyn, Bonita, Quincy, Tiffany, and Catherine

Tiffany, Lewis Jr, Latonia, Quincy, Emanuel, and Bonita

Esther, Helen and Anna Marie

Left: Helen and Lewis Hyde Jr.

Andrea Mitchell

Shirdine Harris, Clinton and Howard Hyde Jr.

Randy and June

Karen B. Jasper and Missy

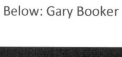
Below: Gary Booker

Randy, Quincy and Monica

Alvin Hyde

(January 19, 1908 - June 17, 1978)

He was born in Amelia, VA and later moved to Akron, Ohio to live with his great uncle Royal. Alvin, enlisted in the United States Army. After his service in the Army, Alvin moved to York Pennsylvania. He married Otha Purnell and adopted Otha's nephew. Alvin was a butler and would visit his family in Amelia every summer and would often bring oranges and peanuts. Alvin had no children.

Emanuel Ambrose Hyde Sr.

(May 11, 1911 - July 3, 1976)

He was born May 11, 1911 in Amelia, Virginia. He was known as simply "Manuel or Ruff Rooster". After the death of his mother, Emanuel was raised by his aunt Lottie Person and also his aunt Rosa Robinson. On December 25, 1941, Manuel married Alice Augusta Granger (1921 – February 1954) pictured below, was the daughter of Rosa Woodfin Granger Goode of Moseley, Virginia.

Emanuel worked for Charlie Gryder. He was a carpenter and He always maintained a garden. He did a lot for people in the neighborhood and did carpenter work for Mr. V. Y. Scott among others. Manuel had a path for almost everywhere he went rarely did you see him walking the roads. Emanuel was a good friend of William Mondrey Sr, Mike Banks, John Allen Ruffin and others in the neighborhood. Manuel was very respectful to the elderly, as well as the young and few if anyone ever heard him curse. Evelyn Harris recalled that Manuel had a lot of respect for her mom Mrs. Emma Wilson. He would often visit her, and tell her things. Mrs. Evelyn and Alice "Gussie" was very close. She recalled stories of traveling to Moseley with Manuel and Gussie and spending weekends at Gussie sister Arletha Jones home. They would often visit Gussie's family the Granger, Francisco, Woodfin and Goode families in Moseley, VA. Manuel enjoyed dancing at Tyler's store especially while drinking. Cousins Edwin Wilson, Estelle Wilson Green and Eliza Jones also remembers the many times his mom Louise would play the Victrola and Manuel would start shouting (dancing) in the middle of the floor. While living in the brick church area, he would often

walk the path to Lou house. Manuel and others made liquor at the Steele near the river. He would definitely drink his part. He wore Bibb overalls and wide brim hat. He raised pigs, and his own garden that his sons worked by hand. He cut trees with crosscut saw. He dug a vegetable storage in the ground to store vegetables for the winter. He had a nickname for each of his children. Emanuel Jr. remembers his dad nicknaming him Six.

Children of Emanuel and Alice Hyde

William McDaniel Hyde (December 16, 1947 - April 11,1971) Pappy as he was affectionately called was the oldest son of Emanuel and Alice Augusta Hyde. Evelyn Harris remembers how excited my grandmother Alice Hyde was about the birth of her son. In earlier years, Pappy had polio which he quickly recovered from. As Pappy grew he became a skillful worker helping out on farms. He also worked for a time at Tyler's store. Pappy received his education at Brick church school and Russell Grove High School where he was taught brick masonry by Mr. Joseph Wilson. Pappy graduated in June 1967. As a youth Pappy worked for Frank Tyler. He was

well known at school as well as in his neighborhood. For a time, he drove the school bus and wouldn't mind laughing with you or cursing at you. He also didn't mind leaving you if you were late. Pappy, graduated from Russell Grove High School on Friday in June 4, 1967 and enlisted in the United States Army three days later. He received his basic training in Fort Jackson in South Carolina. He was deployed to Vietnam and was wounded in action after being hit by a hostile grenade. He was medivac to Zama Japan. He was later sent to U.S. Naval Hospital. After being discharged, with a cast on his leg, Pappy hitched hiked his way to his sister Rose house in Richmond, VA. On Easter Sunday morning, he died in an automobile accident in Washington, PA on Highway 1. His body was sent back to Amelia and laid in state at Tyler's Funeral Home. Pappy's body was guarded by the Army representatives that stayed until after his funeral service. His funeral was held at the liberty Baptist Church in Amelia, VA. It was said to be one of the largest funerals remembered at the old Brick Church.

Blanche Rosa Victoria Hyde Jefferson "Rose" attended Brick Church school and graduated from Russell Grove High School in 1968. Her home has always been a second home to all of her nieces and nephews. For many years Rose has always had a great love for children and along with her sister, has took an active role in the lives of all her nieces and nephews and cousins. She is married to Mr. Charles Jefferson and has four sons; grandchildren; and great grandchildren.

Anna Marie Hyde Bowers attended Brick Church School; Russell Grove High School 1971. She is married to Willie Bowers and two children and grandchildren. She is a retired nurse and has affection and concern for the sick and the elderly. She has also been a motherly figure to her nieces and nephews doing whatever she can for them and always willing to help out in any way she can. She is a faithful

member of Ebenezer Baptist church Lenexa VA.' She makes the best sweet potato pie on this side of heaven.

Elder Emanuel Hyde Jr. (left) aka June born October 18, 1951. He married Betty Minter October 20, 1972 daughter of Arthur Lee Minter Sr. of Sanford, NC and Dorothy Eldridge Minter of Richmond, VA. He is the father of three children (I am the youngest of them) and he has a granddaughter. All of my life he has spoken about growing up in Red Lodge. He has always talked about growing up and how in spite of obstacles he was determined to overcome. When he was a small boy, his father Emanuel Hyde Sr. gave him his first job duty. While his cousins John Robinson and Robert Robinson was sawing wood his dad told him to sit on the wood to keep it in place. Ever since that day, he has not been a stranger to hard work. He learned carpentry work as most of the Hyde men did, and farming working for Frank Tyler. He always said that Mr. Bubba Tyler taught him how to drive a tractor and his cousin Mary Jones (Jane) drove him to DMV to get his license. Since the early days my dad has worked for Matthews Tires, Woodfin Oil, and spent many years at Exxon until the 1990s. Since the inception of this project, he has been a driving force always encouraging me to finish strong. He is a great husband, father and grandfather who has made many sacrifices for his family.

Betty Minter Hyde

Marshae Minter

Dargenaba M. Anderson

Left: Brittany and her grandfather Elder Emanuel Hyde Jr.

Right: Emanuel Hyde III (author)

Pappy

Anna Hyde Bowers

Blanche "Rose" Hyde Jefferson

Emanuel Hyde Jr in the early 1970s

Willie Sr., Anna H. and Katrina Bowers

Charles Jefferson Jr.

Anna, Emanuel Jr, William, Charles III and unidentified girl

Pam Jefferson and Charles Jefferson   Chamberlayne and William Jefferson   Katrina Bowers

Katrina and Willie Bowers Jr.   Terry and Latonia Jefferson   Christopher Jefferson

Donte, Terry, Emanuel III   Mr. & Mrs. Charles and Blanche Jefferson   Jayden Gaskins

Terry Jr. and Charles III

Family of Emanuel Hyde and Alice Augusta G. Hyde

William Jefferson and daughter

Terry Jefferson Sr. and sons

Charles III, William, Donte, Terry Jr, and Terry Jefferson Sr.

Sons of Donte Jefferson

daughter of Willie Bowers Jr.

Robert "Bob" Hyde

(March 7, 1914 – May 1, 1979)

While still a teenager Robert left home migrating to Philadelphia, PA. He enlisted into the United States Army from Fort Meade in Maryland. He later married Beatrice Dorsey and fathered three children. Elaine Williamson, Charlotte Dorsey, and Juanita Dorsey Lipton. It is said that Robert became a store owner in Philadelphia and although he only returned to Amelia, VA for his father's funeral in 1951. Robert would often send his nieces and nephews packages. I can remember the late Junius (Junie) Robinson recalling a story with me years ago, he said in the 1960s while visiting friends in Philadelphia he went to a bar. While sitting at the bar a guy walked in and sat beside him, the guy ordered his drink and started a conversation. As the guy was talking Junie started to recognize who he was so he asked him was he Bob Hyde, he said he was and the first cousins sat for hours drinking and talking about old times. Robert died in 1979 and was buried in Merion Cemetery in Pennsylvania. His wife Beatrice became a minister at the New Jerusalem Living Church of God on Aspen Street in Philadelphia until her passing.

Howard Burdette Hyde Sr.

(October 3, 1916 - January 2, 1998)

The youngest son of Royal Hyde and Fannie Kyle was born October 1916 months before his mother death. After Fannie's passing Howard was reared by his grandmother Jennie, his father and his aunt Rosa Hyde Robinson. Growing up, Howard was nicknamed "Fessor" short for Professor. He later stayed for a time at the former home of his aunt Lottie where his brother Emanuel and his first cousin Richard Person Sr resided. Mrs. Evelyn Harris remembers her visits to Manuel house and at the time Howard was real quiet and shy. He moved to Washington D.C to live with Lottie for a while and later on June 20, 1941, he enlisted in the United States Army and served World War II. Howard toured Africa. Upon returning home, Mrs. Evelyn remembered him being more outgoing. On December 18, 1948 Howard married Rachel Helen Robinson daughter of Leon and Lucy Robinson of Chula, VA. Howard worked various occupations during his lifetime. He worked as a cook and resided in Richmond, Howard was employed with Lucky Strike Tobacco Factory, Charlie Gryder, Whittington, E.F Chimney, Roy Whittington and Matthew Tires. Howard's cousin Rev. Daniel Jones officiated the wedding ceremony. I can remember Uncle Howard was very close to his cousin Oakie. They would ride to the Chula store together then called Exxon. They would argue and disagree yet they remained close. I can recall a time Oakie and Uncle Howard decided to work on a lawnmower. Mr. William "Stiff" Mondrey was also there telling Oakie how to fix it. Oakie had enough he said "Let me tell you the John Brown truth, I know what I'm doing." As far as I know that lawn mower never ran again. Uncle Howard was a

quiet man that said what he meant and meant what he said. For many years, Howard Hyde stood as the patriarch of the family. He was the last surviving child of Royal and Fannie Hyde. He and his wife Rachel Hyde believed in keeping the family united. Sunday dinners was always a great time with good food from one of the greatest cooks in the world, Aunt Rachel. I can remember the Easter Egg hunts and other activities at the home of Uncle Howard and Aunt Rachel Hyde. Aunt Rachel was a part of the Robinson family of the Chula Amelia VA. Children of Howard Hyde Sr: Carolyn Louise Hyde Carroll has been an asset to this project. Carolyn is also a researcher in her own right. She was formerly married to Lawrence Baker and had four children and three grandchildren; One son is deceased, Lawrence Baker Jr. In 1994 Carolyn married Henry Carroll who has two sons, one deceased; Henry also has grandchildren and great – grandchildren. 3. Lucy Hyde Ross (November 12, 1953 – May 7, 1999) married Charles Ross on July 28, 1973. From this union, 3 sons and grandchildren; One son is deceased Kermeth Ross (1976 – 2009) who married Andrea Harper. Howard Hyde Jr. is married to Lynnette Terry and has three daughters and two grandsons. Mary Hyde Harris married Lonnie Harris and has two children and grandchildren 6. Clinton Hyde who married Virginia Hayes. Clinton is the father of three children and has several grandchildren; 7. Clyde Hyde married Delores Green Hyde who had two children, One deceased, Rayshawn D. Hyde (1986 – 2000).

CERTIFICATE OF MARRIAGE
COMMONWEALTH OF VIRGINIA

No. 35438

CITY / COUNTY OF: Amelia.
CLERK'S NO. 69

FULL NAME OF GROOM: Howard Burdette Hyde.

PRESENT NAME OF BRIDE: Rachel Helen Robinson
MAIDEN NAME: single--same.

	GROOM				BRIDE		
AGE	RACE	SINGLE, WIDOWED, OR DIVORCED	NO. TIMES PREV. MARRIED	AGE	RACE	SINGLE, WIDOWED, OR DIVORCED	NO. TIMES PREV. MARRIED
32	Col.	single	none.	16	Col.	single	none.

OCCUPATION: Laborer.
OCCUPATION:

BIRTHPLACE: Amelia County, Virginia.
BIRTHPLACE: Amelia County, Va.

FATHER'S FULL NAME: Royal Hyde
FATHER'S FULL NAME: Leon Robinson

MOTHER'S MAIDEN NAME: Fannie Kyle.
MOTHER'S MAIDEN NAME: Lucy Helen Archer.

RESIDENCE: 810 S. Randolph St., Richmond, Va. 2430
RESIDENCE: Amelia County, Chula, Va. 0040

Date of Proposed Marriage: Dec. 18, 1948.
Place of Proposed Marriage: Amelia County.

Given under my hand this 18 day of Dec., 1948.

Clerk of Circuit Court.

CERTIFICATE OF DATE AND PLACE OF MARRIAGE

I, Rev. Daniel F. Jones, a Minister of the Baptist Church, or religious order of that name, do certify that on the 18 day of Dec., 1948 at Amelia City or 0040, Virginia, under authority of this license, I joined together in the Holy State of Matrimony the persons named and described therein. I qualified and gave bond according to law authorizing me to celebrate the rites of marriage in the county (or city) of Amelia, Commonwealth of Virginia.

Given under my hand this 18 day of Dec., 1948.

Address of celebrant: Mattoax Va

Rev. Daniel F. Jones
(Person who performs ceremony sign here.)

Clyde and fam

Lucy H. Ross

Howard Jr, Lynnette and daughters

Howard Hyde Jr

Carolyn, Wesley, and Monica

Henry and Carolyn Carroll

Mary and Lonnie

Mary Harris

Clinton and Virginia Hyde

Family of Howard and Rachel Hyde

Hyde Family   Clinton Hyde and Timeka Watson

Lucy Hyde Ross   Howard and Rachel Hyde with grandchildren

Clinton Hyde

Kermeth and Andrea Ross with daughter   Kevin, Kermeth, Karl Ross   Krystal and Karl Ross

Stephanie, Heather, and Morgan   Lena Jackson and Anna   Morgan and Orlando

2014 Hyde Family at Reunion   Aunt Blanche (Rose) and Emanuel H. III

Harrison "Harry" Hyde Sr.

(1887 – 1946)

Harry Hyde "also known Buck" was the second child born to Robert and Jennie Jones Hyde in Amelia County. His nickname was Buck Hyde and some say he would live up to his name. According to the 1910 census Harry was living in Richmond, Virginia and worked as a packer at the lumber company. Harry married Rosa Morton (abt.1894 – August 11, 1930). Junius Robinson told me when I was young that Uncle Harry was a quiet man but did not play around Buck resided in Richmond until he passed. Mrs. Evelyn Harris recalled the day of his funeral and burial the weather was so bad, the cars that left the church, were sliding heading back to Richmond, VA. Harry's Children:

Louise Johnson was the daughter of Harry and Josephine Johnson Brown: She married Raymond Wilson son of Rev. Jeff Wilson and Margaret Goodman Wilson in Amelia County, Virginia. Raymond was a skillful barber and learned carpentry skills while helping Royal Hyde. Raymond always had gardens, and was a very hard worker. He passed on his wealth of knowledge to his children. Louise was an active member of Liberty Baptist Church and worked at the Willing Workers Club. Her son Edwin says his mom was a great cook and would often bake for Holidays such as Christmas and Thanksgiving. She would make deserts like pies, cakes, and Jello. In a 2013 interview with her former daughter-in-law Mary Woodson Wallace, she remembered Louise as a sweet humble lady that loved her family.

Children of Raymond and Louise Wilson: Ethel Wilson (deceased) lived in New York had a daughter and grandchildren. James Raymond Wilson (1928 – 2002) was formerly married to Mary Woodson Wilson Wallace (1931 – 2014). His nickname was Tee. He later moved to Philadelphia and would usually visit during the summer. He served in the United States Army. Tee was the father of three children. Two sons, one deceased James "Junnie" Wilson, and one daughter Margrett Owens. Deacon Harrison Wilson for many years has been a faithful member and serving on the deacon board at Liberty Baptist Church in Amelia, VA. He is married to Evelyn Willis of Powhatan County, Virginia. Estelle Wilson Green was married to the late Willie Green. She is a proud mother and grandmother. Estelle resides in New Jersey and always makes it a point to come back home during Homecoming and revival on the third Sunday in August along with her sister Eliza. Eliza Jones lives in Connecticut. Eliza's first born was Arnold Wilson (1957 – 2004) who was also the son of Joseph Goode Jr. and has two sons. In 1961 Eliza married Elder James Jones and from this union, several children were born. Eliza has many grandchildren and great – grandchildren. Clarence "Lee" Wilson (deceased), and Edwin Wilson who has one son.

Ethel Wilson

James Wilson

Estelle Green

Dr. James and Eliza Jones

Edwin Wilson

Clarence Wilson

Mary and Junie

Deacon Harrison and Evelyn Wilson

Junie and Margrett

Harrison "Harry" Hyde Jr. (Jan 11, 1920 – August 17, 2007) was raised in Richmond, VA. He enlisted in the army on December 30, 1942 and married Adeline Hyde (1928 – 1982) on October 31, 1947 in Richmond, Virginia. After the death of his wife, he later married Cora Ann Willis Hicks (1936 – 2012) Harry and his first wife Adeline, had six children: Gail, Harry Jr., Adeline, Barbara, Rosa and One deceased, Irving Hyde. Harry has many descendants many are in the Richmond Area of Virginia. In later years Harry Jr. house was on Gordon Avenue. His car which he normally parked on the end of the street, had Hyde on the license plates.

Harrison "Harry" Hyde Jr.

Harry Hyde Jr. and children: Gail Hyde Williams   Harry Hyde III   Rosa Wyche

Lizzie Bettie Hyde Jones

(September 21, 1889 - July 7, 1964)

Lizzie was born in Red Lodge Virginia. She was baptized and joined the Liberty Baptist Church. On February 15, 1910 Lizzie married Mr. Edwin Twine Jones the son of Phillip and Matilda Dixon Jones of the Pleasant Grove area of Amelia, VA. Edwin was a farmer who raised pigs and cows. Edwin was also a faithful deacon at Liberty Baptist Church. Many times he would walk the path near his home to the church. Lizzie was a good cook and along with Edwin, raised her children in a Christian upbringing. Evelyn Harris remembers the many visit to "Aunt Liz" who was a close friend of her mother Mrs. Emma Wilson. Liz, was a very sweet lady. Edwin and Lizzie lived in Amelia County, Virginia for many years before living in Richmond, VA for a time until they passed away.

Edwin and Lizzie Hyde Jones children

Louis Edwin Jones (September 27, 1911 - March 19, 1999) married Blanche Callaway and he later married Clara Lancaster Johnson. He was skillful in carpentry, welding and brick masonry. Louis enlisted in the United States Army in 1942 and later was honorably discharged. He was involved in the NAACP many other organizations. He accepted Christ at an early age and like all of the children of Edwin and Lizzie Jones, Louis attended Liberty Baptist Church and later joined Ebenezer Baptist Church where he was a faithful member and served on the deacon board.

Jennie Jones born (1914 - 2013) moved to Richmond, VA and became a seamstress.

Katie Beatrice Jones Harris (April 7, 1916 - February 1, 2003) married Linwood Harris on April 18, 1947.

Rosa Matilda Jones (December 30, 1918 - October 15, 2001) On November 24, 1940 Rosa married Arthur Hicks son of Elijah and Perline Lacy Hicks. Arthur and Rosa was a faithful deacon of Liberty Baptist Church. She loved her church, and was very close friend to another Deaconess Margaret C. Bannister. They were both a wealth of wisdom. Arthur and Rosa's home was filled with love, Arthur raised chickens and pigs. Rosa kept her home clean and enjoyed keeping her yard clean. Rosa had a special smile and love for everyone. At her home going, I can vividly recall, everyone was given a piece of candy. During the Eulogy Rev. Neal Jackson asked everyone to put their candy in their mouth in remembrance of the sweetness of this lady. After Rosa's death, Deacon Arthur Hicks would often stop by my home and tell me a lot about the people of the past and about his upbringing. Children of Arthur and Rosa Hicks: Thomas Hicks married Ella Lee Archer. From this union two children were born, one deceased, Kevin Hicks (1977 – 1986). The couple had two grandchildren, one deceased, D'Ajah Braxton Hicks (1998 – 2015). Gertrude Alice Hicks (1914 – 2013) married William King. Herbert Hicks married Joyce Ann Giles daughter of Arthur and Rosa Giles on August 30, 1969. Arlene Hicks Johnson married Isaac L. Johnson on June 13, 1968. Joanne Elizabeth Hicks (February 5, 1954 – July 30, 1954) Louis Hicks married Marjorie Drummond in 1974. Marilyn Hicks. The descendants of Arthur and Rosa are many.

Phillip Garfield Jones (August 10, 1920 - August 26, 1997) was married to Mary Susie Banks on June 28, 1947. The couple had five children; Judy, Cynthia, Phillip, Charlie, Donnie Jones.

Charlotte Jones Hobson married Willie Hobson and from this union three children were born: Douglas Hobson, Leon Hobson and Charles Hobson.

Edwin Jones and Lizzie Hyde Jones

Arthur and Rosa

Louis Jones

Arthur Hicks and Rosa Jones H

Katie, Phil, Rosa

Louis

Louis and Phil

Charlotte and Willie Hobson

Jennie Jones

Charlotte Hobson

Rev. Manning and Hicks/Jones family

Arthur and Rosa's wedding Anniversary

Arthur and sons

Arlene and Isaac

Viola Hicks

Herbert Hicks and family

Gertrude Hicks

Gertrude & grandchildren

Louis Hicks

Arlene Hicks

Larry Jones

Cynthia

Timeka and daughter

Rosa Hyde Robinson

(1888-1965)

She was born and raised in the Red Lodge Community on January 1888. She was baptized at an early age and was a member of Liberty Baptist Church

She met Emmett Robinson and the couple was married July 25, 1916 in Richmond, VA and resided on Lee Street in Richmond, VA. In the 1920s Rosa returned to Amelia, Virginia. Emmett and Rosa had four children; Emmett, Lenora, Junius, and Elizabeth. In the same household, she raised her nephew Howard. Rosa also played a very vital role in helping her sister with the upbringing of anther nephew, Manuel. Emmett worked for the Riley's, and the Tyler Family.

For a time after her husband's death, her son Emmett and his family lived with her. In 1954 after the death of her nephew Manuel's wife Alice, Rosa raised his sons William "Pappy" and Emanuel Jr. "June" Hyde. From that point on she was called Grandma not just from her own grandchildren but Pappy and June loved and respect her just the same. Rosa had one-bedroom house with a living room that was also a bedroom. There was 10 people living in the home at that time. The people were her son Emmett and his wife Ethel Robinson, Elnora R. Coleman, John Robinson, Robert Robinson, Mary Johnson, John Johnson Jr (aka Boo), William and Emanuel Jr. Rosa cooked, cleaned and could make the best biscuits, many children in Red Lodge would make their way to Mrs. Rosa house for a biscuit. She was well loved in the community. On January 24, 1965 Rosa Robinson passed away but her memory lives on in all the generations of all the people who lives she touch.

Emmett and Rosa children

Emmett Nathaniel Robinson Sr. (February 14, 1918 - May 21, 2008) was born in Richmond but was raised in The lodge. Emmett was called Champ by family and friends started his journey of life learning the skills of farming and carpentry. Emmett, was baptized at an early age under Rev. Sadler and became an active member of Liberty Baptist Church where he served many years as a Deacon, Sunday School Teacher, Church Treasurer, Choir member, Trustee and the church sexton for many years. Emmett married Ethel Hicks the daughter of Elijah and Perline Lacy Hicks on November 22, 1939. Uncle Emmett as I called him, told me once the first job he had in Richmond was at a factory. His job was keeping the boiler running down in the basement. One day while he was preparing for work that night, he heard a voice say "Don't go" he decided to follow God's voice and not work that day. He soon found out the boiler in the basement of the plant exploded killing and injuring plant workers. He realized God had spared his life, he said he would always listen to the voice. During his lifetime, he worked for the U.S Highway department and Whittington family. I can remember him riding a bicycle up to the Whittington's. Uncle Emmett was no stranger to hard work in his lifetime he raised pigs, cows, and horses. He had the best vegetable garden and found joy in canning his vegetables and fruits from his fruit trees and vines. Emmett had pear, cherry, and persimmons trees. He also had a grape vine. Each day that the weather was permissible, he would start his day early working on the land. He would always take an hour or more to eat lunch read his devotions, sing and pray. He had a special bond with his siblings and his first cousins that were unmatched. Emmett was a faithful sexton. He kept the church clean and cut the grass on the church grounds and the cemetery. In the winter months he would shovel ice and snow from the church steps and ramps. Emmett supported the Quentin Robinson Memorial Scholarship Fund which was named in the honor of his son who died at the age of 17. He was a devoted husband and had a special love for Aunt Ethel whom he called Bunche. He took care of his wife Ethel in sickness and in health until she passed away in 1990. He loved his children and always enjoyed the homemade pound cakes and other dishes his daughter, Elnora would prepare for him. Emmett invested a lot of his time in his nephew John Jr, and also in June and Pappy showing them what he knew about working. His wisdom was God given and anyone that had an opportunity to talk with him was blessed.

Children of Emmett and Ethel Robinson

Elnora Robinson Coleman who is married to Rufus Coleman and has a daughter. Her grandson Alfred L. Thompson passed away in 1994.

John Robinson; Rev. Robert Robinson married Brenda Elliott and has three sons and one grandchild. Ronald Robinson has two sons; Quentin Robinson (1962 -1977) Quinton was a good kid and attended Liberty Baptist Church. Wayne Robinson married Penny and has one son.

Lenora Clarisel Robinson

(November 7, 1921 - August 11, 1961)

Bell as she was affectionately called, attended Brick Church and Russell Grove School. She married Allen Washington son of Irvin and Callie Washington in Richmond, VA by the Rev. George W. Manning on September 26, 1950. She was a beautiful lady and a great mom. The couple resided on 1705 N. 24th Street in Richmond, VA. Allen and Lenora had 3 children; Rosalind Washington Nelson who is married to James "Jimmy" Nelson, Evang. Renee Washington Walker is married to Arthur Walker; Allen Washington Jr.

Allen Washington Sr. and Lenora Robinson Washington also has grandchildren.

Junius Emanuel Robinson

(March 15, 1924 - February 28,1998)

Junie as he was called grew up like the rest of his siblings in Red Lodge. He was baptized like many others in the old baptism pond at Liberty. He enlisted in the United States Army from Richmond, VA January 31, 1944 and was discharged April 27, 1946. He later married Emily Robinson (December 8, 1919 - December 26, 1998) He was a strong man and was definitely someone that would keep you laughing. Junie told me stories of how he would hide out in the woods at the branch to skip school. He did not like school! He later joined the United States Army and moved North. My memories of him traveling home from Brooklyn, New York wearing a fatigue or just a plain shirt with a pipe hanging from his mouth or in his shirt pocket as in the picture. When I was young I asked him why he walked with a limp. He said he was thrown from a horse. Uncle Junie as my father called him, always told me stories of my grandfather, his father, mother, Uncle Harrison Hyde and others. He was very close with his siblings, first cousins, Mike Banks, John Banks just to name a few. In the late 1970s - 90s When he would come home to visit his brother Emmett and his sister Lizzie (who moved back to Amelia after living in New York for many years.) I can remember walking with him down the old dirt road from Uncle Emmett's house to visit Mrs. Nolie who lived behind the church. He would tell me stories of the old people and things he used to do.

He was a lot of fun. During his visits, he would always get my dad to take him to Red Lodge to see his family and friends. Uncle Junie had great wisdom and survival skills. He could make anyone laugh and often would speak his mind. His most used word he would often say was "Hell yeah." His love for his family is still cherished to this day.

Elizabeth Robinson Walls

(May 14,1927-October 4, 2004)

She was the youngest child of Emmett Sr. and Rosa Hyde Robinson. She attended Brick Church school. She also attended, Virginia State University and Maggie Walker School of Nursing. She was formerly married to John Johnson. From this union two children were born, Dr. Mary Johnson Mills and John Johnson Jr. (deceased) aka Boo. She later married Edward Walls (died in August 1993) while living in New York. According to her son Elder Edward Walls, she always had a big dream of returning to Amelia. It was in 1993 - 1994 she made the dream a reality and returned home. The couple had three children Paula Walls Mays is married to Darryl Mays. Pastor Edward Walls Jr who is the Pastor of Church of Faith and is married to Shelia M. Walls, and Rosetta Walls McBride (1956 – 2014) Rosetta was married to Thomas McBride. Around 1993 -1994 Lizzie returned to Amelia County where she attended Liberty Baptist Church where she enjoyed being on the Willing Workers Club at the church. Aunt Lizzie had a good heart and she loved her husband, Edward Walls Sr. and her family. She was a great mother, good cook and very close to all of her grandchildren. She was definitely a pillar to the family she was always there to listen and give you advice. She would often say "I trust God" she had a deep and committed faith in God. Lizzie had a very close relationship with all of her grandchildren; However, she had a special relationship with her granddaughters, Shante Meyers and Roni Carrington. She has many grandchildren, great grandchildren and great-great grandchildren.

Rosa and Elizabeth enjoying church

Mr. and Mrs. Edward Walls Sr.

Junius and Lenora

Lenora Belle R. Washington   and   husband Allen Washington

Arthur and Rosa Hicks, Emmett, a cousin, and Elizabeth   Emmett and Elizabeth

Pastor Edward and Sheila Walls   Shante ad cousin Timeka   John Johnson Jr.

Elnora Coleman   Robert Robinson   Wayne Robinson   Quentin Robinson

Rosalind Nelson, Roni Carrington, Elnora Coleman, Dr. Mary Mills Rev. Deborah Thompson, John Robinson, Paula W. Mays, Sharetta McBride, Rosetta McBride, and Ronald Robinson.

Shante, Roni, Paula, and I   Roni and A'shantia   Rosetta Mcbride

Lottie Hyde Person Stalks

(March 10, 1891 – March 5, 1956)

Lottie Hyde was born March 10, 1891. She worked as a maid at the home of the Winston and Leary family in Richmond, Virginia. Later she married Percy Person June 17, 1914 from this union two children were born, Percy Person Jr. (died young) and Richard Stansbury Person. Lottie joined the Liberty Baptist Church at an early and later served as the church pianist. She also would sing songs like "Come Follow" and "There is a fountain filled with blood drawn from Immanuel's veins and sinners plunge beneath that cross loss all your guilty stains". Mrs. Evelyn Harris remember Lottie and her siblings, Lottie and her family lived on the land given to her by her sister Lizzie which was right off of route 604. Evelyn remembers the closeness of Lizzie and Lottie and recalled that both of them were very nice. She often remembers the friendship they had with her mother Mrs. Emma Wilson. After the death of her sister in-law Fannie Hyde, Lottie raised one of her nephews Emanuel Hyde Sr. During the days when work was hard and proven scarce, Lottie's friend Mrs. Emma G. Wilson, worked for a white family in Maryland. She returned home and told Lottie about the position. Lottie was hired and moved to District of Columbia while working in Maryland. Giving a helping hand was Lottie way, her nephew Howard moved to District of Columbia to live with her and later William Lewis, her great-nieces Fannie Hyde Baylor and Helen Hyde Phillips followed. Her grandson, Elco and Richard stayed for a while with her as well. During that time, Lottie worked as a waitress at the Peoples Drug Store and was a member of Mt. Carmel

Baptist Church on NW 5 street and Lottie's home address was 505 NW L street in Washington, D.C (the house is pictured left) In later years, Lottie was married to John Stalks who preceded her in death.

Lottie would often return to Amelia County to visit family and check on her home. During her stay she would always worship at her home church the Liberty Baptist Church. Lottie died March 5, 1956. Her body was sent home to be buried at Liberty Baptist Church cemetery.

Lottie's family

Richard Stansbury Person (May 3, 1920 - March 2, 1997) On September 29, 1944 he enlisted in the U.S Navy serving until June 1, 1946. He married Gladys Patterson. Richard was a quiet man. Richard lived in New Jersey for a while and later returned to Virginia where he resided until his death.

Richard and Gladys Person had children; Elco Person who is married to Aileen Ruffin Person, Richard Person who was married to Betty Banks Person and had two daughters and a step - daughter, Sharron Person Archer, James Person, Germaine Person Harris. Rex Person, Kelly Person, and Ycola Person Smith. Richard and Gladys has many grandchildren, and great – grandchildren.

Richard Stanberry Person Sr.

Gladys Person and family

Richard Person Jr and Emanuel Hyde Jr

Pictures of the Hyde Family

Estelle, Helen Hyde Phillips, Eliza Jones Smith and Lucy Hyde Ross

son of Rodney Booker

James Wilson, Rosa, Gail, Anna, Howard, Eliza, Ernestine, Emanuel Jr. (dad), me, and Estelle

Lawrence Baker   Gail, Anna, Rosa Hyde Wyche, and Blanche Rosa Jefferson

Tracy Hockaday		Mary Ann Jenkins and Wendy H. Anderson

Cynthia Edmonds		Carroll Hockaday

Ashantia, Roni, Paua, Shante, Joey

Rev. Royal Allen Jones

Psalm 37:23-24 (KJV) The steps of a good man are ordered by the Lord: and he delighteth in his way. Though he fall, he shall not be utterly cast down: for the Lord upholdeth him with his hand.

The son of ex - slaves Reverend Preston Jones Sr. and Nancy Brown born in the Lodge in Amelia County, Virginia. He married Ms. Mattie Lee daughter of Henry and Mary Wilkinson Lee Gaines. Royal moved to Wadsworth, Ohio and was employed with the Doylestown Coal Mine and Loomis Coal Mines in Wadsworth, Ohio. In 1892 he moved to Akron, Ohio and worked at the Tappan Rice Foundry. After the recommendation of Rev. Cheatham, he was called to Pastor a congregation of eighteen members of the newly founded Second Baptist Church. With a great desire for learning, he attended private night classes for three years at Buchtel University which he later quit to fulfill the plan God had chosen for his life. In a time when pastors were called upon in grievances, to be lawyers in court, acting doctors and to help others in any capacity needed. Rev. Jones and his wife Mattie, name quickly was known throughout Akron and Second Baptist Church membership grew quickly. The Second Baptist Church which at the time was situated on the corner of Hill and James Streets, soon became one of Akron's greatest churches. There were countless functions and events that were highly attended at Second Baptist. For a short period of time Rev. Jones served in politics. After the death of his sister -in- law, Angelina Kyle in 1897, Rev. Jones and his wife Mattie raised Angelina's children: Mary, Fannie, Royal, and Esther Lee Kyle while he maintained his duties as pastor. Within a few years, the Second Baptist Church congregation grew to hundreds and Rev. Jones had a national reputation. In the early 1900s with low pay, lack of education, and the mistreatment of Blacks (called Negro during that time) many leaders such as Booker T. Washington visited Akron to speak on Solving the Negroes Problem.

In 1909 Rev. Jones spoke out at the Men's League of the First Universalist Church he stated: The only real solution to the Negro problem is through education to Solving the Negro Problem and address was written and spoken by Rev. Royal A. Jones: A story is related of a family in the West that owned a donkey which was too old to do any kind of work. How to get rid of this burden was a puzzle they could neither sell nor give him away, and because of the good service rendered by him they did not have the heart to kill him. One day, the farm hands were digging a well on the place. When it had been sunk some 30 feet the men were called to dinner. During their absence the old donkey walked too near the edge of the well and it caved in with him. The family was somewhat elated over the accident and exclaimed, "We have gotten rid of the donkey at last, for we cannot get him out of the well, so we will bury him and dig another." When the men began to shovel the dirt on him he would, with great vigor, shake it off and trample it under foot. This process continued until the donkey tramped his way to the top of the well, walked out, and went to grazing with the rest of the stock. The negro is in the pit He has had the dirt of slavery, ignorance, superstition, fanatic, poverty, inferiority and minority thrown upon him by the so called superior race, but the negro like the donkey in the story with his brawny muscles and acute intellect, is shaking off all of this trash which is intended to bury him, trapping it under his feet, making them stepping stones by which he reaches the plain of prosperity, intelligence and noble manhood. Towards the end of 1913 Rev. Jones and the Second Baptist Church held a program to celebrate the semi centennial of the freeing of four million slaves. Other churches and organizations came from far and near to make sure the services and the festivities that followed was a success. In 1914 he wrote and published a book "Second Baptist Church embracing the history from 1890 to March 30, 1914 also the numerical and financial history in the darkest and most prosperous times. The book is about the humbling beginnings and success of Second Baptist Church. In the book, it is recorded that his niece Lottie Hyde Person, Fannie Kyle Hyde and her sons Pleasant and Alvin visited from Virginia and was given a great reception at the church. His wife Martha was a leader of an organization called The Daughters of Jerusalem and helped many people. She also was president Northern Ohio Baptist Association. In 1915 his wife Martha passed away, and was known as one of the best known colored women in Akron, Ohio. In 1919 Rev. Jones married Ms. Flora Randleman and by 1920 with a membership of over 1000 the Second Baptist Church entered into a new church which was paid off and mortgage burned in 1928. Rev. Jones who has been celebrated with appreciation services and banquets had received many accolades for his work. Mayors, Governors, and ministers has travel the world preaching the gospel was loved by many. Rev. Jones never forgot his family at The Lodge, he would always return to Amelia to visit his family and in the 1930s his great – nephews Alvin and Pleasant Hyde stayed with his wife Flora, and an adopted daughter. According to the Pittsburgh Courier 1938, The nationally known reverend had 468 couples, blessed 150 babies and baptized thousands and eulogized many. He kept on preaching, teaching and leading the people of Second Baptist until 1938 due to his failing health. On Friday January 24, 1941 Reverend Royal Allen Jones passed away. His funeral was held on Monday January 27, 1941 at 1 pm many attended to pay homage to a man who gave his all to God and mankind while he lived. In 1906 during the time of Rev. Jones 13 year anniversay celebration as pastor of the Second Baptist Church, a member Mr. William Greene wrote a poem entitled the Life of Second Baptist Church.

The Life of Second Baptist Church

Thirteen years ago a band of Christians met, The Lord's name for to praise, and to tell all sinning creatures of a savior that would save. They were few, but they were mighty, for God their strength did lie, And they would said "We'll build a Baptist church in Akron by and by. Oh there struggles they were many, And there victories were few, But they were good Christian people and they knew just what to do. They read their bibles daily and in god they did pray, For they faithfully believed that He would open up a way. So god blessed them with a leader, who like Moses in his day, Led the children out of Egypt from the bondage so they say. Of course their were some weak ones, and their faith indeed was small, but their leader reasoned with them Jesus died for one and all. And they prayed to God for courage, and for hope, faith and pluck, and God gave them what they asked for though the scornful said "T'was" luck. Though starting with an handful, in a poor mans humble home, God looked down upon earth and blessed them, aswella s the finest church in Rome. Soon the flock of ten began to grow, and many sinners did repent; God just kept on blessing them, and a guardian angel sent, Some are dead and gone above who started with that band., and under a good leadership the rest go hand in hand. So let us praised the God we loved and Jesus, who was crucified, that we are allowed to live witth the faithful and the tried. But let us not forget the led us all the rugged way. By Gods own power each darkened hour He taught us to watch and pray. At church we would always find him there. And lo, when death came in our homes, Twas our thoughts were all of him Gods humble servant Rev. Jones.

WIFE OF COLORED MINISTER IS DEAD

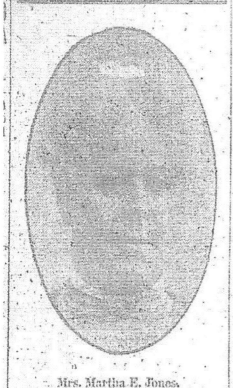

Mrs. Martha E. Jones.

Mrs. Martha E. Jones, 56, wife of Rev. R. A. Jones, pastor of the Second Baptist church, and one of the best known colored women in Akron, died Saturday afternoon at her home of the grip and rheumatism after six weeks' illness.

Mrs. Jones had lived in Akron 25 years. She was president of the Northern Ohio Baptist association for several years.

Surviving are her husband, a daughter, Mrs. Esther L. Johnston; two brothers and two sisters.

Funeral services will be held Wednesday at 1 p. m. at the Second Baptist church, Rev. B. K. Smith, of Cleveland, officiating, and Rev. Edward H. Smith, assisting.

TAKEN BY DEATH

Organizer Of First Negro Church Here Is Mourned By His Community

Akron's Negro community mourned today the passing of a leader and pastor.

Rev. Royal Allen Jones of the Second Baptist church died at his home, 286 Scott av. late yesterday after an illness of two years. He had kept on with his church duties until a year ago.

Rev. Mr. Jones was born in Virginia between 75 and 80 years ago, and after several years spent in the coal mines in Doylestown and at the Loomis Coal Co. in Wadsworth, and brief employment with the Tappan Rice Co., he took up the ministry here about 40 years ago.

Akron was without a Negro

REV. MR. JONES
death ends career

church at the time and Rev. Mr. Jones, who had studied in the south and at old Buchtel college, started the first church here with 18 members.

Today that church, the Second Baptist, has between 500 and 600 members.

Became Leader

Rev. Mr. Jones soon became known as a leader among his people, and in the years when there were no Negro doctors or lawyers here, they went to him for advice on all matters.

He was the only Negro minister ever admitted to the Baptist Ministers Alliance and at one time served as moderator of the group. He was moderator of the northern Association of Negro Baptist ministers for the past 35 years.

He leaves his wife, Mrs. Flora S., and one daughter, Mrs. Esther Wimbish.

Funeral services will be conducted at 1 p. m. Monday at the Second Baptist church. Rev. C. T. Isom of Dayton will officiate. Burial will be in Mt. Peace cemetery.

Flora S. Jones

Flora S. Jones, 91, of 414 Pine, Apt. 31.

She was born in Surry County, N. Carolina. She was a member of the Second Baptist Church, and wife of the late Rev. Royal Allen Jones. She participated and prepared the communion table for over 30 years for the church.

She was a Sunday School teacher, and chairperson of the flower distribution for 20 years, the treasurer of the Women's Auxiliary of Northern Ohio, District Convention.

She is survived by a devoted niece, Mrs. Virginia Spencer, of 414 Pine St., Apt. 35, where condolences may be sent; three great-nieces, Barbara McBeth, New York City, Mrs. Jean Spencer Dixon, and Miss Ethel Spencer, both of Akron; foster daughter, Mrs. Chanie Warford, of Cincinnati; two first cousins, Mrs. Hester Davis, of Akron, and Oscar Sawyer, of Winston-Salem, N.C.; other relatives and friends.

Funeral Services Wednesday, 1 p.m., Turner Memorial Home, 1101 Palmetto Ave., Rev. Lynton assisted by Rev. E. E. Morgan. Interment Mt. Peace Cemetery. Body may be viewed Monday, 7 to 9 p.m., and Wednesday until time of services. (Turner, 724-1202.)

Children of Preston Jones and Nancy Brown Jones

Millie Jones Thompson

Millie was the youngest child of Rev. Preston and Nancy Jones. After the passing of her mother, Millie was reared by her eldest sister Elizabeth Jones Stiger. She migrated with Lizzie and her family to Westmoreland County, Virginia where she married George Washington Thompson on February 26, 1885. Her husband, George was a founder of Salem Baptist Church in Montross, Westmoreland, VA which is pictured right. Millie died February 17, 1929 in Cople, Westmoreland County, Virginia and is buried at the Salem Baptist Church in Erica, Virginia.

Nine Children of George and Millie Thompson

Daniel Thompson (1885)

Eliza Jane Thompson Tyler (August 5, 1888 - September 18, 1954) She was raised in Westmoreland, VA moved to Amelia, Virginia where she married Matt Tyler Sr. After his death, Eliza moved to Ambler, Pennsylvania where she lived until her death.

Jeremiah "Jerry" Thompson (May 18, 1890 - December 31, 1968) was married to Mary Thompson and was a farm laborer. They had a daughter, Alice Thompson Dixon who married Charlie Esau Dixon (1914 – 2009) and a son Esan Roosevelt Dixon (1939)

Allen Thompson (March 1891 - June 15, 1919) He was a farmer and died at the age of 25.

John Archie Thompson (February 2, 1895 - January 8, 1950) married Lucy Thompson

Solomon Thompson (January 7,1898 - March 20,1942) born in Philadelphia, Penn. Solomon married Rose Lipscomb and from this union several children were born; Solomon Thompson (1928) Clarence Thompson (March 3, 1928 - April 15, 1998), Elizabeth Millie Thompson (November 25, 1930 - September 11, 2000) and Rose Mary Thompson (1934)

Nena Thompson Lane (August 1, 1899 - August 14,1968) married Joseph W. Lane March 10, 1918) in Westmoreland, Virginia. Children of Nena: Benjamin Lane (1920 - 1970); Joseph Lane (1924 - 1993); Geraldine Lane (1927); Gladys Lane (1930); Daniel Webster Lane (1933 - 1959) and Leola Lane (1936)

Lucy Thompson Wimbish (1901) married Moses Wimbish

Siblings of Nancy Brown Jones

Russell Brown born in 1829 was the son of Davy and Chloe Brown. He was born and slave and after slavery became a landowner. Russell married Eliza Johnson and from this union nine children were born. Russell was a farmer. There is no documentation of his death but it is believed that he died between the years 1880-1900.

Russell's children

David Brown (1864) married Jennie Smith and later Rebecca Ruffin (1878 - 1936) daughter of Humphrey Ruffin and Ellen Archer Ruffin on December 29, 1897 in Red Lodge. After David's death Rebecca married Peter Johnson. Rebecca lived in Richmond for a while then returned to Red Lodge. Children of David and Rebecca: 1. Mary St. Clair Brown (1896 – 1926) who married Willie Harris and had three children; Daisy Harris Barnes (1920 – 2002) who married John Barnes (1925 – 1986) and had one son; David Harris (1940 – 1996); Elizabeth Harris Taylor (1923 – 1979) married Floyd Taylor; Viola Harris Calvin Brown (1899) Samuel Brown (1901) married Eva Brown from this union three children were born Joseph Brown (1923) Samuel Brown Jr. (1933) and Annie Brown Blount (1935) married Layton Blount and had one son Kermet Wayne Blount. 4. Richard Brown

Fannie Brown (1867 - 1933)

Bettie Brown Flood (1870) met William Flood (1866 - 1926) and they were married March 27, 1896 lived in Richmond, VA.

Lettie Brown

Archer Brown (1874) married Jennie Taylor on December 4, 1895. Only one child was found during this research. Annie Brown Banks (October 1893 - August 5, 1936) grew up at the home of her grandparents Russell Brown and Eliza Johnson Brown. She married Joseph "Joe' Banks the son of Frank Banks and Caroline Brown. (Joe Banks and Annie Brown Banks descendants are later in the book)

Rosa Brown (1875)

Russell Brown Jr. (1876-1955). At the age of 25, Russell married Virginia Davis daughter of Franklin and Lizzie Davis on September 30, 1901. The couple lived at 27 West Jackson St. Richmond, VA. He worked as a laborer.

Ezekiel Brown (December 9, 1877 - May24, 1939) He married Josephine Johnson in 1905. His second marriage was to Frances Goodman (May 7, 1892 – May 31, 1942) daughter of Jordan and Phoebe Banks Goodman on December 26, 1906 in Amelia, VA. The couple divorced on July 23, 1919. Ezekiel lived in Richmond, Virginia and passed away at the home of his nephew, Samuel Brown.

Beverly Brown (1879 - July 12, 1935) married Estelle Carey (1883 - 1963) the daughter of Robert Carey and Eliza Giles Carey on November 11, 1903. Stella was a midwife and after Beverly's death, Stella later married James Bland son of Willie Bland and Martha Giles on September 21, 1947. James Bland was employed as a laborer for Owenby Auctioneer. It should be mentioned that Stella raised James from childhood. Beverly Brown and Estelle "Aunt Stella" Carey had one child Rosa Brown Jasper (1908 - 1958) she married Carey Jasper Jr. (May 9, 1890 - 1958) son of Carey Jasper and Lydia Bannister of Amelia.

Stella Carey (Aunt Stella – The midwife)

Moses Brown

Moses Brown (1820 – August 1890) a slave of the Red Lodge Plantation. Moses was a farmer. He was married to Harriet Johnson. From this union seven children were born at the Lodge. Like his siblings, Moses land was also a part of the Chancery suit at the Lodge.

Moses and Harriet Brown children

Annie Brown (1857)

Patty Brown (1868 - March 1887)

Patience Brown (1869 - October 22, 1935) on June 2,1883 married Stephen Banks (1855 -1928) son of Warner and Betsy Banks. From this union four children were born. 1. Pattie Banks Brown (1888 – November 17, 1962) married David Brown of Chesterfield, VA on October 1, 1918 and resided in Richmond, Virginia. From this union, several children were born; Abram "Bootsie" Brown (October 13, 1909 – November 9, 1969) was married to Betty L. Brown and had two sons, Robert Brown and James Brown. Rev. Wilson Edward Brown (1912 – 1991) married Florence Verla Gilliam. His second marriage was to Inez Arrington Thompson on Oct. 26, 1985 in Richmond, VA. Wilson and his first wife Florence had one daughter Doris Elizabeth Brown who married Charles Lee Shannon and later Charles Thompson Jr on September 1, 1980. From the union of Doris and Charles Shannon several children were born: Rev. Charles Lee Shannon born October 10, 1954 is the pastor of Mount Level Baptist Church in Ford, VA. Wilson Edward Shannon who pastors in Centralia VA, Rev. Charles Lee Shannon III is married to Shirley Shannon. Joann Elizabeth Shannon, Rev. Michael Ellis Shannon who was a pastors in Ashland, and Naomi Ruth Shannon. David Lee Brown (August 10, 1924 – September 23, 2003) who served in the U.S. Navy during World War II and is buried in Quantico Cemetery. Arthur Brown (1925 – 1975) married Idella Elizabeth Ross on April 15, 1950 in Richmond, VA. The couple divorced on October 5, 1967. Edna Mae Brown Johnson Blakes (1926 – 2001), Anna Brown (1929), James Brown (1929), and Linwood Brown (1931)

2. Harry Banks (January 1892 - January 30, 1963) he married Maria Greene on September 30, 1912 in Richmond, Virginia. He later married Nettie Jones in Richmond, VA. 3. Mary Cobb (September 27 1895 - May 13, 1959) married Jeff Cobb and resided in Richmond, VA. 4. Linwood Banks (June 20, 1985 - December 18, 1985) was a member of Liberty Baptist church. Linwood married Geneva Ruffin. (see descendants on the Brown/Ruffin family)

Moses Brown (1870 – August 1890)

Mary Brown (1872-1890) died at the age of 18.

**Martha Brown Bannister Gibson** (1878 – October 14, 1943) a faithful member of Liberty Baptist Church. She is remembered for her singing in the church. Evelyn Harris remembers Mrs. Martha singing "Jesus is on the mainline tell him what u want". Her granddaughter Della Montague remembers her singing an old gospel hymn "Precious Memories." She married Joseph Bannister (1850 – 1917) on February 19, 1903 in Amelia, VA. Joseph was the son of Jordan and Rosena Bannister. He enlisted as a private in Company H 5th regiment of the Colored Infantry in the US Army. He received an honorable discharged in North Carolina, on April 26, 1865. He passed away in 1917. For many years, Martha Bannister was a sexton of the Mattoax Presbyterian Church until a debilitating stroke left her unable to continue the job. Her daughter-in-law Margaret Bannister and also her granddaughter, Della took over the position. She later married James Gibson of Amelia, VA.

Leona, Joseph Sr., Joseph Jr, and Harriet (baby) Bannister

Leona Bannister (July 1905 - August 8, 1965) married Landon Jasper and later married Andrew Askew. From the union children were born; 1. William Roosevelt Jasper (May 21, 1922 - October 11, 1982) married Virginia Best. 2. Monroe Arthur Bannister (October 23, 1923 - November 11, 1955) married Ethel Lee Vauters on June 28, 1950 in Richmond, VA. 3. Ecclesiastes Lyons Jasper (1925 – 2002); 4. Thaddeus Jasper (October 21, 1926 – March 16, 1988) 5. Shirley Jasper 1929 and is still living, and 6. Charles Jasper (1932) is still living.

Isaac Bannister (March 26, 1906 – October 20, 1971) according to the 1940 census, Isaac and his wife Mae Bannister (April 7, 1907 – June 1995) lived on 1222 David Hill Avenue in Baltimore, MD. He worked as a chauffeur. At the time Mae was a maid but later became a photographer.

Deacon Joseph Bannister (May 12, 1910 - April 23, 2004) was a lifelong faithful member of Liberty Baptist Church. He married Margaret Chambers on June 24, 1934. Deacon Bannister was a hardworking man he worked for Sonny Anderson, Charlie Gryder and also worked on the Council farm. He also raised pigs and cows, and had one of the best gardens. Deacon Joseph and Margaret Bannister children: Dallas Bannister (1932) Martha Bannister Ellis, Dorothy Bannister Bradley, Joseph Banister Jr., Margaret Bannister Everett, Della Bannister Montague and Nancy Bannister Wallace.

Mrs. Della Bannister Montague lived in New Yok for many years and later returned to Amelia, VA. Upon her return, she was steadfast in taking care of her parents until they passed away. She has been a great help since the inception of this project. Mrs. Della, has been a positive role model in the lives of many people. Her faithfulness at the Liberty Baptist Church has been shown down through the years. She has helped many youth and has served faithfully as a choir member. She is a pillar in the community and I am blessed for all the years she encouraged me. Nancy Bannister Wallace a family historian and researcher in her own right gives the Bannister genealogy see the book Our Stories Our Struggles: A history of African Americans in Amelia County, VA. Vol.2 written by Dr. Henry Featherston.

Harriet Bannister Johnson (1912 - 1978) she was a faithful member of Liberty Baptist Church and was married to Cyrus Johnson (1908 - 1993) son of Martha Johnson Epps. Five children were born to this union, Cyrus Johnson Jr (October 22, 1929 – May 26, 2013) who was married to Mary Ward. From this union one child was born, Juliet J. Morales, six grandchildren and two great- grandchildren; Julia Johnson who has two sons, Kenneth Johnson and Keith Johnson who has a son; Alease Delphine Johnson (1933 – 2015) who has one son Roderick; Virginia Johnson (June 10, 1935 – March 21, 1977) married Leroy Wade (1936) on June 16, 1956 in Amelia, VA. They had one son, Leroy Wade Jr. who has one daughter. Isaac Johnson Jr. who is married to Arlene Hicks and has one daughter Tammy J. Tyler and a grandchild.

The Home of Cyrus and Harriet Johnson

Cyrus and Harriet

Joseph Bannister daughters (Della Bannister Montague (far right) and Alice Lewis

Deacon and Mrs. Joseph Bannister & Family

Deacon Isaac Bannister

Cyrus Sr, Harriet, Arlene and Isaac

Leroy Sr, Leroy Jr, and Virginia J. Wade

Cyrus Johnson Jr.

Moses Brown Descendants

Gerald, Cyrus Jr, and Isaac Johnson

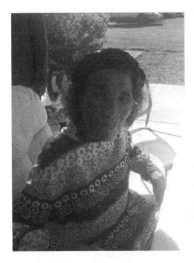
Julia Johnson

Isaac, Arlene and Tammy

Alease J. Hagwood

Daughters of Deacon and Mrs. Joseph Bannister

Mr. and Mrs. Joseph Bannister Jr.   **Martha Bannister Bradley and husband**

The Finney Family

A few years ago Carolyn Carroll mentioned to me that while at Food Lion in Powhatan County, Virginia her husband introduced her to a man named Essex Finney. After conversing with him he told Carolyn that his father told him that he was related to the Hyde family of Amelia. Carolyn and I spent hours trying to find the connection. She found a picture on ancestry of a man named John Finney who my father favors a lot. Little did we know it wasn't from the Hyde side that the family ties with the Finney's connect it is with the Brown family. After I made the connection through the documentations of Senator Archer estate. One of my DNA cousins Garland who has ties to the Lodge connected with a Finney descendant Moriah Adams. It was Moriah and her mom Samone that invited me over to the Finney's Family gathering. I quickly asked my dad and Dale Hyde to ride with me and all three of us where amazed at how nice and receiving they were to us. We were also amazed at the family resemblances and on August 19, 2015 the Hyde family were blessed to have Samone and Moriah Adams join our family cookout. It was there Fannie Hyde Baylor recalled the time her and Samone's grandmother Fannie Johnson Finney used to visit her grandmother Martha Reid. Essex and the Finney Family has a great Legacy and I am most fortunate to say I am connected to such an awesome Family.

Essex, Emanuel III and Emanuel Jr. **Dr. Maurice Finney** **Carlton Finney**

Siblings of Nancy Brown continued.

Julia Ann Brown

(1823- December1869)

Julia Ann Brown was born in 1823 and was a slave of the Red Lodge Plantation. She was the ancestor of the Epps, and Finney Families. Her name was listed on the Slave Inventory Records of Sen. William S. Archer in the 1855 court document. She was married to Cyrus Mariah Epps (1795 - 1869) and was the mother of four children Susan Finney, Edmund Epps, Ann Epps Rison, and Cyrus "Sye" Epps (1858 - March 2, 1935).

Susan Epps Finney (April 1842 - July 9, 1921) was born at "The Lodge" and later served as a nurse there. The Finney oral history states that Susan was sold to John B. Harvie who owned Gilliam -Harris Plantation in Powhatan, Va. It was during this time, Susan met and married Essex Finney (1843) son of an Indian John Finney and Mary Dixon of Mill Quarter Plantation which was also owned by the Harvie Family. Essex was a farmer, carpenter and a millwright. According to the Finney family book, he did extensive work for the Jones family who owned a mill. From my research it is known that the owner of the mill name was Samuel Jones of Jones Mill. The mill was formerly named Giles Mill which was owned by Gov. William Branch Giles. Essex was an expert on the water wheel that powered the mill. According to the Finney family book, Mary Dixon is a descendant of an African King. It is known that many of the Dixon family were once owned by the Tabb Family in Amelia, VA. Essex Finney was a carpenter which caused him to travel for days at a time. According to the United Census 1870, Essex and Susan lived in Amelia, Virginia. It is documented that Susan Epps first cousin Preston Jones, lived with them at the time. After the war, Essex and his brother purchased 30 acres of land which was deeded on January 4, 1874. The land is between The Fighting Creek and the Lodge. Mr. Essex Finney told me there was a bridge that crossed over the river into the lodge. Essex and Susan are buried in the family cemetery on the Finney's land. The descendants of Essex and Finney are numerous however, here are the first 2 generations of the Finney Family.

Children of Essex and Susan

Mary Ann Reynolds (1864 – 1913) she had two children; A daughter 1. Julia Reynolds (1897) and lived in Philadelphia, Penn. 2. Samuel Reynolds lived in Cleveland, Ohio.

Julia Finney (1866)

Essex Finney Jr. (1869 – 1933) was a carpenter and a farmer. Essex married Alice Mosby and had a daughter named Ann Finney (1887) After Alice death, Essex married Bertha Robinson and had a son, George Carroll Finney (1905 – July 13, 2000) who was married to Odessa Finney and lived in Long Island, New York.

John Finney (April 1, 1870 – January 3, 1951) a man of Integrity purchased an extensively farm where he farmed his own land. John married Fannie Peyton Johnson (May 4, 1877 – July 5, 1950) from the Pleasant Grove communities of Amelia. 12 children were born from this union. John was a member of Liberty Baptist Church Amelia, VA. Fannie attended St. Paul College, Virginia State College and Hampton Institute. was a teacher and a member of Pleasant Grove Baptist Church. Fannie also served for many years as teacher at the Pine Hill Elementary School which was an all-black school in Powhatan, VA. Fannie taught the first grade to the sixth grade. John later purchased 100 acres and later the Finney family owned up to 650 acres of land in the Macon District of Powhatan County, Virginia. John and Fannie are both buried at Pleasant Grove Baptist Church in Amelia, VA. Today John Finney House is still standing and is in great condition. Each year many of the Finney family travels near and far for their family gathering at the home of John Finney.

Children of John and Fannie Johnson Finney

Clifford Finney November 18, 1900 – 1963 moved to Long Island, New York and married Lessie Parker (1907-1980) in 1925. They had nine children: 1. Cleotha Grant (1927 – 1990) married Claude Grant. From this union two children were born, Cynthia Grant and Claude Grant. 2. Clifford Finney Jr. (1928 – 2001) was in the United States Army and served in Korea. He married Helen and had two children, Charles and Cecil Finney 3. Ruth Finney (1929 – 2004) 4. Gerald Finney (1931 – 1960) was a 1950 graduate of Bridgehampton High School. He served in the United States Navy and later worked for Ford Motor Company in New Jersey. He married Barbara Rogers in 1960. From this union two children were born, Tara and Gerald Finney Jr. 5. Carleton Finney was born March 18, 1934 he moved to New York and enlisted into the United States Navy in 1952. During his tenure in the Navy, Carlton, served in Morocco, Guam, Texas, San Francisco, England, Portugal, France, Spain and Italy. Carlton married Flora Jackson on June 15, 1962. The couple had two children, Electra and Robin. Carlton retired from the Navy after twenty-two years of service and lived in Morocco until he returned to the United States in 1985. Since that time, he lived in New Jersey and Powhatan County, Virginia where he lives today. Now in his 80s Carlton is a man of great wisdom. I am glad I had the opportunity to meet him. 6. Mary Finney Woodson (1938 – 1990) called Peggy attended Bridgehampton High School. She married Charlie Woodson and was the mother of three children, Eileen, Patricia and Dennis. 7. 8. Donald Finney born in 1940 is a retired veteran of the United States Army where he served as a Military policeman and served in Germany. He married Jolean and the couple has three children; Craig, Kenneth and Tanya 9. Gary Finney born in 1941 owned and later retired from his own Typewriter Repair business. He married Ann Lucas in 1956 and they have two children, Ann and Gary Finney Jr. 10. Faye Holmes (1944) was a 1982 graduate of Bridgehampton High School and received

several college degrees in Education. Faye taught Spanish to Elementary school students in Richmond, VA and retired in 1999. She has one daughter Tracy.

John Finney "Jack" (January 2, 1902 - August 18, 1968) married Fannie Darden (August 7, 1907 - February 13, 1969) They had four children: 1. Helen Finney Gilliam born in 1930 was a graduate of Southampton High School in Long Island, NY. Helen married Charles Gilliam in 1951 and from this union 5 children were born, Paul, Cynthia, Thomas, Vivian, and Christine. 2. Ursula Finney Stephens born in 1931. She graduated in 1949 from Southampton High School. She married Haywood Beverly in 1951 and later in 1975 she married Cecil Stephens. She is the mother of two daughters, Patricia Banks and Denise Beverly. 3. Lawrence Finney born in 1934 married Cornelia Mealy on July 24, 1955. The couple had three children, Lawrence Finney (1958 – 1995) 4. Curtis Finney born in 1935 he obtained several degrees in music and served as Minister of Music at University Methodist Church in Syracuse, NY. He also worked as Chorus Master for the Syracuse Opera Company. Professor Finney has received many awards and grants in honor of his hard work and accomplishments. He is married to Nancy.

Annie Nita Finney Willis (August 20, 1903 – August 22, 1981) married James Arthur Willis (1896-1972) They had five children 1. Phyllis Snow Talbot (July 19, 1923) married Dr. David Talbot on June 4, 1946; 2. Fannie Key (October 14, 1924) married Richard Key; 3. Maria Louise Manson (October 13, 1925) married Roger Manson 4. Pattie Goode Smith (August 5, 1927) was married to Joseph Smith; 5. Annie Juanita Finney Harrison (September 27, 1928) married Moses Harrison on April 2, 1953.

Junius Finney (April 1905 - 1912)

Constancia Finney Hunter (November 6, 1906 - 1949) married Harold Hunter was a school teacher in Powhatan, Virginia.

Albert Finney (August 1908) married Nellie Hubbard had two children 1. Virgil Finney (1930) married Gertrude 2. Lawrence Finney married Ji Suk

Margaret Finney Valentine (January 12, 1910 – December 3, 1986) married Nathaniel valentine and had one son; Nathaniel Finney Valentine (May 9, 1953 – December 6, 1975)

Jeanette C. Campbell (July 11, 1911 – October 20, 1990) married Robert Dean Campbell (1911 – 1975)

Essex Eugene Finney Sr. (July 9, 1912 – February 21, 2003) married Etta Burton (1916 – 1954) They one son Essex Finney Jr. born May 16, 1937 (see page 122)

Emory Morris Finney (October 11, 1913 – August 8, 1985) married Mary Dabney on December 27, 1938. He was owner of Finney's grocery store in Powhatan, Virginia. He also was a member of the NAACP. They had two children Joan Gilbert graduated from Powhatan Public School System in 1958. She graduated from North Carolina Central University in 1962 and later received a Masters of library Science from the University of Maryland in 1984. Joan worked as a patient librarian at the VA Hospital in Lebanon, PA. She also served as an elementary school librarian in both Virginia and Detroit, Michigan. She was later employed as a Technical Information Specialist for the Department of Defense in Washington DC. Rev. Maurice Dabney Finney who resides in Charlotte, VA. Maurice is a retired educator serving as a teacher, assistant principal, principal and Superintendent during his career in Education. He is married to Mrs. Beatrice Womack. Maurice is the pastor of the St. Andrews Baptist Church in Cullen, VA and also the Aspen Hill Baptist Church in Brook Neal, VA.

Novella Finney Ambrose (March 11, 1915) was a school teacher in Powhatan County, Virginia. She was married George Ambrose Jr; one son George Spencer Ambrose.

Paul Finney (March 28, 1916)

Lillian Johnson (June 3, 1918 – October 20, 2000) married Julian Johnson on June 16, 1948

Hettie Finney Hewitt (1872) married Dudley Hewitt and lived in Powhatan, VA. She was a school teacher in Powhatan, Virginia. Dudley and Hettie Children: Essex Hewitt, Milton Hewitt, Bernice H. Mathias and Blanche Cannady.

Robert Louis Finney (1875-1966) graduated from Virginia Normal and Collegiate Institute (now Virginia Union University) in Petersburg, VA in 1898. Robert was a man of great determination, the Finney's family book states that once Robert walked 40 miles from Petersburg to Powhatan County, Virginia. Robert worked various jobs to pay his way through school. He was employed by the Powhatan County School Board in (1898-1899) and taught at a number of schools. He married Nannie in 1903 who was also a teacher and he moved to Cumberland, VA where he acquired a farm. Robert and Nannie Finney Children: Mary Flournoy, Robert Alvin Finney (1905 - 1987), Ernest Finney (1906 – 1992), Nannie McDaniel, Essex Bernard Finney (1909 – 1994), Claude Finney, Bertha F. White, Edward Finney, and Otelia F. Darling.

Martha Finney Mergison (1876 - 1967) lived in Richmond, VA.

Lillie Finney Goode (1879) lived in Richmond, VA. Lillie had one son, Oliver Goode married Pauline who lived in the Bronx, New York.

Maggie Finney Eubanks (1882 - 1949) lived in Baltimore, MD. She married Robert Eubanks and had three children: 1. Walter Eubanks (1906 - 1982) and Robert Eubanks Jr. (1911) who also lived in Baltimore, MD. Maggie.

Spencer Finney (December 25, 1885 - 1975) was married to Edmonia Finney, He was a faithful member of Pine Hill Baptist Church serving as a deacon and the church clerk for many years. And served in other capacities at the church. Spencer and Edmonia Finney had a son, Colonel Finney who married Alberta Finney. A granddaughter, Geraldine Morris and many other descendants.

Daisy Finney (1889 – July 7, 1971)

Certificate of Death
Commonwealth of Virginia
Bureau of Vital Statistics
State Board of Health

Form No. 12

16205

1 PLACE OF DEATH
- County of: Powhatan
- Magisterial District of: Spencer
- Or Inc. Town of: ___
- Or City of: ___

Registration District No. 121A Registered No. 6

2 FULL NAME: Susana Finney
- (A) Residence: No. ___ Macon, Virginia

PERSONAL AND STATISTICAL PARTICULARS

3 SEX: Female
4 COLOR OR RACE: Negro
5 SINGLE, MARRIED, WIDOWED, OR DIVORCED: Widowed
5A HUSBAND OF (OR) WIFE OF: Essex Finney, Sr
6 DATE OF BIRTH: ___ 19__
7 AGE: 77 years

8 OCCUPATION OF DECEASED:
- (A) Trade, Profession: At Home

9 BIRTHPLACE:
- City or Town: Amelia County
- State: Virginia

10 NAME OF FATHER: Cyrus Eppes
11 BIRTHPLACE OF FATHER: Amelia County, Virginia
12 MAIDEN NAME OF MOTHER: Julia —
13 BIRTHPLACE OF MOTHER: Amelia County, Virginia

14 INFORMANT: Essex Finney, Jr.
(Address) Macon, Va

15 FILED: July 21, 1921 W. R. Davis, Registrar

MEDICAL CERTIFICATE OF DEATH

16 DATE OF DEATH: July 9th 1921
17 I hereby certify that I attended deceased from July 4, 1921 to July 9th, 1921
That I last saw her alive on July 7th, 1921
And that death occurred on date stated above, at 1 A.M.
The cause of death was as follows:

Cerebral Hemorrhage

(Duration) yrs. ___ mos. 5 ds.

Contributory (secondary): ___

18 Where was disease contracted if not at place of death? —
Did an operation precede death? No
Was there an autopsy? No
What test confirmed diagnosis? No Test

(Signed) R. D. Tucker, M.D.
July 9th, 1921 (Address) Powhatan, Va

19 PLACE OF BURIAL: At her residence
DATE OF BURIAL: July 10th 1921
20 UNDERTAKER: Essex Finney, Jr.
Address: Macon, Va

Essex Finney the son of Essex (Eugene) Finney and Etta Burton was born in the Macon community in Powhatan, VA on May 16, 1937 and was raised on the 200-acre family farm owned at that time by his grandfather John Finney. It was there Essex and his family raised tobacco, wheat, corn, hay, and livestock. Essex attended the Pine Hill Elementary School where his grandmother Fannie Johnson Finney taught school the first through six grades. He attended and graduated from Pocahontas High School in 1954. Essex furthered his education being of one of the eight blacks to enroll in Virginia Tech University. Essex graduated in 1959 with a degree in Agricultural Engineering. It was that same year, he attended and graduated from Penn State in 1960. He later in 1961, began his PHD program at Michigan State East Lansing. In 1963 he received his PHD and later entered the Military in 1963. Essex continues to be the glue that holds the Finney family together as one. Essex was employed with Beltsville Research Center which is the largest research center for Agriculture. In 1973 selected to go to Princeton as a Princeton Fellow from 1973 – 1974. In 1977 Essex was appointed as the Assistant Director at the Beltsville Agricultural Research Center. has served in the Office of the Science Advisor to former President Jimmy Carter in Washington D.C from July 1980 to June 1981. In 1988 Essex went to Philadelphia as an associate director of one the Agricultural Research Service. He returned to Beltsville as director of the Agricultural Research Center in 1989. In 1992 he worked as the associate administrator for the Agricultural Research Service in Washington, D.C. for the nationwide programs and research. He has shaken hands with President's and other officials and has been honored and interviewed by History Makers. Beyond all the prestigious honors he has received, Essex remains humble and his love for his family and the legacy of his Ancestors shines bright. Every year he continues to keep this Legacy alive by having the annual family gathering. Essex also is responsible for the Finney Family book which has been an asset to this project. This only a brief representation of the accomplishments of Essex Finney there is so much more accomplishments, and achievements that Mr. Finney have made.

Essex is married to Mrs. Ellen Finney and has two children: Essex Finney III and Karen Shelton and has several grandchildren.

All photos of the Finney Family are made courteous by Essex Finney and family. Excerpts of this page was taken from two interviews of Essex Finney Oral History with Essex Finney: University of VA Tech and History Makers.

John Finney, Mrs. Fannie J. Finney, Connie and Maggie

Spencer, Margaret, and Jeannette

Novella, Eugene and Etta B. Finney

Edward Finney

Emory and Mary D. Finney

Dr. Maurice Finney

Joan Finney Gilbert

Novella Ambrose with students at Pine Hill School

Pattie, Etlee Carrington and Maria

Essex Finney

Essex Jr. and Ellen Finney

Mary Finney

Phyllis Willis Talbot and Family

Nita and Novella F. Ambrose

Pattie and children: Arthur, Ben, Quentin, Carroll, Samone, Joseph Jr., and Alma

Descendants of Messiah Epps and Julia Brown

Edmund Epps (1846-) married Johanna Johnson of Nottoway, Virginia on February 18, 1870 and resided in Amelia County, Virginia.

Randall David Epps (December 14, 1865) married Matilda Washington while residing in Richmond, Virginia and later married Mattie Fuller.

Emma Baylor (January 5, 1872 – April 15, 1955) married John Baylor of Richmond, Virginia on September 23, 1930. The couple lived in Richmond, Virginia.

Spencer Epps (Dec 1873) married Mollie Hobbs in 1898 and lived on 306 Stephenson in Richmond, VA. He remarried on October 10, 1901 to Perline Jackson. In 1904 he resided at 400 Monteiro Avenue in Richmond, VA. Spencer worked as a butler for many years.

Harriet Epps (1882) married Reuben Ruffin on July 26, 1905 from this union five children were born:

1. Esterine Ruffin (1906 – 1928), 2. Ruby Ruffin Falls (1908 – August 1, 1988), 3. Lottie Ruffin Falls (1907) 4. Willie Ruffin (1914) was a butcher and 5. Emma Ruffin (1920). She later married Gillis Dunn (1881-1956) in Richmond, VA on March 18, 1944.

William Epps 1886

Lottie Epps Daily (1886) lived in Richmond, Virginia.

Leila Price (May 25, 1887 – March 9, 1950)

Edmund Epps (1887 – 1961) married Martha Johnson and raised step son Cyrus Johnson. The couple lived in the Pleasant Grove Community. He is remembered most for his farm and his white horse and fancy buggy that was his transportation. He is buried at Liberty Baptist Church.

Mary Epps (1888) married Field Bland (1883) on November 24, 1908 in Amelia County, Virginia

Robert Epps (1892) lived in Amelia Virginia

Sallie Epps (January 1894) married John Bailey November 17, 1915 in Richmond, VA.

Calvin Epps (1896)

Joseph Epps (1897) lived in Richmond, VA.

George Brown

(1846)

A slave on the Red Lodge Plantation married Flora Johnson (1850) daughter of Billy Johnson and Fannie Johnson. The couple had five children.

Gifford Brown (1874 – January 30, 1953)

Washington Brown (1875 - 1943) grew up in Red Lodge later moving down the road to the. He worked for Mrs. Mason and after being fired and put off the land. Wash Brown lived not far from Brick Church School. Late in life, Wash was an amputee but that didn't stop him from working. Wash worked for Mrs. Mason who lived at Mason Corner. He died December 25, 1943 in Amelia, VA.

Edmonia Brown Johnson (March 1875 – February 8 1916) married Wash Johnson in 1897 and from this union one child was born; Flora Johnson Jones wife of Rev. Daniel Jones.

Hampton Brown (1888 – June 14, 1956) On November 27, 1913 Hampton married Lottie Bell Watson daughter of Richard and Agnes Watson of the Brick Church Area in Amelia, Virginia. Hampton and Lottie had four children; 1. Gladys Brown Shepperson (May 7, 1911 - November 7, 1960) married Roy Glen Shepperson (1913 – 1996) on June 20, 1936 in Amelia County, Virginia. The couple were divorced on November 30, 1948. She later moved to Philadelphia, Pennsylvania where she died and was buried at Mt. Lawn cemetery. 2. Dorothy Brown Booker (October 3, 1914 – February 16, 1995) married Robert Booker (1914 – 1977) son of Fred Booker and Rebecca Hyde Booker in Amelia, Virginia on March 26, 1965. 3.George Brown (1916) 4. William Brown (1919)

Martha Brown Wilson (1892 – December 25, 1942) lived in the Brick church area of Amelia, Virginia. After the passing of her niece Flora, Martha helped raised her great- niece Mary. In later years, she married Rev. Jeff Wilson Sr. in Amelia, VA.

John Brown

John Brown (1845) was a farmer he married to Louisa Venable daughter of Tillman "Archer" Venable and Lydia "Archer "Venable on October 20, 1875. It is said that the Archer's gave him 50 acres of land which is still in his descendants, The Ruffin family name. From this union four children were born Westley, Ada, Mack and Lettie Brown. After the death of Louisa, John married Georgianna Washington daughter of George and Mary Washington of Prince Edward County, Virginia on October 20, 1876. Mike Banks named his daughter Georgia after his aunt-in-law Georgianna. There is little information on John's children other than Westley and Ada. Westley Brown who married Judy Conway on February 23, 1899 in Amelia, VA.

Ada Brown (March 11, 1877 – December 19, 1961) is pictured right. She married Ottoway Ruffin the son of Humphrey and Ellen Ruffin in Amelia. Catherine Hyde Booker, vividly remembers Mrs. Ada sitting on the porch at her home singing There's a Bright Side Somewhere and other hymns. Children of Ada and Ottoway: Louise Ruffin married Coley Wilson and lived in the Brick church area of Amelia, Virginia. John Allen Ruffin aka "Weeks" married Geneva Banks daughter of Joseph and Annie Brown Banks. He was a hardworking man who worked for the Anderson Saw Mill. Mrs. Helen Bannister remembers her father working all week for little pay like most African Americans during that time. According to Mrs. Ethel S. Morris, Weeks lived in several locations when and his wife were younger. The Couple resided on Murphy's place off of route 609. He also lived on Genito Rd in the Mattoax area before returning to his birth place at the lodge. At home Weeks raised pigs and chickens and other types of livestock. Children of John and Geneva: James Ruffin, Latifah Aileen Ruffin married Elco Person. Mrs. Lateefah better known to her grandchildren and so many others as "Big Momma." She helped raised many children and is loved by all. Mrs. Lateefah is the mother of five children. Alvin Ruffin who married the late Geneva Watson Ruffin (1953 – 2016) Mrs. Freda Ruffin Porter who married Percy Porter and Bernice Ruffin Hueston Jefferson who married William Hueston and later George Jefferson. Aileen has many grandchildren. Helen Ruffin who is married to Dallas Bannister they have three daughters and one son who is deceased Garland Fitzgerald Bannister (October 20, 1965 – December 2, 2000) was married to Deleah White. Wilson Ruffin married Hattie Patterson. Allen Ruffin married Fannie has two daughters, Christine Ruffin and Patricia Ruffin and, Clarence Ruffin Jr. (Sad was his nickname) was married to Martha Woolridge. They had four children and several grandchildren. Virginia Ruffin was married to Charles Mitchell and the couple has three children and grandchildren. She later married Glen Smith. Virginia and Charles has three children and several grandchildren. Thelma Eggleston married Franklin Eggleston the couple has three children and several grandchildren. Frances Ruffin McCoy was married to Phillip McCoy and two children and grandchildren. Joseph Ruffin married Margaret Middleton and has six children and he has grandchildren. Geneva Dorothy Ruffin (June 23, 1911 – Jan 15, 2005) known to many as "Ms. Peach or Grandma Peach." She was raised in the Lodge and married Linwood Banks. Her cooking was unmatched and she was loved by many especially her family. She had a special love for the children of the community and would often host the annual Easter Egg hunt at her home. Her children: Robert Banks (May 3, 1933 – March 18, 2016) resided in Clarksville, TN served in the United States Army and was employed as a machine operator at the Zinc plant. He was a member of Walnut Grove Baptist Church. Robert, was married to Frances Banks. They had two children, Roderick

Banks, Christopher and Toni Banks. Robert has several grandchildren. William Westley Banks Sr. (October 13, 1938 – February 14, 2003) married Vivian Bell and he later married Martha Reed. William served in U.S Army in Korea. Chidren of Westley Banks: Deacon Gloria Banks Williams has two children and Grandchildren. 2. William Westley Banks Jr. and has two children; Brian Banks married Aurora and has children and grandchildren. 3. Eric Banks married Margaret Palmer and has children; 4. Kerry Banks; Harold Banks married Flora Irene Jones on February 20, 1965 has three children one of them is deceased Wanda Spratley and has several grandchildren. 5. Marvin Banks who is retired from the Healthcare field.

John and Louisa has many descendants

Marriage License and Death Certificate for Ada Brown Ruffin

Name:	Ada Brown
Gender:	Female
Marital Status:	Single
Race:	Black
Age:	22
Birth Date:	1877
Birth Place:	Amelia Co., VA.
Marriage Date:	28 Dec 1899
Marriage Place:	Amelia, Virginia
Father:	Jno.
Mother:	Louisa
Spouse:	Ottoway Ruffin
FHL Film Number:	30474
Reference ID:	Pg 91

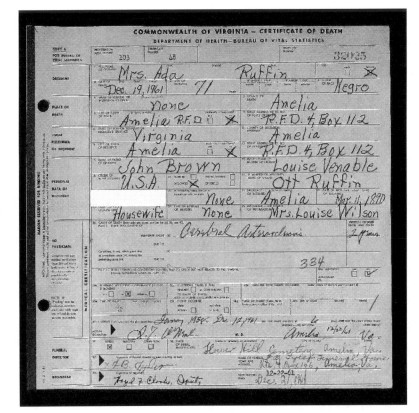

Linwood and Geneva Ruffin   William "Wes" Banks   Bernard, Gloria and Jennifer Williams

Alvah (Bootsie) Mitchell, Virginia, and Clarence Ruffin   Clarence Ruffin and friends   Wilson Ruffin

Bernice Hueston   Coley Wilson along with Mr. Buck Harris   Robert Banks

Helen Ruffin Bannister

Helen and her sister Frances

Alvin and Geneva

Amy Bannister

Travis Ruffin

Garland Bannister

Freda Ruffin

Richard Brown

(May 1854 – July 22, 1929)

Richard was born the youngest son to Davy and Chloe. He was a farmer and a laborer. On December 31, 1879 Richard married Betsey Crump (1858) daughter of ex – slaves Madison and Caroline Crump the couple had three children and lived in Red Lodge. After Betsey death Richard married Sarah Ruffin on May 23, 1885. Sarah was the daughter of Humphrey and Ellen Archer Ruffin. Like the majority of blacks during Richard lifetime, he could not read and write but he worked hard. In 1929 Richard moved in with his daughter Clara Brown Booker where he resided at 1218 ½ Parkwood Avenue where he died.

Richard Brown and Betsey Crump

James Brown (1874)

Caroline Brown (October 1879)

Children of Richard Brown and Sarah Ruffin

Ellen Brown (May 1884)

William Brown (October 1885)

Chlorie Brown (October 1887 – August 1890)

Clara Brown Booker (1888)

Armstead Charles Brown (July 4, 1890 – January 8, 1958) was married to Sadie Brown and lived in Richmond, VA. In the 1940s the couple lived at 750 9th Street in Richmond, VA.

Eliza Brown (1894)

Elisha Brown (January 1894)

Elijah Brown (February 5, 1895 – November 28, 1978) worked for the Garnett family in The Lodge. He was married three times first to Grace Magnolia Davis on March 29, 1957. His second wife was Mary Melissa Hubbard and they were married on March 29, 1957. His third marriage was on April 29, 1960 to Marie Jones.

Daniel Brown (October 18, 1899 – April 2, 1957) received fourth grade education which was normal for blacks during the time. According to the 1920 census, Daniel and his brother Elijah worked as farm hands and lived with Joseph Garnett Family. Daniel was married to Mary Lillie Richardson (1900 – 1993). In 1930 Daniel and Mary lived briefly in Richmond, Virginia where they rented a house for $10.00 a month at 95-A Price Street and Daniel worked at the Jank shop. During the 1930's Dan and Mary returned to Amelia and lived on Rt. 609 and later returned to Red Lodge and moved into the former home of the Scott Family. Children of Daniel and Mary Brown: 1. Carrie Bell Brown (1924 – March 18, 1945) married Mike Banks Sr. and had Mike Banks Jr. (deceased), Roosevelt Banks (deceased) and Helen B. Moseley; 2. Robert James Alfred Brown (1993) was a member of Flower Hill Baptist Church enlisted in the United States Army on June 15, 1943. On July 4, 1946 he married Rev. Luvenia Brown in Amelia, VA. Rev. Daniel J. Jones officiated the wedding ceremony. 3. Adele Goodman born 1927. She resides in New York and is the mother of two children, Robert Kimbrough and Frederick Kimbrough (who is deceased)

4. Daniel Brown Jr. married Lee and resided in New York 5. Dorothy Lee Brown (May 23,1930 – September 28, 1997) was the second wife of Mike Banks Sr. Children of Mike and Dorothy: Mary, Bethel, Archer (deceased), Georgia, Zaccheus (deceased), Doris, Linda and James Banks (see the Banks section); 6. Willie Lee Brown (June 21, 1933 – June 1982) was married to Martha Reed daughter of Joseph Reed and Martha Mitchell on June 10, 1953 in Nottoway, Virginia. At the time of his marriage, Willie occupation was listed as a farmer. He later resided in New Jersey. They had three children; Willie Brown Jr. who is deceased; Shirley Ann Brown who has three children; and Terry Brown who has three children. Chlorie Brown (October 1887 – August 1890) 7. James Edward Brown 8. Charlie Brown married Bell and has four children; Charlie Brown Jr, Theresa, Vickie and Deborah Brown. 9.Lucille Brown Carruth who married Allen Carruth, and has five children, Allen Carruth, Bryant Carruth, Andrea Carruth, Andre Carruth, and Avery Carruth.

Nellie Brown Jasper was married to Haskins Jasper. Nellie had two children: Victoria Leila Jasper (April 1, 1917 – October 9, 2001) who married Tyler and had two children: Nellie Jasper Harris, and James Tyler.

Clara Brown Booker (1888)

Armstead Charles Brown (July 4, 1890 – January 8, 1958) was married to Sadie Brown. They resided in Richmond, VA and had one daughter Mamie Brown (1903 – 1951) who received a college degree and became a school teacher for Richmond Public Schools. Mamie married Thomas Brown (1898) of South Carolina. Mamie lived on Idlewood Avenue and later at 2415 Lamb Avenue Richmond, VA. Mamie Brown had Five daughters, Nannie Brown Christian (April 5 1926 – May 19, 2003) was a former school teacher at the Richmond Public Schools. She was married to Sgt. Harold Randolph Christian (May 28, 1920 - July 10, 1967) a World War II veteran. The couple had one daughter, Cheryl; and one grandson. Clara Brown Henderson, Edna Brown Woolridge, Delores Brown Richardson.

Florence Brown

Reuben Brown (May 9, 1916 – May 1962)

Daniel Brown

Lillie Brown

Robert and Luvenia Rison Brown

Dorothy Lee Brown Banks

Daniel Brown Jr

Nannie Christian

Rev. Luvenia Brown

During an event over the summer at the Nash home in Red Lodge, Darlene Lewis who had been researching all of her family lines was talking about Red Lodge. Carolyn Hyde Carroll suggested to her that she should talk to me. After our first conversation, I was amazed at her and her son's information on history especially slavery. She shared her history with me and after finding out she was a DNA testing match on Gedmatch sharing cm which is in the bracket of 5th cousin. We exchange kit numbers and realize although its low we share a 5th cousin relationship and researched mutual matches. From all of my information and documentation we concluded that her ancestor Ben Brown was my ancestor Nancy's uncle. Apparently, he was sold from the Red Lodge and his son returned after slavery. Since that time, we have found other Brown descendants together and met one Chris Harris who is from the Brown and Ward family. We have talked it through, analyzed documents and even compared chromosome. We've concluded it's a Brown thing! I'm thankful for all of her efforts and encouragement during the process of research and writing this book.

Me, Darlene Lewis Robinson and her great-niece

Ben Brown and Rachel Brown

There is very little information on Ben Brown but it is believed he was sold at Prince Edward from The Lodge plantation. Ben had a son named **George Brown** (1835) married **Violet Banks** (1841 – 1880) daughter of Warner and Betsey Smith Banks of the Lodge Plantation in Amelia, VA. After Violet's death he married her sister Frances Banks (1855) one child was born who died as an infant; Emeline Brown (1887 – 1887)

Children of George and Violet Banks Brown

Willis Brown (June 1860 – December 28, 1914) married Betsie Carter of King William, Virginia and lived in Richmond, Virginia. He worked as a farm laborer in King William, VA and in New Kent, County. The couple adopted a son; George Brown (1902)

Israel Brown 1863)

James Brown (1867)

Lavinia Brown (1871 – July 21, 1918) lived in Richmond, Virginia

Sarah Brown

Molly Brown (1875 – 1939) married **Scott Branch** (1863 – 1921) son of Thomas and Hannah Branch on December 29, 1883. The couple had five children: Violet Branch (1884) Cleveland Branch (1887) According to the United States Census, Cleveland worked as laborer at the sawmill and he also was a farmer. Cleveland married Fannie Jackson daughter of Andrew Jackson (1840) and Matilda Sherman (1840). From this union six children were born: 1. Lula Jackson (1902) 2. Carrie Branch (1919 – 1967) married Mathew Ruffin (1908 – 1984) son of Robert Ruffin and Lucy Tinsley. Matthew was a farmer who raised cows, pigs, goats, chickens and tobacco. He worked at the saw mill. He was a Deacon at Flower Hill Baptist Church and was a Mason. Matthew always had a big garden each year. Mathew Ruffin and Carrie Branch children: Ophelia Ruffin Robinson married Marvin Edward Robinson and had children; Marvin Edward Robinson Jr.(deceased) married Sylvia; Lonnie Garland Robinson married Beverly Christian, Donna Paulette Logan, Sandra Robinson, Rudolph Robinson, Teresa Robinson. Josephine Ruffin Anderson (died 1978) married Leslie Everett Anderson had children; Adele Anderson, and Leslie Anderson is married to Linda Thornhill. Josephine also has grandchildren. Alease Ruffin Murray married Benjamin Murray Sr. From this union four children were born; Raymond Murray Sr. and is the father of four children and grandchildren; Russell Murray is married to Joyce Ann; and Sandra Scott is married to Lynzra Scott. Benjamin and Alease Murray. Eleanor Rebecca Ruffin was married to Samuel Lewis; Chidren of Sam and Eleanor Lewis: Charlene Lewis Yates is married to Ernest Yates; Samuel Lewis is married to Gloria Yancey, Gloria Lewis Nelms was married to the late Min. William Nelms; Thomas Everett Lewis; Rev. Nathaniel Lewis is married to Camilla Faye Lewis; Darlene Lewis Robinson. Gladys Marie Ruffin Clements married William "Sonny" Clements. The couple had two children; Lorraine Clements Patrick was married to Richard Patrick and had three children; 2 deceased. William Clements Jr. who is married to Shauna Clements and has two sons. Catherine Ruffin Epps married John Henry Epps and had a daughter; Jacqueline Epps. Ercelle Ruffin (June 20, 1942 – March 14, 2016) at an early age joined the Flower Hill Baptist Church in Amelia, VA. She later moved to Richmond where she lived for years and attended the Trinity Baptist Church. In later years, she returned home to Ruffin Lane in Amelia, VA and returned to her home church Flower Hill Baptist Church. She was employed as a dietician and retired from Johnston – Willis Hospital. On March 19, 2016 many family, and friends filled the Flower Hill Baptist Church to say their goodbyes to Ercelle. Many relatives and friends gave testimonials to her good heart and sweet personality. Ercelle has one daughter Barbara Byars. Matthew Ruffin married Carolyn Ross and had four daughters. He later married Gloria Robinson. Matthew and Carolyn children: Valerie Ruffin Giles married Sammie Giles; Amenta Ruffin married Wayne Johnson; Sherry Ruffin Ward; and Terri Ruffin. Fannie May Ruffin Carey who is the mother of Renita Archer Jordan, Henry Lee Archer; and Katrice Carey. Deacon Andrew Truman Ruffin married Evelyn Epps; Patricia Ruffin. The descendants of Matthew and Carrie are too numerous to name.

3. Garfield Scott Branch (July 9, 1917 – October 23, 1963) enlisted into United States Army July 9, 1942 in Pittsburg, Pennsylvania. He was a World War 2 Veteran and his service ended on July 9, 1946 and resided in Philadelphia, Pennsylvania. He was buried at the Long Island National Cemetery. 4. Daisy Lue Branch Edwards (September 29, 1920 – February 15, 1992) After finishing High school, Daisy moved to New York City and at the age of 20 she worked for the Rabinowitz Family on Sumner Avenue in New York. She lived in the Bronx until she passed away. 5. Mollie Branch (1922) 6. Cleveland E. Branch (August 23, 1923) 7. Louise Branch (1925);

Julia Brown (November 3, 1876)

Kate Brown Randolph (1875 – 1938) married John Randolph and from this union several children were born, Junius Randolph (July 4, 1894), Mary Randolph (1895) Luvenia Randolph (1895) Murry Randolph (died October 22, 1918) lived in Chester PA, Easter Randolph (1898) married James Frasier a farmer on December 27, 1916 in Amelia, VA. James Randolph (April 4, 1900) Marion Randolph (1902) Cora Randolph Foote (1905 – 1982)

Emma Brown (1877)

Carrie Ruffin

Matthew Ruffin

Eleanor Ruffin Lewis

Ercelle Ruffin

Eleanor Ruffin Lewis

Matthew and Carrie Ruffin

Gladys Ruffin Clements grew up on her father Matthew 100-acre farm on Ruffin lane off of Rt. 609 in Amelia County, Virginia. She is a lifelong member of Flower Hill Baptist Church where she has been active on the choir for many years. Gladys Clements, remembers being baptized at the creek behind her grandmother Fannie Jackson Branch home. Life on the farm wasn't easy, Gladys remembers growing up and working on the farm alongside her sister Eleanor. Each morning Gladys and her sister Eleanor, would get up before going to Brick Church school and milking two cows in the morning and two cows after they returned home. They worked the tobacco fields and tie up the tobacco. They also worked the gardens, the worked in the fields and shuck the corn. She vividly remembers cutting wood with her sister Eleanor with a cross cut saw. After marrying William Sonny Clements in 1956 she moved to Clements Lane right off of Genito Rd. in Amelia, VA. Gladys has made several drawings. Living on Clements lane, she remembers Mr. Ben Clements who had a wagon that was driven by two black steers. Gladys is a gifted lady pictured upper right is a drawing that Gladys produced in the 1960s.

When it comes to singing Gladys has been faithful in uplifting the name of Jesus she has sung in various groups including her Aunt Lizzie Ruffin Group and the Home Gospel Singers. Out of the many people I've met Mrs. Clements has been and remains one of the nicest person I could meet. Her loyalty to God, her family and friends is indescribable. She tries to help any and every one, she is well loved by all who ever has come in contact with her.

Home Gospel Singers   Gladys and Eleanor   Gladys

Richard Jr. and Richard Sr.   Daniel Patrick   William Clements Jr.

Darlene, Gladys, and Christian   Fannie and Catherine

Gladys Ruffin Clements   Katrice Carey   A Branch/Ruffin descendant

Barbara R. Byars   Terri, Matthew Ruffin Jr, Valerie Ruffin Giles   Lorraine C. Patrick

Note: These are only a few pics of the many descendants of Matthew and Carrie Branch Ruffin

George Brown and Heartly Brown (1830)

The name George Brown is seen numerous time in the neighborhood of Red Lodge during the late 1800s. He is believed to be close kinship to all of the Browns of the Lodge but the exact relationship is still uncertain.

George Brown (1830?) was the husband of Heartly Brown and they had five children; Sallie Brown Branch (March 1860 – February 6, 1940) married Charlie Branch and had several children; Ida Branch (1889), Atwood Branch (September 15, 1891 – April 30, 1956) married Ada Frazier (December 14, 1891- April 18, 1968) on April 24, 1913 in Amelia, VA. From this union several children were born; Robert Branch (1914 – October 1971), Estelle Branch Hilliard (May 30, 1915 – June 1979) Columbus Branch (1916), Helen Venable Branch Bell (March 21,1917 – January 15, 1996), Ephray Branch (1919), Bethel Sallie Branch Covington (August 24, 1920 – January 31, 2002) lived in New Jersey and worked for the Rice Family as a maid in 1940. Charles Branch (1923) married Mary Miles on March 23, 1940 and they were divorced on June 27, 1964. Bettie Cornelia Branch (1924 – 2003), Emma Jane Branch (April 8, 1926), and Pricilla Branch (1929); Charles Branch (1892) James Ellis Branch (1897 – 1956), Waddie Branch (1900 -1972), and Lee Branch (1902).

DNA Connections to the Brown Family

One of the greatest accomplishments of the modern Era is the advancement of DNA analysis through Ancestry.com, 23 and me, Family tree DNA and Gedmatch. While researching my mother maternal lineage, her 4th cousin DNA match (researcher) Garland Ervin a Texas native decided to test his mother's Lottie L. Ervin. After her DNA was complete he gave me access to view his DNA as well as his moms. While he was going through his DNA matches and his mother matches, he saw a lot of matches with the last name Goss, and Brown. He said that he grew up in the area of Texas and there were many Brown living in that area. From his research he reported that his ancestor, Alice Means may have been from Virginia. After much research, comparison of DNA matches, and other documents. It is certain that Garland is also a descendant of the Brown family of the Lodge and the Wigwam plantation. Alice was the daughter of Aggy Brown Hill and according to the generation pattern it appears that Aggy has a close family relationship to my ancestor Nancy Brown. Garland are one of the many DNA matches I chose to work with to compare DNA matches and try to confirm DNA matches. According to Garland Ervin, Alice Means and her family moved to Texas and were freed possibly upon arrival. What I have confirmed, is that there was a Thomas Means who was a plantation overseer for the Giles plantation during slavery and a farm manager in 1870 who later moved to Kansas as well as other places. There is also a connection with the Lusk family from Amelia, VA. After these findings, Garland asked me if the Giles family who last name is a familiar one in Amelia County history. I told him there were several Giles families that I know of in different parts of Amelia they may all be one family. I was told of the Giles family of Giles Distric in Amelia that lived not far from the Lodge who later migrated behind Liberty Baptist Church on to what was then called Horse Pen Branch. It is said that this family moved away many years ago and no one knew where they went. He quickly recalled to me that when he was younger he had a teacher named Mrs. Giles who said her family was from a place near Powhatan, VA and that she

was related to the Browns in Troupe Texas. The Giles family originated as slaves of Governor William Branch Giles of the Wigwam plantation and the Featherston Plantation which was near Genito Rd to the Brick church area. After great research and DNA analysis it also certain there is a DNA kinship with the Giles as well. Garland and Mrs. Lottie's DNA has been an extra blessing to this project.

Alice Means (1868) pictured left: married John Thomas known as Jim (1868- 1936) eight children: Lee Thomas (1877 – 1942) Texana Thomas Veneer (1882 – 1937) Palenstine Alice Thomas (1884 – 1960) Johnnie Walker (1887) Jim Thomas (1888) E.D. Garfield Thomas (1889) Harriet Thomas (1892) Jessie Thomas (1897) Bonnie Thomas (1900 – 1983).

Palenstine Alice Thomas (March 11, 1882 – 1960) referred to as Palace was raised in Troupe, Cherokee, Texas. She was married to James Walker and from this union 11 children were born. Lennis Walker (1900 -1976) Ruby Walker (1902 – 1976) Pearl Walker (1904) Sarah Walker (1907 – 1929) LT Walker (1910) Gertha Walker (1912 – 1986) James Walker (1914 – 2005) Curtis Jackson Walker Sr. (1916

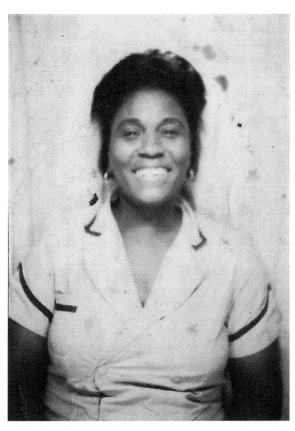

– 2012) Flossie Mae Walker (1919) Dorothy Walker (1923 – 1993) Hartford Walker (1925 – 1984) married Golden Rodgers and had one daughter Naomi Rogers (1926 – 2010).

Pearl Walker (1904) was the grandmother of Garland Ervin. She was born in Pittsburg, Camp, Texas. She was married three times and was the mother of Silent Cummins Sr. (1926 – 1976) Elvin Cummings (1927) Almeda Parks (1934) Jetta Mae Parks, Etta Parks, Fred Nelson Harrell (1939 – 1982) Lydie Lottie Latimer the mother of Garland Ervin was born in Tyler, Texas. She married Garland Ervin Sr. on December 3, 1961. From this union six children were born: Michelle, Marcel, Gale Benjamin Ervin (March 20, 1970 – March 3, 1976) Garland, Geoffrey, and Garfield Ervin.

There were many unsung heroes before and during the Civil Rights movement. Many were tired of racial laws and brutality; Pearl Walker was one of them. Before Rosa Parks refused to give up her seat in the 1940s. There was Pearl Walker who lived in Texas that also refused to get up. After an argument with the white driver, and a fight occurred and of course, she was arrested. When Alice was released she quickly got back on the bus and refused to give up her seat. Pearl displayed the strength and character that Black America needed. Pearl, was a Pilar of strength during a time of racial hatred towards African Americans. I was told by her grandson Garland that she drove in the middle of the night to save her sister and brother-in-law from getting lynched. She was a great business woman who brought large quantities of land, divided it up and sold each share. She turned her home into a café and took care of her mom until her death. She later moved to San Joaquin, California. In later years, she moved to Vallejo California Garland remembers he and his grandmother's conversation and the letters that they wrote each other. They kept in contact until her death.

Lydie "Lottie" Ervin and bottom pic: Garland Ervin owner of Nomadic Communications

On August 19, 2015 after a successful reunion the previous year The Hyde Family Committee spearheaded by Monica Jackson, Timeka Hicks, Carolyn Carroll, and myself, decided to have a Family Cookout. Thankfully because of recent DNA connections, many came from far away to attend the event. We all assembled at the Hyde home place where approximately 200 family and friends came together. The cookout kicked off with Family historian Carolyn Hyde Carroll telling our family history as far back as three generations. After Carolyn's awesome presentation, I spoke of the Red Lodge Plantation. I shared with the crowd the importance of the land in which we stood and the family ties that we really did not know about. Then Garland Ervin spoke of his connection to our family. We were happy to have Dr. Henry Featherston, Garland Ervin and his family along with Samone and Moriah Adams of the Finney family and all other guest. It truly was a blessed event.

Clinton Hyde and Garland Ervin

Blanche, Deloris, and Andrea

Anna H. Bowers and Brianna Gaskins

Another Close Connection to The Brown/Branch Family

Margie Bates who is a great researcher in her own right has been researching her family line. Her mother Mrs. Tessie Bates roots are traced to the Brown family. According to several Brown descendant DNA matches it is proven that their family relationship between her ancestor John Brown of Cumberland, VA and the Brown family of Amelia. While comparing Margie's family tree it is apparent that the same first names that are in her family tree are seen in the descendants of Red Lodge Plantation. Slaves used names a code for family relation. It was the only way to trail family relationships mainly because of selling and division of slave families. This name trail repeated itself for many decades after slavery. It should also be mention that Margie's father the late Deacon Floyd Bates, was my grandmothers second cousin. My grandmother and Deacon Bates mutual ancestors was The Hardaway's originates in the Brick Church Area and were former slaves of the Hardaway family and also worked at the Dykeland Plantation.

John and Lucy Brown of Cumberland, VA

Son of John and Lucy Brown: **Addison Brown** (1830) married **Louisa Brown** two children were born Caroline Brown and Richard Brown. and later **Addison** married **Fannie Jones** and to this union several children were born namely; Matthew Brown, Samuel Brown, Thomas Brown, John Brown

Caroline Brown (February 1860 – March 25, 1931) resided in Powhatan, Virginia. Caroline married Andrew Branch in 1882. From this union 4 children were born: Richard Branch (1878) Molly Branch Hobson (1879 – 1946), Lucy Branch (1882) Linnie Wood Branch (1889 – 1969) who married Rosa Hudson. He was a farmer and lived in the Belona, Powhatan, Virginia. Children of Linnie and Rosa Branch: Dorothy Branch, Carrie Branch, Richard Branch, John Branch, Lucille Branch, Linwood Branch married Elizabeth Branch Evans, Rosa Branch, Andrew Branch, Arlene Branch, and Tessie Branch.

Lennie Wood Branch and have many descendants.

Caroline Brown Branch

Andrew Branch

Linnie Wood Branch

Another DNA match, Christopher Harris (pictured with his mom), has been researching his family lines thoroughly and has a wealth of information. I was introduced to Chris through Darlene Lewis who along with Howard Hyde Jr. also matched him through DNA. He has also been helpful to the history project.

He has researched his family as far back as the 1700s – early 1800s. Chris is a native of Gary, Indiana. He has been working in Richmond and since his stay he has been researching every chance he can. I am grateful to have met him and his mom. Twice I showed him around, to the areas from where our ancestors once lived. Thanks to Chris, I was able to obtain several documents that would have probably been over looked. Chris is an avid researcher and has a wealth of knowledge.

Chris' family line originates from Amelia, VA although he is still researching his lines; what is known is that at one time, his family was owned by Seth Ward Jones, an Amelia County, Virginia native who moved to Yalobusha, MS. DNA confirms his findings since he is genetically related to Seth W. Jones and the Jones family of Virginia. The eldest ancestor Chris was able to research was Simon Brown and Patsy Jones of Amelia, VA. According to a document Chris was able to retrieve, Simon was from Richmond, VA. While I was researching the will and inventories of the Wigwam Plantation in Amelia, VA I found a document stating, slaves Simon and Patsy were in his plantation in 1831. It is believed that at some point Simon and Patsy were in this plantation before being sold and later relocated to Tennessee. Christopher is constantly tracing his ancestors and I believe he will soon fulfill his desires and trace his roots back to Africa. Pictured below; Simon Brown, son Ulair and wife Pency Brown.

Ancestors and Descendants of the Banks Family

Warner Banks Sr. was the husband of **Betsey Smith (**1815 – March 28, 1915) whose parents Harry and Lydie Smith were a part of the Red Lodge Plantation during the lifetime of Major John Archer. According to Betsey's death certificate she is buried in Red Lodge; exact location is still unknown. Warner and Betsey had children; Violet, Frank, Jane, Frances, Stephen, Phoebe, Warner, and Peggy Banks.

Below is the death certificate of the eldest Banks ancestor, Betsey Smith Banks

Here are the children and descendants of Warner and Betsey Banks. It has been said that one of the descendants of Warner and Betsey was sent to Georgia.

1. **Violet Banks** married George Brown (1841 – 1880)
2. **Frank Banks** (1851) was married to Nancy and had two children. On November 23, 1886 Frank married Caroline Brown who is the daughter of Joe and Phyllis Brown in Amelia, VA.

Children of Frank Banks first marriage

1. **Michael Banks** (1874)
2. **Lela Banks** (1879)

Children of Frank and Caroline Brown (his second marriage)

3. **Joseph Banks** (1884 – 1964) married Annie Brown (October 1893 - August 5, 1936) daughter of Archer Brown and Jennie Taylor. Joe as he was called, lived on Wood farm owned by his employer Mr. Wood. His occupation was working in the dairy barn among other job duties. Like most of all of the people of The Lodge, he was an active member of Liberty Baptist Church where he was a faithful deacon and trustee. After church, all of his grandchildren would go to his home for Sunday dinner that was prepared by his daughter, Mrs. Annie Banks Jackson. His granddaughter Doris Booker and Helen Bannister remembers their Papa would call all of the grandchildren in the house and give all of them candy he had locked in his trunk. He had a special love for his grandchildren, his granddaughter, Mary Banks Johnson still remembers the moving Eulogy; Rev. G.W Manning delivered during Joseph's funeral service and spoke highly of Mr. Joseph Banks. My aunt, Blanche Jefferson remembers being a flower bearer that day.

Children of Joseph Banks and Annie Brown Banks

Eliza Banks Smith (March 25,1914 – September 25, 1982) was the wife of John Sidney Smith (1912 – 1983) they were both hard working and devoted parents and grandparents. According to the 1930 census, Eliza at the age of 16 worked as a maid at the home of William P. Wood who at that time lived on 434 Monument Avenue Richmond, VA. For a time, she worked at a factory and other jobs along with her husband to continue taking care of the family. Their daughter Ethel remembers the day her parents had electricity installed in their home. She said she still remembers how she felt when she "saw the lights in her eyes." From the union of John Sidney and Eliza, children were born: Ethel Priscilla Smith Morris, born June 16, 1932, grew up in Red Lodge and spent a lot of time with her grandmother Nannie T. Smith. Ethel met her husband Horace Morris of Moseley, VA at her great uncle Charlie Banks' baseball game. The couple married on June 27, 1953; Rev. Manning officiated the wedding ceremony. From this union 3 children were born. Marion Morris, Jaqueline Morris, and Dale L. Morris who married Gerald Johnson on July 3, 1976. Mrs. Ethel Morris has helped me tremendously, sharing countless stories of the people, and events that took place years ago. She has definitely been an asset to this project. Children of John and Eliza Banks Smith: Junius Smith, born October 22, 1933. He was formerly married to Martha Mondrey and from these union children were born. Rev. Junius Leon Smith born married Evang. Sandra Evans Smith of Amelia, VA. Curtis Orlando Smith (August 6, 1959 – August 25, 2007) married Annie Mae Booker of Cumberland, VA. Malcom Smith is married to Brenda Smith, Ronnie Smith and Kimberly Smith. John and Eliza has many great grandchildren and great – great grandchildren. Carrie Smith Lawson who married Robert Lawson.

Carrie Banks Bolden (November 21, 1912 - May 15, 2002); On October 10, 1942 Carrie married Calvin Bolden (October 1, 1916 – February 12, 1998) son of David Bolden and Edith Woodson. Rev. S.S. Wilkinson officiated the wedding ceremony. At that time Calvin worked as a helper at the sawmill. He later worked as a sawyer at the saw mill. They lived in the Pleasant Grove Area of Amelia County, Virginia. Calvin loved to fish and Carrie was a great lady that loved her family and friends. She loved to talk about the old times and loved to talk about God; and sing old hymns. Carrie's grandson, Michael Jones remembers his grandmother's love for God. He remembers the many times he would hear her praying and singing around 3 am. He said the anointing would be so strong he would have to get up. Carrie often encouraged the youth, and she had an intense love for her family. Calvin and Carrie had one daughter, Rebecca Bolden Jones, who married Archer Jones Jr. The couple had 3 children and several grandchildren and great – grandchildren.

Mike Banks (May 2, 1915 – August 30, 1995) A man of great wisdom and had a good heart. He was willing to help anyone he could at any time. He was baptized and joined the Liberty Baptist Church in Amelia County, Virginia. Mike worked at the sawmill in Powhatan County, Virginia and at home. His daughters, Georgia and Doris, recalled how they had to work in the fields, not just their own. They also would help work in other fields as well. Mike Banks had crops in the field; chickens, horses, a pony, cows, goats, and fruit trees were also in the field. Mike married Carrie Bell Brown on August 6, 1938; the wedding ceremony was officiated by Rev. Edward Gilliam. From this union three children were born; Mike Banks Jr. who worked for the OK Foundry in Richmond, VA; Roosevelt Banks (August 20, 1940 – October 25, 2007). Helen Banks Moseley married Winston Moseley. Mike Banks Sr. (February 19, 1939 – February 22, 2002) who later married Dorothy Lee Brown (May 23, 1931 - September 28, 1997) on November 20, 1948; she was also the daughter of Daniel and Mary Lillie Richardson Brown in Amelia County, Virginia. Rev. Isaiah Wilkinson officiated the wedding ceremony. From this union seven children were born; Mary Johnson, Bethel Banks, Archer Banks (1950 -2000) who served in the U.S. Army and married Evangelist Vinnie. Georgia Banks, Zacchaeus Banks who married Sheila Pemington, and Doris Banks Booker who has been an asset to this project. Linda Banks, and James Edward Banks, also known as Jimmy. Mike also has a daughter; Mary Ann Evans Person. Mike and his wife Dorothy Lee, whom her grandchildren and so many others called "Big Momma", including me. They always made you feel welcome in their home. I remember I used to walk to their home to visit them. I would ask Big Momma questions about the older people like her father, and several others who died long before my time. One day, Big Momma told me to remember her great uncle was Beverley Brown, and Aunt Stella Brown, who was a midwife; she said, their grave which was in the woods at that time, had an old tombstone on it. In recent years it has been cleaned off. I always wondered why she told me about Beverley Brown, but since the recent discovery of distant kinship, now I understand. She loved to sing and could really sing well; she loved the old hymns and whenever she would lift her voice in church she would rock the house. To their credit, they helped many people and would always share their wisdom. She was a great cook and made the best homemade souse you can ever imagine. I remember well how Dorothy Lee took care of her mother in her final days, and at the same time took care of her husband while he was sick as well. Thank God for the memory of Mike Banks Sr. and Dorothy Lee Banks. Her daughter, Doris, remembers after her older siblings had moved from her home. Doris and her two younger siblings Linda and James "Jimmy" would sing and praise, while backing up their mom who took the lead. They would sing songs like, "This Little Light of Mine" and "God Is Able to Carry You Through". They would always have a good time. The grandchildren, great and great – great grandchildren of Mike Banks Sr. are too numerous to mention. There are several that are deceased: Anthony Martin, Jaquan Anderson, Carolyn Banks, Gale Banks, and a great grandson, Antony Martin.

Geneva Banks Ruffin (December 4, 1917 – March 1, 2000) wife of John Allen Ruffin (see Brown Family section)

Annie Banks (1920 - December 10, 1995) was married to Royal Jackson on June 24, 1972. She was a faithful member of Liberty Baptist Church and often would sit near her good friend, Mrs. Evelyn Harris during services. She was the mother of Shirley Banks Givens (1942 – 1984) who was married to Walter Givens and has two children and grandchildren; Soloman Banks who married Martha and has four children, Rosa Banks Broadnax who married Marvin Broadnax and has one daughter, and Annie Belle Banks Booker. Annie also raised other relatives. She was a major pillar in our community and was well loved by her entire family and church family. She loved all of the children of the neighborhood and they definitely loved her. She was well loved by her children, grandchildren, and great – grandchildren. In fact, she was so well loved by all the neighborhood, people that were not related to her also called her Aunt Annie or simply Grandma.

Phyllis Banks (June 4, 1921 – March 12, 2005) she was well loved and was a lot of fun Phyllis lived in Richmond, VA for many years before returning to Amelia after the death of her sister Annie. She told me that she used to work for Richmond Times Dispatch years ago; and she showed me a scrap book with all the obituaries and other articles she collected of the people of the Lodge. She was well loved by her family. Joseph Banks (April 2, 1922 – July 4, 2016); Joe was married to the late Lester Mae Banks. From this union two children were born; Joseph Jr. and Phyllis Banks (deceased); and he has two granddaughters. Archer Banks (May 5, 1923 – September 21, 2001); He lived in Newark, Worcester, Maryland

Elder Banks (April 21, 1926 – February 18, 1997) lived in Newark, Worcester, Maryland

4. John Henry Banks (December 1888 – November 4, 1939) was married to Mattie Jackson of Hanover, VA on December 31, 1916 in Richmond, Virginia. He resided in Richmond until his death. He had one son William Banks (1922)

5. Sallie Banks (1890 – 1919) married Albert Ruffin son of Humphrey and Ellen Ruffin on November 24, 1906 in Amelia, VA. The couple had five children; 1. Rev. Frank Ruffin (1907 – 1993) married Lucy Lee on September 10,1938 and lived in Richmond, Virginia. The couple had three children; Lawrence Ruffin, Shirley Ruffin and Louis Ruffin; 2. Ottoway Ruffin married Helen 3. James Alfred Ruffin

Rev. Frank Ruffin

Eliza Banks Smith

Geneva Ruffin

Carrie Bolden

Mike Banks Sr.

Dorothy lee Banks

Mike Banks Jr

Archer Banks

Roosevelt Banks

Shirley Givens

Carolyn Banks

Gale Banks

6. Phyllis Banks Friend (March 1892 – October 18, 1965) married Joe Friend. The couple lived on 211 A Leigh Street Richmond VA and had six children; Mattie Friend Robertson (April 17, 1917 – September 27, 1997) married Stephen Friend (1920 – January 16, 1945) who was a laborer and lived in Richmond. Phillis Irene Friend Smith (September 8, 1921) married Clinton Smith on July 21, 1945 in Richmond, VA and Robert Friend (February 14, 1923 – August 29, 1937); Rose Friend (1926); and Clara Friend (June 5, 1928 – October 10, 1943)

7. Charlie Banks (February 6, 1896 – May 6, 1976) Booty as he was called, by the people that knew him. He enlisted into the United States Army on October 29, 1917 and was discharged on March 8, 1919. According to the 1930 census, Charlie was a farmer and worked at the saw mill. Mrs. Ethel Smith, remembers her uncle Charlie was the first resident in Red Lodge to have a baseball team and made a ball park across from his house. As time passed, his son John and later his grandson Leslie had teams and operated the ball park. He was married to Alberta Perkins (1899 - 1978), the daughter of Wilson and Dena Perkins; Mrs. Alberta used to sell candy to the children of the neighborhood. Children of Charlie and Alberta Banks: Ethel Lee Banks McDonald (March 5, 1921 – June 4, 2006) was married to Clarence McDonald (1944– 1964) They lived in New York and had two sons; Charles McDonald and Clarence McDonald. John Henry Banks (December 9, 1922 – May 8, 1996) who started life early working on the farm in Amelia, VA. On March 12, 1949 John married Eloise Harris, the daughter of Geddes Harris and Rosa Scott Harris in Amelia County. John worked for Richmond Foundry for many years. He later worked as a supervisor for McGuire Hospital. It was said that John had a baseball diamond many years ago, across from his father house. Years later, his son Leslie also held baseball games there that would always be highly attended by the people of Amelia and from various counties. John also served as a security guard for Amelia County High School games. Mrs. Eloise has been and still is today a very strong lady. She is truly a woman of great wisdom and I've learned a lot from her. She is one of the eldest of the Red Lodge Community. John and Eloise Banks had seven children; Cerelia Banks "Cee Cee" (1947 – 1958), Deloris Banks "Pig" (1949 – 2009); Arlene Banks Brown "Boogie" (1950 – 2006) who was married to Charles Brown and has two children and grandchildren; John Banks "Big Boy", Leslie Banks "Jimmy" (1953 – 2016) served in United States Army and retired from McGuire Hospital. He has one daughter and two grandsons; William G. Banks "Gee" has two children and grandchildren; and Constance Banks "Connie" has two children and grandchildren. Frank Wilson Banks (January 6, 1926 – October 11, February 8, 2016) also known as "Boobie" Hardaway Banks (August 7, 1927 – August 9, 1927) was only two days old when he died. Dena Banks (January 24, 1929 – October 8, 2002) Iredell "Jack" Banks (1931 – 2012) I remember he would come back home to visit every third Sunday of August. Ernest Garfield Banks (July 22,1932 – June 24,1992) was called "Acie" and James Banks (August 12, 1937 – February 1993) also known as "Boatman" married Estelle Mondrey the daughter of William and Annie Gilliam Mondrey of Amelia, VA. He was the father of three children Sherry Pilar Banks Fouch (November 9, 1964 – April 24, 1993), Tyra and Delta Banks.

Mr. and Mrs. Charlie Banks and family

John Banks   John and Eloise Banks and family   James "Boatman" Banks

Leslie Nathaniel Banks   Eloise Banks and grandchildren

Warner Banks

(May 2, 1898 – April 8, 1972)

Warner Banks, the eighth child of Frank and Caroline was only twelve years old when his mother died. He married Bessie Johnson, daughter of Baylor Johnson and Alice Smith. Warner was a farmer and a laborer. In the 1930s Warner worked 50 hours a week. He had cows, mules and horses. Warner was a good man, who believed in taking care of his family and keeping them together. Warner, was a faithful member of Liberty Baptist Church. His daughter Sarah, recalls the many times her father and the family would walk to Liberty on third Sundays. He would also ride a bicycle to Second Antioch Baptist Church in Powhatan, VA. On the Sunday Pleasant Grove was having service, Rev. Nunn, who pastored the church, would pick him up for morning service. Like many of the men that would come together to slaughter hogs. His daughter Sarah, who we call "Ms. Lou", remembers the many times Warner and Emmett Robinson would kill the hogs together. It's been said that Warner had two mules and he used one at a time to plough the fields at Dr. Rucker's farm. When one mule would tire, he would let him rest and get the other, but he never stopped working until the work was done. Warner worked for Dr. Rucker, The Mennonites and for Roy Whittington. Warner invested a lot of his time in raising his grandson Gerard. He taught him a great work ethic. It has been said that Warner always worked; and if you would be around him you couldn't just stand, you had to work. He was firm and didn't play, especially with his children. His wife Bessie, was a firm but loving mother to her children. She was a great cook and loved her children and grandchildren. Warner and Bessie loved welcoming people with open arms into their home. Many people have been blessed to taste

the delicious food Mrs. Bessie prepared. She was also a faithful member of Liberty Baptist Church. Like most blacks of his time period, he had very limited education but, he would give his best with what he could do. He always was willing to give what he could to his church. The house that Warner and Bessie lived in, was once her father's, Baylor Johnson's home; and it stood for 100 years before being dismantled. When hearing of the humble beginnings of Warner and Bessie, you can't help but appreciate their legacy, which lives in the lives of their children and descendants. Warner and Alice's children were: Alice Banks (January 11, 1921 – Jan 23, 1971) who married Deacon Archer Jones Sr. on August 12, 1939 in Amelia, VA. (for more info see Archer Jones line page), Charlie Banks (1922), James Banks (1925 – 1927), Grace Banks Roberts (1928 – 1986), Mary Susan Banks Jones (1930 - 2014), Gladys Leola Banks (February 7, 1935 – March 22, 2002) who married Herbert Junior Henley Sr., son of Albert and Alice Bell Henley, on June 6, 1959. Helen Banks Goode (living). Sarah Louise Banks was born in 1937, who has been most helpful in assisting me get this project done. Sarah and James Mason has been a blessing in aiding with pictures and countless stories. She is a great mother of two children; grandchildren and great- grandchildren; Queen Victoria Banks (1939 – 1939) and Pearl Banks Booker (living) married Simon Booker. Warner and Bessie have many descendants including children, grandchildren, great – grandchildren, and great - great grandchildren.

Helen Banks Goode

Susie Banks

Sarah Banks

Gracie Banks Roberts

Charlie Banks

Gladys Banks Henley

Louise Banks, Leilia Patrick and Gloria Henley

Pearl Banks

Lelia, Dontavia P. Ray "Tu Tu" and Louise

Antonio Squire   Stephanie   Frances   Gloria Henley

Cornell Banks   Gerard Banks   Lou at work   Ronnie Henley

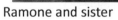

Ramone and sister

Pearl Booker and family

Lelia Banks Patrick

Bessie Banks

Cornell, Jancis and Family

Brenda Henley

Dinner at Warner and Bessie house

Herbert Henley

The Johnson twins, Kenneth and Keith Johnson, Gerard Banks, and Clara Jones Squre

Children and descendants of ex-slaves Warner and Betsey Smith Banks continue

Jane Banks (1853 – July 1882) resided with her mom Betsey in the 1870 and 1880 census.

Children of Jane Banks

Bettie Banks (1871 – 1928) worked as a house servant.

Otha Banks Conway (1877) married Jesse Conway in 1894 and moved to the Leigh District of Amelia, VA. From this union five children were born: 1. Josephine Conway Brooks August 18, 1895 - February 2, 1955 was married to Solomon Brooks (February 15, 1892 – September 17, 1988) and resided at 1235 Parkwood Avenue in Richmond, VA. She is buried at East End Cemetery in Richmond, VA. Solomon Brooks and Josephine Conway Brooks had four children: Jessie Cassandra Brooks Rhone (1913 – 2009) lived in Richmond, VA. Solomon Thatcher Brooks Jr. (1921 - 1995) lived in Hopewell, Virginia. He served as Sergeant in the United States Army and married Mary Bragg in Williamsburg, Virginia on July 18, 1943. Ernest Brooks (March 31, 1922 – July 29, 1975) married Clara Britt December 2, 1949 in Richmond, Virginia. Ernest was a World War II veteran and worked as a truck driver. Robert P. Brooks (March 20, 1936 – August 1, 1994) Richmond, VA. 3. Stephen Conway (March 30, 1899 – February 19, 1948) married Rhoda Conway and worked as a farm laborer.

Lula Banks (1879) no info available on descendants

Frances Banks Brown (1855) married George Brown, see page and had one daughter Emeline Brown (1887-1887)

Stephen Banks (1855 – 1928) was a farmer and married Patience Brown, daughter of Moses and Harriet Brown on June 2, 1883 (For descendants, see Patience Brown Banks family) which consist of Linwood Banks, the Shannon family and others).

Name:	Stephen Banks
Gender:	Male
Marital Status:	Single
Race:	Black
Age:	27
Birth Date:	1856
Birth Place:	Amelia Co., VA.
Marriage Date:	2 Jun 1883
Marriage Place:	Amelia, Virginia
Father:	Warner Banks
Mother:	Betsy Banks
Spouse:	Patience Brown
FHL Film Number:	30474
Reference ID:	Pg 59

Phoebe Banks Goodman (1858 – April 3, 1952) married Jordan Goodman (1852 – 1933) on June 1, 1879 in Amelia, Virginia. From this union five children were born: 1. Frank Goodman (1886 – August 26, 1931) married Emma Johnson on January 29, 1907 in Amelia, Virginia. They had two children, Elizabeth Goodman (1908 - January 10, 1919) and Arnetta Goodman Carter (April 7, 1909 - March 31, 1962) was married to Richard Carter and lived on 1525 Claiborne St. Richmond, Virginia. Frank and Emma also adopted several children. 2. George Goodman (July 1883) married Linda Robinson on July 15, 1915
3. Frances Goodman Brown (May 7, 1892 – May 31, 1942) received up to a 7th grade education and was the second wife of Ezekiel Brown (see Brown Family section) whom she married on July 23, 1906. The couple were divorced July 23, 1919 in Richmond, VA. 4. Alma Goodman (1894) married Percy James on April 21, 1915 in Richmond, Virginia and moved to Philadelphia, Pennsylvania. Percy and Alma's children; Purcel James (November 19, 1917 – December 15, 1975) who resided in Philadelphia, Pennsylvania. Wilbur James (March 29, 1919 – January 15, 1996) resided in Philadelphia, Pennsylvania and Victor James (November 14, 1922 – November 7, 1946) resided in Philadelphia, Pennsylvania.
5.Madeline Goodman McNeal Coles (January 13, 1894 – May 1987) lived in Richmond, VA and married Claiborne McNeal (1892 – 1961) on May 10, 1913. She later married Zachary Coles on April 29, 1945. Three children were born to the union of Claiborne and Madeline; Ollie McNeal (1914), Evander Alexander McNeal (1915 – 2004) married Sarah Barcroft (1916 – 1991) on July 5, 1937 and lived on Elkridge Ln, Richmond, VA. John McNeal (1917) lived in Richmond, VA.

Children and descendants of ex slaves Warner and Betsy Banks continued

Warner Banks Jr. (November 1859 – June 12, 1913) married Onie Green (1874 -), the daughter of Daniel and Eliza Green on August 18, 1898. The couple lived on 216 West Duval Street in Richmond, Virginia and Warner worked at a Feed Store. Warner and Onie had two children; and after Warner's death, Onie and her children moved to New Jersey. She later returned to Richmond, VA where she died. Children of Warner and Onie Banks: George Banks (1890) and Bessie Banks (1902)

Peggy Banks Harris (October 1860 – January 15, 1942) was the youngest child born to Warner and Betsey Smith Banks. In 1883 she married Overton Harris and resided in Red Lodge. Overton and Peggy had three sons. 1. Violet Banks (1882 – 1882) 2. John Harris (August 20, 1887 - February 21, 1952) He lived in Richmond, Va. 3. Willie Harris (1893 – 1955) married Mary St, Clair Brown.

The Bates Family

Another family line that was identified with the Lodge Plantation were the Bates Family. They have a connection with the Harris Family and possibly other families that originated from the Plantation. This connection was first discovered in September 2015. Deacon Floyd Bates who was related to me on the Hardaway line, was the great grandson of former slave Charlie Bates. He had been very helpful in my research of family history. I was glad to share my findings with him, especially the name of his eldest Bates ancestor, Julia Harris. She had two sons, **Charles Bates** and **Wilton Harris** who in 1855 were slaves of The Red Lodge Plantation. Charles Bates (1845 –1915) was a farmer who married **Frances Hicks;** the couple remained in Amelia County after slavery and lived there until the late 1880s. Charlie and Frances then moved to Powhatan, VA where they lived on Route 13. In the 1930s, her son Charles and two of her cousins, Dorothy Grey, and Louise Grey lived with her during that time. Frances Bates great-grandson, the late Deacon Floyd Bates, recalled once that he remembered his grandmother Frances, whom he called Fannie. He told me that she passed away in the 1940s and she lived to be 100 years old.

Children of Charles and Frances Bates

Kate Bates (1865) married Archer Bentley on September 27, 1899 in Richmond, VA. The couple lived in Richmond, VA. Katie died before 1910.

Julia Bates Stewart (1872 – 1958) married Robert Stewart (1882 – 1966). The couple lived in Richmond, VA on Leigh Street.

James Junius Bates (1867 – March 17, 1936) married Charlotte Hardaway on December 26, 1895 in Powhatan, VA. They lived in the Moseley area. From this union seven children were born: 1. Florence Bates Turner (1886) 2. Charlie L. Bates (1901 – 1969) married Bernetta Jackson (1902 – 1969) on Oct 13, 1924 in Powhatan, VA. From their union six children were born. Robert Bates (1923 – 1987), Melvin Bates (1924 – 1994), Floyd Bates (1927 – 2016) married Tessie Branch on March 26, 1949 in Powhatan, VA. The couple had five children: Glenn Bates, Larry Bates, Margie Bates, Melody Harris and Michael Bates. Geneva Bates; Leon Bates married Cora Bonaparte on June 27, 1964 in Midlothian, VA. Leon was known to all as "Mickey" and was a store owner. He had two children who are both deceased. Junius Bates (1935 - 1993) 3. Robert Bates (April 3, 1903 – June 1985) married Carrie Braxton; raised two of Carrie's children from a previous marriage. Children: Herbert Bates (1925 -1985) and Herman Bates Jr. (1925 – 2008) 4. Ella Louise Bates (1908) 5. Milton Bates (1910 – 1986) 6. Ella Bates (1908) 7. Milton Bates (1910 – 1986).

Reuben Bates (March 17, 1873) lived on 218 West Cary St. Richmond, VA. He owned a shoe repair shop.

Ellen Molly Bates married Jefferson Scott in Powhatan, VA. There are two known children: Florence Scott (1894) and Everett Scott (1898)

Rosa Etta Bates (1874) married Thomas James on August 23, 1899 in Powhatan, VA.

Eliza Bates Johnson (1890 – 1973) married Andrew Johnson on February 25, 1914 and resided in Powhatan, VA.

Nanny Bates (March 6, 1883 – September 15, 1963) married Robert Hicks and the couple lived in Powhatan, VA. Molly Bates and William Bates

Charlie Bates

Melvin, Robert and Floyd

Floyd Bates and Sons

Geneva Helen Bates

Robert Bates

Junius Bates

Leon (Mickey) Bates

Margie Bates, the daughter of Floyd and Tessie is a great researcher in her own right. It was her family tree that enabled me to put some of the links together in the Bates and Brown families of this book. I was blessed to be a part of the family.

There are many other Bates descendants that are too numerous to name; however, I will mention two: Towanda Cox (a researcher), and Henry Carroll.

Top: Deacon Floyd and Tessie Bates and below: Melody and Margie Bates

In August, 2015 my father agreed to take a DNA test from ancestry.com. I took a DNA test as well. In a few weeks, the results were back. I noticed my dad had a close match; a fourth cousin. After several correspondences, I learned that the match was Selissa Brown. Selissa was adopted, but she told me her father's name was Herman Bates, and that she was born in Maryland. I looked at my family tree and discovered he was my grandmother's cousin. I quickly contacted Deacon Bates and told him the story. Deacon Bates gave me a telephone number, and told me to contact Harriet Penny of Baltimore, MD. After talking to Harriet, it was confirmed that Selissa was a part of the Bates family. I called Selissa, who resides in West Virginia; I told Selissa that I had found her father's immediate family in Baltimore, with the help of Deacon Floyd Bates. Soon after, she united with a brother, sister in law, and cousins she didn't know. On October 16, 2016, Selissa, her daughter Brittani, her brother Herman Jr., his wife Niko Bates, and her parents spent the weekend in Amelia and Powhatan. What was amazing to me, was that I had two parts of the family history in my possession at the same time. The Hardaway line, which I descend from, and the Bates who came from Red Lodge. That weekend they had the opportunity to meet family, such as Deacon Bates, Lloyd Fleury, and the Goode family. On Sunday October 18, 2015 we worshiped at the Second Antioch Baptist Church in Powhatan, VA. I am thankful to God that I was able to bring this great family together.

Miles/Baugh/Perkins

The Miles were one of the oldest families of The Red Lodge Plantation during the early 1800s. The Miles family were apart of other plantations as well. A few miles from The Lodge as it was sometimes referred to as, was another plantation, The Oak Plantation, it was owned by the Harrison brothers Edmund and Nathaniel. Today, some of the descendants of The Miles family still reside in Red Lodge.

<u>Daniel and Jane Miles and descendants</u>

Daniel Miles was born in 1810 a slave of John Archer and his wife Jane Miles (1812) was also a slave. There's not much information on Daniel however, what is known is that Daniel was a farmer and they raised their children and grandchildren. Daniel died shortly after 1880 in Red Lodge. Jane Miles was blessed with a very long life and lived to be 100 years old. Daniel is buried in the Miles/Perkins cemetery in Red Lodge. It is not known how many children the couple had however there is one daughter, Dianna Miles Baugh that is documented.

Dianna Miles Baugh (1830 - March 11, 1920) married James Baugh (1822) from this union ten children were born

1. **Jane Baugh Tyler** (1857 - June 1887) who married Matt Tyler (1867 – 1934) and had one child Eliza Jane Tyler White (March 1, 1890) married Timothy White and resided on Dean Street In New York City. Eliza had one child Alice Mae Foster (1911), she did bead work in New York.
2. **Eliza Baugh** (1862)
3. **Dena Perkins** (1863 – January 29, 1955) married Wilson Perkins (1863 – July 8, 1947) of Powhatan County, Virginia in 1880. Wilson was the son of Wilson Perkins Sr. and Martha Scott Perkins. They both originated from Amelia, VA. Wilson was a farm laborer. Mrs. Dena lived in Red Lodge and was remembered for being a good cook and making ashcakes from her fireplace. From the union of Wilson and Dena Perkins eight children were born, James Perkins (1884), Blanche Perkins (April 1887 - July 1887), Lizzie Perkins (1889 - 1978) lived on 1321 North 28th street Richmond, VA; Ernest Perkins (1891 -1940), Ardell Perkins (1893 – March 1896) Hardaway Perkins (1895), Alberta Perkins Banks (1899 -1978) who married Charlie Banks; Daniel Perkins (August 29, 1899 – May 16, 1967) He was a janitor and lived on 425 North 31st Richmond, VA. and Cathleen Perkins (1903)
4. **Lucy Baugh** (1864) married Matthew Hobson (1854) and they had several children, Minnie Hobson Houston (1895-1928) lived in Goochland, VA and married Samuel Houston; Florence Hobson Henley (June 17, 1896 – July 18, 1977) She was married to Oley Henley and had five children; Lucille Beatrice Henley Smith (November 11, 1920 – November 21, 1993) lived in Richmond, VA. Jennie Henley (1922 – July 23, 2007); Juanita Henley (1923 – 2005); Oley Henley Jr., (1924 – 1975); and Emma Henley (1927)
5. **Alfred Baugh** (1867 – 1893)
6. **Alice Baugh** (1869 – October 28, 1937) was a social worker and married James Alfred Seay
7. **Minnie Baugh** (1870 – June 1889)
8. **Daniel Baugh** (1871)
9. **Charlotte Baugh** (1877)

The Gray Family

The Gray Family's amazing history is believed to be Native American, African as well as white heritage. The Grays were listed in the Lodge Plantation. When I was young boy I heard the elderly family members mention that the Archers of Chula are descendants of William Segar Archer Family. After in depth research it is believe that many others are descendants as well. The connection is thought to be through the Gray Family. It is suggested that this connection is from William Gray and Mary Bolling whose daughter Virginia "Jincy" Archer bears a striking resemblance of Senator Archer in his later years. It has been said that the Gray family came from Southampton, VA, and some of them took part in the Nat Turner Rebellion in 1830. I'm uncertain what year the Grays of Red Lodge entered the plantation but what is known is that this line of Grays was in the plantation in 1855 and more than likely, many years before. According to an early map of Amelia County, there was a Mr. Gray who owned land beside The Lodge. The Gray family descendants like all of the other descendants of The Lodge were free from the shackles of Slavery and arose from the ashes of the Era Reconstruction to become pillars in their state and community. Many descendants of the Gray families became successful land owners, teachers, preachers and business men and women. I salute the ancestors of this family who became great at a time when blacks especially mixed race people, could not find a place in society. Mixed race people were not appreciated or recognized by whites and also by some blacks, due to the stigma and discrimination between light-skin and darker skinned African American. The ancestors who knew their trade that was learned from their native land and through slavery, illuminated their minds and honed in on their skill which overtime, set the pace for their descendants through education. Today the descendants, stand on their shoulders.

Slaves Children and Descendants of William Gray and Mary B. Gray

William Gray Sr. and Mary Bolling Gray were both former slaves of The Red Lodge Plantation. William Gray Sr. (1796) married Mary Bolling (1802) They were listed as mulatto (mixed race). According to the 1870 and 1880 United States Census, William was a carpenter and was still working at the age of 80. From my research, William and Mary had six children, Betsy Gray Smith wife of John Smith, Sallie Gray Archer Robinson, William Gray, Virginia (Jincy) Gray Archer, George Gray, Octavia Gray Thompson, and Lucy Gray.

Sallie Gray (1831 -1915) first marriage was to **John Wyatt Archer.** They had one son. After slavery she moved from The Red Lodge, but remained in Amelia County. Her second marriage was to John Nelson Robinson (1825 -1912) in 1861. The children of Sallie Gray Archer Robinson: 1. **Junius Freeman Archer** (July 11, 1854 -April 8, 1940) son of John Wyatt Archer. and Sallie married Frances Miles (August 10, 1858 – March 23, 1889) daughter of Mr. and Mrs. Reuben Miles on May 23, 1878 in Amelia VA. From this union four children were born. Junius worked as a wheelwright (he would build or repair broken wheels for carts and wagons and he also had his own farm and land. After Frances death he later in 1893 remarried to his second wife Johanna Harris (May 1859 - April 17, 1929) the daughter of Jack Johnson and Caroline Harris in Amelia, Virginia. They resided in Amelia, Virginia until their death. The Children of Junius F. and Frances M. Archer: Thacker Franklin Archer (October 13, 1877 – October 7, 1931) was raised in Amelia, VA by 1910, Thacker moved to Richmond, Virginia and resided on 1201 West Moore Street. He was a retail employer owning his own store. On January 14, 1914, Thacker married Carrie Ransome (1882) He later became a realtor in Richmond, Virginia and later Amelia, VA where he lived until his death. John Wyatt Archer (May 1883 – July 22, 1940) married French Dennis (1888 – 1934) they had seven children, 1. Hazel Archer (1921), 2. Richard Kendall Archer (Jan 30, 1923 – August 8, 1945), 3. Julius Archer (1925), 4. John Percy Archer (April 20, 1927 – November 23, 1984). 5. Sadie Archer Taylor (1886 – 1962), 6. Frances Archer and 7. Richard Archer (1898 – 1904); Christopher Columbus Archer (April 1881 – July 1927) married Queen Victoria Harris and had four children: Mary Archer, Frances Turner Archer (September 8, 1911 – January 28, 1975) who married Homer Thompkins Sr. (June 20, 1908 – April 20, 1976) on March 21, 1936 in Nottoway County, Virginia. From this union three children were born; Homer Thompkins Jr married Eleanor Wheat and has three children, Carrie Thompkins and Joyce Thompkins Medley married Leonard Medley Jr. They have three children. Mrs. Joyce Medley has served faithfully in the Amelia County Public School System. She was the first black teacher and the first black principal in Amelia, VA. The Lineage of Homer and Frances also consist of grandchildren and great – grandchildren. 3. Lawson Smith Archer (May 25,1915 – November 1976) who married Clara Perry (1915 – 2002) they had two sons, Ronald and Christopher Archer; Fannie Archer Winkler (1884) married Willim Winkler on December 22,1915 in Amelia, VA; Bettie Elizabeth Archer Moore (1885 – 1959), Julia Estelle Archer (1889 – 1931) married Oscar Scott on December 27, 1916 the son of Anderson and Henrietta Epps Scott and the brother of Vanderbilt Yates Scott (1895 – 1981) of Amelia, County. The couple had a daughter Doris Russell Scott (June 16, 1918 – July 9, 2002) married Orville L. Giles (February 14, 1917 - May 1992) on October 25, 1938 in Alexandria, VA. and adopted daughter, Sadie Woodson.

Emmett Robinson (July 1861 - 1912) married Kate McNeil of Robeson, North Carolina on June 6, 1888 in Amelia County, Virginia. After Emmett's death Kate later lived with her daughter in New York. Chilldren of Emmett and Kate: Cameron Robinson (1879), Geneva Robinson (1889) Nelson Robinson (1890) Salomon Robinson (1891 – 1891) Louisa Robinson (1892) Henry Evander Robinson (January 31, 1895) served in the United States Army and served in World War 1 and lived in White Plains, New Yok. Frances Louise Robinson Archer (1895 – 1970) was married to Irving Archer; Janice Robinson (1896), William Junius Robinson (March 1, 1897) Ann Elizabeth Robinson (May 20, 1899), Emmett Robinson (November 7, 1898 – May 10, 1961) married Naomi Thompson. Children of Emmett and Naomi Robinson: James Edward Robinson (November 21, 1921 – December 20, 2001) Walter Silvester Robinson (May 10, 1929 – December 27, 1994) Josephine R. Vanderveer (May 20, 1901 - May 20, 1978) Charles Howard Robinson (February 25, 1904) Laura Robinson Easley (March 12, 1908 – August 12, 1977) married William Palmer Easley and lived for a time in Westchester, NY and also Buffalo, NY. The couple had a daughter Dorothy Joan Easley Dryer who was married and had children. 3. Judy Robinson (February 22, 1864 - 1951) married John Wyatt Archer. John N Robinson Jr. (1869 – 1953) who married Dora M. Harris (1875-1953) on April 20, 1892. 5. Willie Robinson (1872 – 1941) who married Lottie Dixon Archer (1875 – 1960) they had six children, Wilmer Robinson (1894 – 1961) who married Sarah Wingo; Nettie (1895 – 1927) married Milliard Leathers, Florence Robinson (1903 – 1918), Egbert Jesse Robinson (1906 – 1970) who married Catherine Conway Buxton (1908); Ella Robinson (1875 – 1949)

Laura Robinson Easley

Dorothy Joan Easley Dryer

William Gray (October 1842 – March 28, 1919) the second child born to William Gray and Mary Bolling Gray he was also a carpenter. In 1870 he married Martha Ann Robertson (1838 – April 1891) From this union nine children were born. Some of the descendants of William and Mary Gray changed their name to Grey.

Children of William and Martha R. Gray

William Gray Jr (1860) married Georgie Ella Gray (1870 – April 26, 1961) on December 27, 1887 in Richmond, Virginia. In the 1900s William and Ella lived at 429 West Golden Street Richmond, Virginia. He worked as a Pullman porter. William and Georgie Ella Gray had several children; 1. Maggie Gray (1899), 2. Margaret Gray (1890 – 1969) Georgie Gray (1891 - 1961), 3. Louise Gray (1894) and 4. William Gray (1894 – 1950)

Armstead J. Gray (1861) married Caroline Gray (1863) on October 18, 1894 in Washington, DC. The couple moved to New Jersey where Armstead lived at 542 Mercer Street and worked as a Pullman porter. Armstead and Carrie's children; 1. Alice Gray (1899) 2. Armstead Gray Jr. (1901 – 3. Kathryn Laurene Gray Rodgers (July 1, 1906 – January 18, 1997) was born in New Jersey

Dandridge Gray (1863)

Henry Gray (1865)

Wilson Robert Gray (1867) married Mary Ann Peachy Burrell on August 8, 1889 in Richmond, VA. The couple moved to New York City. Children of Wilson and Mary Ann Gray: Colista Viola Grey (October 8, 1899 – January 1979) was born in New York and raised in Richmond, VA before moving to Washington D.C., Hortence B. Grey (October 12, 1894 - 1947) married William Lafayette Craig (1885 – 1952) They lived in Richmond, VA, Washington DC and Allegheny Pennsylvania. From this union, three children were born: William Lafeyette Craig Jr. (November 12, 1923 - April 4, 2012) he married Mary Elizabeth Roberts (1925 – 2013) in 1948. Carl Ellsworth Craig (February 20, 1927 – November 28, 1950) served in the

United States Army as 1st Lieutenant, Company L 15 Infantry Regiment in World War II Korea. He married Grace Minter in Pennsylvania and later moved to Washington D.C and later Fairfax, VA. They had a son, Carl Ellsworth Craig Jr. (November 20, 1950 – September 3, 2008) and, Linwood Burrell Craig (March 10, 1929 – March 5, 2005) was also born in Braddock, Allegheny, Pennsylvania and later resided in Norfolk, Virginia he had 3 children. Clarence Montague Grey (November 6, 1894 – December 20, 1956) He was a carpenter and enlisted in the United States Army on June 18, 1918 and served for one year. He married Julia on August 30, 1917 and the couple lived in Roanoke, VA. Clarence and Julia later moved to Pennsylvania and later divorced in 1941. He married Thelma Stinson in 1942 in Brooke, West Virginia. Clarence and Julia was the parents of Clarence Gray (July 9, 1918 – April 27, 1977) he lived in Pittsburgh, Pennsylvania. Robert Wilson Gray (December 4, 1920 – April 9, 1982) lived in Columbus, Ohio.

Martha Gray (1870)

Henry Gray (1872)

Robert Gray (1874)

Mary Gray (1876) born in Amelia County, Virginia. On December 26, 1895 she married Walter T. Jones The son of Gustavus and Charlotte Jones who were at one time slaves of Governor William B. Giles at the Wigwam. Later owned by Giles nephew Samuel Jones and was later taken to The Oaks plantation was owned by Nathaniel Harrison. Mary Gray Jones and Walter Jones lived in the Mattoax Area of Amelia, County and later divorced on June 27, 1918. On December 5, 1918, Mary married Mr. Henry Ford who lived and owned a blacksmith shop located on Genito Rd. Mary had a daughter by her first husband, Charlotte Jones Hatcher Smithson (May 31, 1903 – September 4, 1957) who married Harry Hatcher and later Smithson. She is buried with her family the Grays in Pleasant Grove Baptist Church. Charlotte had one daughter Margaret Ann Hatcher known to all as "Woodsie." Margaret was reared near the Brick Church Community by her grandmother Mary and step grandfather Henry Ford. She married Mr. James Arthur Hill and moved to the Chula Area of Amelia County, Virginia. From this union several children were born Floyd A. Hill (November 20, 1948 – April 22, 2015) married Hattie Jones on July 16, 1977. Leon Hill married Mary Robinson, Rev. Bernard S. Hill Sr. who married Consuella Robinson of Amelia, VA. Pastor Hill is the pastor of High Rock Baptist Church. Charlotte Ellen Hill who married Lonnie Henderson, James Hill Jr. who married Florence Staples and Rev. Lorenzo Hill who married Bernice Patrick (deceased). He is the pastor of Little Bethel Baptist Church in Amelia, VA. There are several leaders and ministers of the Gospel who have preached the good news of Jesus Christ that descends from this ancestral line.

**Jincey Gray Archer (**1835 – August 26, 1923) "aka Virginia" was a slave on the Red Lodge Plantation in 1855. She married Thacker Archer. After closely looking at this picture and comparing it to a picture of Senator Archer it is certain that they have a close family Resemblance. She is possibly the granddaughter of Senator Archer. It is uncertain what year Thacker and Jincey met or married but more than likely, it is possible that the two of them connected through the family relationship and business dealings of Senator William Segar Archer and Robert P. Archer. The couple are two of the many slaves that traveled to Tchula Mississippi and worked at Senator Archer Tchula Plantation and Richard T. Archer's Anchuca Plantation before returning to Amelia County, VA. For more information on Jincey and family please see Thacker Archer Family line.

George Gray (July 1845 – August 26, 1923) was a farmer in the Mattoax area of Amelia, VA. In 1865 George married Peggy Lawyer (1853 – February 5, 1927) the daughter of Charles Lawyer and Margaret Lawyer.

Children of George and Peggy Gray

Mary Gray (1868)

Nellie Gray Eggleston (1871 - November 30, 1954) married Cary T. Eggleston (April 1863 - 1912) son of Frances White on March 24, 1894 in Amelia, VA. Mrs. Alberta Person remembers her grandmother who was a very light woman with long hair. Mrs. Nellie Eggleston lived in the Pleasant Grove Community of Amelia, VA and was a member of the Pleasant Grove Baptist Church where she and her husband are buried.

From this union eight children were born to Cary and Nellie Eggleston

Gertrude Eggleston (1893 – 1981), Frank Eggleston (1893 – March 22, 1931), Harold B Eggleston (August 29, 1903 – December 1,1970) received a 5th grade education and by 1940 he was working 52 hours a week as a laborer. Harry as he was called, married Ada Gilliam Johnson (March 15, 1893 – August 1987) who was originally from Chesterfield, VA. They lived at the Dykeland and worked as a housekeeper for the Harvey family for many years. Harry is buried at Pleasant Grove Baptist Church and Ada is buried at the Johnson Epps family cemetery. George Cary Eggleston (May 23, 1904 – Jan 13, 1984) he had a sixth grade education which was exceptional during that time period. By 1940 George was working 40 hours a week as a laborer. He was married to Ophelia Green Eggleston the daughter of William Henry Green and Moriah Green in Amelia, VA. Children of George and Ophelia Eggleston, Cary Thomas Eggleston (1927 – 1982) Viola Eggleston born 1930, Minor Eggleston (1931 – 1966) a successful business man and undertaker in Farmville, VA. He was married to Ruth Eggleston Children: Minor B. Eggleston Jr. (1949 – 2003) was formerly married to Denise Langhorne. Stanley Dale Eggleston (1953 – 2006) was married to the late Bessie Townes, Command Sgt. Harold Timothy Eggleston (1958 – 2012) married Gwendolyn Nash, Carolyn Eggleston Town, Michael Eggleston and Carl U. Eggleston who is a successful business man and director of the Carl U. Eggleston Funeral Home and Oliver & Eggleston Funeral Establishment in Farmville, VA. He graduated from Robert R. Moton High School in Farmville, VA in 1969. Mr. Eggleston received many degrees and honors and is a part of several organizations. Carl married Barbara Nunnally in 1975; Elvira Eggleston Pleasant (1933), Boyce Venetta Eggleston (1934 – 2006), George Eggleston Jr (1936), Helen Eggleston Sauls (1938 – 2003), William Eggleston born in 1941. Franklin D. Eggleston (1943 - May 3, 2016) who married Thelma Ruffin. He worked for Union International Paper and also for Ukrop's as a truck driver. Alberta Eggleston Person, Linda Eggleston who is married to Alvah Mitchell. George and Ophelia Eggleston have many grandchildren and great – grandchildren.

Emery Eggleston (July 14, 1912 – September 9, 1961) married Frances Roberta Thompson on September 16, 1944 in Amelia County, Virginia daughter of Richard Thompson and Florence Tyler. From this union one child was born, Brenda Francine Eggleston (September 8, 1947 - June 11, 2001) was married three times, first marriage was to Christopher Chappell on Dec. 18, 1965; Second marriage was to Jackie Donald Hicks on November 25, 1974; Third marriage was to Charles Phillip Banks on July 7, 1952; Emily Eggleston (1912). The descendants of Cary and Nellie are many and are residing in Amelia, VA, New Jersey and across the world.

Lilly Gray (1888) George Gray (1886) Ellen Gray (1888) Sadie Farmer (1895 – December 26, 1989) married Major Farmer and the couple had two children, Leroy Farmer (1916), and Allen Farmer (1927 – December 26, 2006) who married Vivian Mickens (1929)

Octavia Gray (1852) lived in Amelia, VA

Lucy Gray (1855) lived in Amelia, VA

Harry Eggleston

Boyce Eggleston

Franklin Eggleston

Ruth Eggleston

Stanley & Bessie Family

William Craig

Minor Eggleston

Carl U. Eggleston

Carl Craig

The Smith Family

John Smith (1832) a former slave, and farmer. He married **Betsy Gray** (daughter of William and Mary Bolling Gray. John was raised in Powhatan County, Virginia and Betsey was a slave on the Red Lodge Plantation.

Children of John and Betsy Smith

Catherine Smith (1856) married Griffith Gibson the son of Ned and Fannie Gibson on December 26, 1883 in Amelia County Virginia.

William Smith (1859) married Priscilla Miller daughter of Jim and Lucy Miller of Powhatan, Virginia on April 18, 1882. The couple lived in the Red Lodge. After his death Priscilla remained on the Smith family land and married Walter Anderson the father of Alice Anderson Lewis.

Bolling Smith (1865) died when he was a teenager

Bettie Smith who married Clarence Woodruff. The couple had two sons: Clarence Woodruff and George Woodruff. Mary Susan Goodrich (1869 – June 13, 1931) was married to Moses Goodrich on November 19, 1885 and lived in Washington DC. In the 1920's the couple worked for Charles Bispham. Martha Smith Farrar (1874) moved to Connecticut.

Junius Smith (October 15, 1875 – June 15, 1915) was a farmer and married Nannie Thompson daughter of Fred and Elsie Thompson on June 24, 1903 in Amelia, VA. Nannie was a member of Pleasant Grove Baptist Church. She was a devoted mother and grandmother who helped raised her grandchildren and was very close with her granddaughter Ethel S. Morris. The couple lived in the Lodge and from this union five children were born 1. William Smith (1905 – 1921) 2. Ethel Smith (1907 – January 16, 1969) Had one daughter Lucy Smith (1927 – 1927) 3. Bettie Smith (1908 – 1982) married Theodore Roosevelt Booth on May 6, 1943 in Richmond, VA. The couple had a daughter Joyce Ann Booth a retired school teacher at the Richmond Public School System. who married Earl Granger Jr. Two sons one namely, Theodore Booth Jr. 4. John Sidney Smith (1912 – 1983) married Eliza Banks Smith daughter of Joseph Banks and Annie Brown Banks. The children of John Sidney and Eliza Smith are documented in the Banks section of the book. 5. Freddie Smith (August 17, 1914 – January 1, 1993) married Susan Virginia Lee Clements daughter of Peter Clements and Isabelle Jasper in Amelia, Virginia. From this union six children were born Mocile Smith Trotter, Vivian Smith Thomas, Susan Smith Sanders, Freddie Smith Jr. (April 7, 1948 – August 11, 2010), Isaiah Smith, and Nannie Smith Parham.

Sidney Smith (1877 – 1879) died as an infant

Alex Smith (1878 – 1879) died as an infant

Left: Susan Clements Smith and Deacon Freddie Smith

Children of Freddie Smith

John S. Smith

Jackie Morris, Ethel Smith Morris, and Dale Johnson

Horace Morris

Rev. Junius Smith

Rev. Junius and Sandra Smith

Malcom Smith

Deacon Freddie Smith

The Archer Family

The earliest Archer Family ancestors that have been traced are William and Kate Archer.

William Archer (1792 – 1880) and his wife **Kate Archer** (1803 – abt. 1909) who was said to be an Indian slave in Amelia, VA and Powhatan, VA. This line of the Archer family was first, the property of John and Frances Tabb, and was willed down to her son-in-law's, Bathurst Randolph and William Barksdale families; which later descended to the grandson of John and Frances Tabb, named Robert. P. Archer. Some were also slaves of William S. Archer, who owned a plantation in Tchula, Mississippi, and his cousin who was a major and Quartermaster in the Confederate Army during slavery and lived in Amelia, County and Powhatan, VA. Richard Thompson Archer moved to Claiborne County, Mississippi. Some of the Archer slaves were divided during slavery. After slavery, Kate Archer appeared in 1880 as a widow raising her younger children in Powhatan, VA. According to the 1900 United States Census, she later moved to Richmond, VA appearing with her granddaughter Kate Norrell and her family. It's believed she died between (1901 – 1910)

The Children of William and Kate Archer

James Randolph (1823 - June 14, 1885) son of Kate was born in Amelia, VA and later lived in Ashland, VA. He was married to Rebecca Randolph and the couple had eleven children. 1. **Edwin Archer Randolph** (January 19, 1850 – 1919) married Olive Virginia Crawford on December 14, 1893. Edwin was a lawyer and an author who wrote a detailed book on the life of Rev. John Jasper who was most notably recognized for his sermon, "Sun Do Move." 2. **Henrietta Randolph** (1851) 3. **Warner Randolph** (1853) 4. **William Randolph** (1860) married Mary Quarles (1868 – 1925) on December 15, 1887 in Hanover County, VA. They had eleven children: Henrietta Randolph (1888) James Randolph (1889), Olive Randolph (1892), Ulysses Randolph (1892 - 1977) married Melissa Roberts. The couple had five children: Ulysses Randolph Jr. (April 5, 1917 – October 3, 1922) James Randolph (1919) Mary Randolph (1920-) married Robert Elmore Binford on April 4, 1953 in Richmond, VA. Phyllis Larnester Randolph (December 1921), Constance Augusta Randolph (September 24, 1924), Maude Randolph (1893 – 1978) wife of Bill Gibbons. (all of the children are pictured left; courtesy of Library of VA) Lillian Randolph Pervall (1895 -1979) who married Rev. Robert Pervall Gertrude Randolph Davenport (1899 - 1926), Viola Randolph (1900), William Randolph (1902), Marian Randolph Settle (1904 - 1989) married William Settle. Beulah Randolph (1906). 4. Lillie Randolph Hope (1866 – 1934)

5. **Kate Randolph Glover** (1867 – 1919) was married to Thomas Glover (1862) on August 26, 1914. 6. Lillie Randolph, 7. Nannie Randolph.

Amy Archer (1830 – February 21, 1920) children of Amy Archer: Grandison Archer (1848 – 1881), son of slave owner Robert P. Archer lived in Richmond, VA. Edinboro Archer (1849 – 1907), son of slave owner Robert P. Archer and Amy, married Amanda Seay and lived in Richmond, VA. After Edinboro's death, Amanda moved to New York with her son, Simon and his family. Children of Edinboro and Amanda: Simon Archer (1871) who married Mary White, and later moved to New York. He worked as an engineer for a candy company. Robert Archer (1873 – September 11, 1923) was married to Ella Washington, and the couple lived on 2308 Cersley St. in Richmond, VA and worked for the railroad. Robert and Ella had 3 children: Wilbert Archer (1907 – 1985) was married to Florence Archer. Marie Archer (1910 – March 11, 1964). Robert Archer (December 27, 1910 – May 5, 1961) known as Bob Archer who married Ruby Robinson, the daughter of Cicero and Hannah Robinson on June 20, 1948.

Fernella Archer Steele Futrell (1881) married Emanuel Steele (1867) on July 14, 1903 in Richmond, VA. Emanuel worked as a porter on the railroad. The couple moved to the District of Columbia and had one daughter, Ruby Steele, who later lived in New York. Edinboro Archer (June 17,1881); Arthur Archer (1883) married Clara Archer and lived in Manhattan, New York. Clara Archer (April 19, 1887 - 1948) married Charles Fairfax Mitchell (1884 – 1948) and later married Arthur Thomas. Clara lived in Youngstown, Ohio. Her children: Charles Fairfax Mitchell (September 14, 1914 – April 7, 1998) married Maude Barnes and later, Dolly Harris. Margie Thomas (1918), Thelma Thomas (1921), Arthur Thomas (1923), and Harold Thomas (1926). She also raised Nathaniel Zigler, and Simon Zigler. Grandison Archer (1867) lived in Manhattan, and later moved to the Bronx, New York. Clarence Archer (1876 -1891), and Fendall Archer (1879)

Kate Archer Norrell (1862) who married Albert Norrell (1856), son of Moses and Sarah Norrell. He was a teacher and worked at the Daily Planet in Richmond, VA. Children of Albert Norrell and Kate Archer:

1. Neota Norrell (1879) 2. Barsenia Norrell Trueheart (1882) lived in the Richmond and Madison, Virginia area; and later lived in Atlantic City, NJ where she was employed as a teacher. 3. Juanita Norrell Peterson (1884 – 1888) married George Peterson on November 18, 1909 in Richmond, VA. The couple had two children: George Peterson Jr. (1911) and Ethel Peterson Pierre (1912 – 1980); she married Basil Pierre (1913 – 1982) and the couple lived on 620 Overbrook Road Richmond, VA. She graduated from Richmond Normal School in 1930, and received an undergraduate degree from Virginia Union University; and also received a Master's in Elementary Education from Columbia University. She was in several organizations including, Delta Sigma Theta Soriety Inc. and the National Retired Teachers Association. She was a teacher at Baker, Carver, Whitcomb, and Reid Elementary School retiring in 1973 after 43 years of service. 4. Ethel Norrell (1887 - 1957) was a clerk and lived on 1015 North 7th Street. 5. Moses Alphonso Norrell Sr. (November 24, 1887) worked as a social worker and married Addie Phillips. He lived on 709 East Bates Street in Richmond, VA. In 1917, he worked as a carrier. While married to Addie, they lived in Richmond, VA. The couple had several children: Aline Norrell Vann (1912), Catherine Norrell (1913 –1937), Moses Norrell Jr. (1915 – 1970) married Marian Evans. The couple had children:

Albert V. Norrell (June 23, 1923 – March 25, 2009) received his B.A. degree in History from Virginia Union University; and he also received an M.A. in Elementary Education at Temple University. Albert served in World War II under General Patton. He spent 25 years working with the school district of Pennsylvania. Albert was a catholic and began his ministry first, in the Permanent Diaconate Formation Program for the Archdiocese of Philadelphia in 1979, and later became Permanent Deacon in 1982. In 1984, he began studies for the Archdiocese of Philadelphia at the Seminary at Pontificio Collegio Beda, Rome. Albert Norrell was ordained in Rome on May 29, 1988 by His Holiness Pope John Paul II and named Honorary Prelate to His Holiness on May 29, 1991. In 1989, Albert was appointed Pastor of Saint Carthage Parish, Philadelphia and named Goldie Norrell Williams (1937 – 2002), Moses Norrell III (1938) and Ivan Pastor Emeritus there in 1998; and he was the first African American in Philadelphia to be elevated to Monsignor. Albert, spent his last years at St. Joseph Villa in Darby, PA. In his 2005 interview, Msgr. Norrell gave what could be his own valediction. "When you are as old as I am and you see yourself on the way, you can start rejoicing that you are going to the Lord. That's what you strove for, worked for. You'll be there forever." When he died, he was given two funerals; officials from the state of Philadelphia all payed homage to Albert Norrell. He was buried in the Holy Cross Cemetery in Darby, PA. Coralease Norrell Wilson (1917 – 1983)

Coralease Norrell (1890 – July 21, 1922) was a teacher. Mattie Norrell Paige (1892 – May 26, 1966) married Lavigerie Paige on March 15, 1918. She lived on 3326 Woodrow Avenue in Richmond. The couple had one daughter Gertrude Paige (1933 – 1989). Albert V Norrell Jr. (1896 – 1976), Goldie Norrell White (1898 - 1981), Endinboro Norrell (December 16, 1898 – October 28, 1996) lived in Richmond, Virginia. He was married to Faith Elizabeth Morris Norrell and the couple had a son, Edinboro Aquinaldo Norrell (1938) who lived in California. Irvin Archer was the youngest son of Robert and Amy Archer.

Harrison Archer (1831) lived in Richmond, VA. He was married to Louisa Archer and later, Kitty Archer. He was the father of Harry Archer (1867) and Isabelle Archer.

William Archer (1833) lived in Amelia, VA and later Richmond, VA; he was married four times. His first wife was **Suckey Gray**. He married **Aleze Fund** on May 2, 1870 in Powhatan, VA. He also married Clarinda Tucker on December 4, 1876 in Powhatan, VA. Later, he married **Pariset Jasper** (1854). Children of **William** and **Suckey Archer**: **Isham Archer** (1850), who married Jane Old on June 25, 1881 in Amelia, Virginia. Children of Isham and Jane: Ellen Archer (1888 – 1927), Lee Archer (1889), Charles Archer (1890), and Anthony Archer (1891) lived in Richmond, Virginia. Mack Wiley Archer (July 17, 1894 – March 20, 1994) married Alice and lived in Connecticut where he worked as a janitor. The couple had five children Edith Archer, Alfred Archer, Livia Archer, Pauline Archer, and Gladys Archer. **Field Archer** (1855), **Anthony Archer** (1862), **Isaac Archer** (1866), **Jennie Archer** (1867), **Rebecca Archer** (1867), and **Pattie Archer Randolph** (1869) married Thompson Randolph and lived on South Beech Street in Richmond, VA. From this union 7 children were born: Isaac Randolph (1890), Thomas Randolph (1894), Lucretta Randolph (1903), Willie Randolph (1904), Rosa Randolph (1905), Mary Jane Randolph (1910), and **Willie Archer** (1872).

Bathus Archer (1836 – 1913) was born in Amelia, VA. He married Patsey Drew on December 24, 1967 in Powhatan, VA. The couple lived in Hanover, VA. Bathus later died in Washington, DC. Bathus and Patsey had seven children: Constance Archer (1867) who moved to Philadelphia, PA and worked as a servant for the Rhawn family. Abraham Archer (1869 - 1957) who was a mechanic and an electrician. Charles Archer (1874 – September 22, 1920), and Bathus Archer Jr. (November 1877 – April 4, 1934). He was married to Charity P. Archer and had a daughter, Christine Archer (1921); Napoleon Archer (June 15, 1882) married Emma Archer and lived in Philadelphia, Pennsylvania. Granderson Lee Archer (September 2, 1882 – June 4, 1961) lived in Richmond, VA. Granderson married Elizabeth Johnson and had 6 children: Granderson Lee Archer Jr. (May 26, 1915 – December 12, 1989) married April 13, 1941, Ruth Royster in Richmond, VA. The couple lived in Richmond. Granderson later resided in Philadelphia, PA until he died. Emory Archer (1918 – 1973) married Gladys Johnson on January 16, 1944 in Richmond, VA. They had two children, Frieda Archer and Emory Archer Jr.; and a grandson Emory Archer III. Geraldine Archer Mayo (1918 – 2003), Wilmette Archer (1919 – 1996,) Susie Archer (1920 – 2006), Walter Archer (1924 – 2009), and Evelyn Archer Hemingway. Florence Archer Evans (1884 – 1952) married Abram Evans, lived in Pennsylvania and had four children: Ottoway Evans (1905 – 1992) married Mabel Docket in 1935. He was a teacher and lived in Philadelphia, Pennsylvania. He was married to Mabel Evans and had one daughter Virginia Evans (1937), Leonard Evans (1909), James Evans (1912), and Alphonso Evans (1913).

Thacker Archer (1837 – 1924) (see Jincy Gray Archer) was a slave of the Tabb family, William Barksdale,

Dr. Bathurst Randolph (see slave account page 24), Richard T. Archer, and W.S. Archer. Thacker was sent to work on the Archer's plantation in Mississippi. After 1870, Thacker was given an enormous amount of land by Lewis Harvie. This property was named Chula after Tchula, MS. The Archers were one of the largest black landowners in the county. What is known is the land's former owner, Lewis Harvie, and his brother John were administrators of Senator William Archer's estate in Amelia and Mississippi. John Harvie became owner of the Mississippi estate in which Thacker and several of his family members were sent to work as slaves. Joan Owens once recalled to me, that her father James mentioned years ago how his ancestors worked with the family land in the Chula Area of Amelia, VA. They used picks, hoes and other tools to plant. To this day, Chula remains the home of many of the Archer family descendants. The Archers are best known for their entrepreneurship; not only did they own land but, they basically had their own community as well. The Archers were founding members of Mt. Herman Presbyterian Church and some were also founding members of Mt. Olive Baptist Church. They had stores, funeral homes and like mostly all black neighborhoods before the late 1960s, they had a school house. Many preachers, teachers, administrators, barbers, morticians, and merchants have been birthed out of this great lineage. Today, the Archer legacy still continues. The Archer family legacy and contribution to African American history should never be forgotten. At the time of his death, Thacker was one of the few African Americans to have a will in Amelia, VA.

Children of Thacker and Jincey Archer

John Weyeth Archer (September 3, 1852 – September 25, 1925) married Julia Robinson daughter of John Nelson and Sallie Gray Robinson on December 28, 1887 in Amelia, VA. From this union nine children were born: George Vester Archer (September 27, 1888 – May 1,1948) Virginia Archer (1892) Ella Archer (1893), Charles Oferrall Archer (November 5, 1894 – November 8, 1974) who lived in Amelia, VA., Phillip Southall Archer (1896 – 1987) who was a carpenter for building construction. Robert Johnson Archer (May 24, 1901 – May 21, 1973) who was a farmer; Armistead Archer (July 1, 1902 – August 15, 1973), Lacy Archer (1906), and Morece Archer (1909)

Catherine Archer Gill (1862 – April 14, 1949) married Andrew Gill on August 25, 1886 and

Mary Archer 1864

William Sears Archer (December 6, 1864 – November 24, 1954) was born in Mississippi but, raised in Amelia, VA. Over the years, his granddaughter-in-law would always tell me how he reminded everyone that he was born in Mississippi. He would often tell people, "I'm a Mississippi man myself" reminding other Amelia County citizens, that he was not born in the county. In 1888 William married Fannie Simpson Bass. From this union eight children were born; Mabel Archer Stith (1901 – October 14, 1999) who married Benjamin Harrison Stith (February 12, 1891 – February 5, 1968) son of Peter Stith and Eliza Stokes of Nottoway, VA. Ben was a World War I veteran and was a retired railroad worker. The couple lived in Nottoway, VA. They had one child, Lorone Stith (1931). William Sears Archer (December 17, 1902 – March 12, 1972) married Sallie Baker (1905 – 1961) daughter of William Baker and Mary Robertson. The couple had five children; 1. James Warren Archer (July 3, 1926 – March 21, 1997) who married Victoria Robinson, daughter of Leon and Lucy Archer Robinson on April 24, 1947; Rev. Daniel Jones officiated the wedding ceremony. From this union three children were born: James Archer Jr. who married Nancy Epps and had three children. Franklin Leroy Archer (February 15, 1949 – February 16, 1949), and Sylvia Archer who has one daughter, Pastor Tara A. Owens, who is married to David Owens. Joan Archer Owens, who married Eyser Owens and has three sons. James and Victoria Archer has many grandchildren and great – grandchildren. 2.William S. Archer "Ziek" (May 21, 1927 – March 13, 1982) 3. Mary Louise Archer (January 10, 1929 – May 31, 1999) married George Bunn on October 2, 1953 in Richmond, VA. Ida Vivian Archer (May 2, 1934 – December 22, 1934) living in Richmond, VA. Franklin Archer (1938), and Joseph Rudolph Archer (1943) who is living and has one daughter. Lloyd Archer (1906 – 1974), Julia V. Archer (1908 – 1981), Bettie Archer (1910 – 1999), Freddie Ernest Archer (1912), Vernie Archer (1913), and Rozella Archer McCoy (1915 – 1963). There are many descendants of William Sears Archer and Fannie S. Bass.

George Gray Archer (June 10, 1868 – July 14,1962) was a farmer; and like most of the Archer family, he lived in Chula. He married Wertley Archer in 1896. Later, at the age of 74 he married Lottie Dixon Robinson on August 9, 1945 in Amelia, VA. Rev. Wallace Evans officiated the ceremony. Children of George and Wertley Archer: 1. Ruth Archer Spain (1894 – December 17, 1977) married William Spain (1892) on October 07, 1914 in Amelia County, Virginia. The couple lived in New Jersey and in the 1940s they lived on Wilson Street in Essex, New Jersey. From this union five children were born. William Spain Jr. (1916), Gladys Spain (1920), Horace Archer Spain (December 19, 1923 – September 1980) was born and raised in Essex, New Jersey, Elaine Spain (1929) and 5. Lillie Spain (1932)

Raymond Archer (January 4, 1897 – November 1980) lived in East Orange, New Jersey and was married to Ida B. Archer (1895); and later Ethel Spencer (1905)

Eugene Carrington Archer (January 20, 1899 – October 5, 1960) married Mabel Carter (1901- 1993) and had eight children: Eugene Archer (1922 – 1989), Pearl Archer Brown (May 27, 1924 – July 1, 2014) who married Reginald Brown Sr. the son of Major Brown and Agnes Tyler on January 15, 1945 in Richmond, VA. The couple had two children: Reginald Brown Jr., who is married to Deborah Brown, and Mabel Brown Chavis, who is married to Walter Chavis. Bertha Archer Johnson (1927) married Lovell Johnson on September 10, 1949 in Richmond, VA. Children: Earl Johnson married Princine Lewis (November 8, 1951 – March 29, 2009), Lovell Harrison Johnson (February 8, 1954 – July 12, 2005) married Irene Taylor Johnson; from this union there was one son; Teresa Johnson, Yvonne Johnson, and Jerry Johnson (1954 – May 1, 2009) who was a retired electrician for Phillip Morris. He was formerly married to Vanessa Johnson. Daniel Johnson. Robert Milton Archer (1928 – 2001) married Estelle Hatcher on July 1, 1950, Albert Archer (1931) married Sylvester Featherston (1924), daughter of Clinton and Mabel Venable Featherston on July 30, 1949 in Amelia, VA. From this union, 3 children were born: Albert Archer married Dorothy Gray and Charles Carrington Archer married Sharron Person Archer. Franklin Sonny Archer (1938 – 1997), and Aubrey Vanderbilt Archer (January 11, 1942 - March 16, 2015) who married Vivian Wright, daughter of Garland Thomas Wright and Ethel Edwards on July 15, 1974 in Richmond, VA. There are five children; Lorenzo Archer, Anthony Archer, and Rodney Archer who is married to Erica. Angela Archer Davis is married to Marcel Davis; Lynnette Brownlee is married to Mallory Brownlee

*Also from this lineage is a great researcher in his own right, Mr. Frank Archer

All of the grandchildren, great grandchildren and other descendants of Eugene and Mabel Archer are numerous

4.Gladys Archer (1900 – September 27, 1967) married Edgar Dallas Mason (1892) on September 10, 1918 in Richmond, VA. Lived in Nottoway, VA

5.George H. Archer (May 2, 1902 – December 14, 1965) lived in New Jersey

6. Bennet Hattel Archer (1904 – 1951) married Alice McDonald and lived in White Plains, New York

7. Julian Archer (1906 – 1986) lived in Newark, New Jersey

8. Virginia Archer Webb (September 8, 1907 – April 22, 1994) was married to Everett Webb

9. Wertley Archer West (May 1, 1911 – August 21, 1999) was married to Melbourne West (1913) and from this union two children were born: Leon West (1935), and Sylvia West (1936) Major Harvey Archer (November 1, 1912 – April 17, 1977) lived in Flushing, New York. Consuela Archer McCoy (February 10, 1914 – September 27, 1985) lived in Englewood, New Jersey. Grace Helen Archer Wilson (October 18, 1916 – April 17, 2006)

Lewis Ross Archer (January 1, 1869 – January 30, 1957) was a blacksmith and later, was a mortician and owned the L.R. Archer and Sons Funeral Home. Lewis' signature is seen on many of the death certificates I have researched for this project. Lewis married Kate Robinson (1877 – 1948) on April 7, 1891 in Amelia, VA. From this union four children were born. Charles Irving Archer (1891 – 1944) married Louise Robinson (November 13, 1893 – June 1970) who later became a store owner. In the late 1930's Charles and Louise lived on A4 Barclay in Newark, New Jersey. They later returned to Amelia, VA.

John W. Archer (1894 -1980) Richard Lewis Archer "Mr. Jordon Archer" married Henrietta Crawford. From this union, two children were born; Richard Archer Jr. (1936 – 1941) and Alvin Archer (1935) married Rose Jones of Plainfield, New Jersey. They have children and grandchildren. Sallie Winifred married Cedric Tyler; Laverne Archer Johnson, a former teacher, was formerly married to James Johnson and had one son and two grandchildren.

For more information on this family line see the book: Our Stories Our Struggles a History of African Americans in Amelia County, Virginia Complied by Henry J. Featherston.

Bettie Britton Archer (1875 – Jul 19, 1959) married Granville Harris (October 14, 1871 – April 22, 1937), the son of James and Susan Harris on December 24, 1903 in Amelia County, Virginia. Granville owned his own farm; Granville Harris (1904 – 1966) married Sarah Wingo (1904 – 2002) on March 10, 1941. From this union four children were born: Welford Harris (1942), Granville Evan Harris (1943 – 1992), Theresa Harris Stokes (1908 – 2012), Gregory Harris (1909 – 1972) married Bettie Archer Harris (1910 - 1999) on July 22, 1939.

<u>Children of William and Kate continued</u>

Henry Archer (1847 – 1893) married Julia Williams on August 19, 1885 in District of Columbia.

Mary Archer (1850) married Napoleon Drew on February 20, 1869 in Powhatan VA. They had five children: Mary Drew (1872), Thomas J. Drew (1872 – August 14, 1927) who married Louisa and moved to Philadelphia, PA, and Simon Drew (May 15, 1878 – 1948) who lived in Darbytown, PA where he worked as a butler and also owned and operated an oyster house restaurant and Ice cream shop in Chester, Pennsylvania. He was married to Mabel Felicia Cork (1883 – 1952) and had several children: Mabel Drew Gates (1904), Napoleon Frederick Drew (Oct. 9, 1906 - 1912), and Simon Drew (1909). There were also his siblings; Walter Drew (1879), Hattie Linn, Andrew Drew (1884), and John Walter Drew (1885).

Simon Archer (1851 – February 8, 1913) lived in the District of Columbia and was married to Victoria Archer. Simon was a carpenter and had his own shop in Washington, DC.

James Archer (1855)

Harriet Archer (1864)

Amy Archer death certificate

CERTIFICATE OF DEATH — COMMONWEALTH OF VIRGINIA
Bureau of Vital Statistics — State Board of Health

No. 4051
Registered No. 577

1. **PLACE OF DEATH**
   - County of: Henrico
   - City of: Richmond

2. **FULL NAME:** Amy Archer
   - (a) Residence: 1915-N-?

PERSONAL AND STATISTICAL PARTICULARS

3. Sex: Female
4. Color or Race: Col
5. Single, Married, Widowed, or Divorced: Widowed
5a. If married, widowed, or divorced, Husband of (or) Wife of: —
6. Date of Birth: —
7. Age: About 90 years
8. Occupation of Deceased: Domestic
9. Birthplace: Va
10. Name of Father: William Archer
11. Birthplace of Father: Va
12. Maiden Name of Mother: Kate — ?
13. Birthplace of Mother: Va
14. Informant: Kate C Nowell — (address) as above
15. Filed: Feb 23 1920 — Registrar: [signature]

MEDICAL CERTIFICATE OF DEATH

16. Date of Death: Feb 21, 1920
17. I hereby certify that I attended deceased from 2-14, 1920 to 2/20, 1920. That I last saw her alive on 2/20, 1920. And that death occurred on date stated above at 9:05 A.M.
    The cause of death was as follows: Senility
18. Where was disease contracted if not at place of death? —
    Did an operation precede death? No
    Was there an autopsy? No
    What test confirmed diagnosis? —
    (Signed) E. S. Roane, M.D.
    2/21 1920 Address: E. S. Roane

19. Place of Burial: Woodland — Date of Burial: 2-23-1920
20. Undertaker: A D Price
    Address: 210-12 E Leigh

No. 2758 Record for Bartlett Archer

Date of Application, March 27th 1871
Where born, Amelia Co. Va
Where brought up, do
Residence, Cor 8 & Canal
Age, 37
Complexion, Br
Occupation, Hostler
Works for,
Wife, Patsey
Children, Constance & Abraham

Father, William
Mother, Kate
Brothers, Wm, James, Thacker, Simon, Harrison, Henry
Sisters, Amy, Mary, Harriet

Signature, Cannot write

Thacker Archer and Jincey Gray Archer

This couple was one of the first major black land owners in Amelia County, Virginia; and Jincey perhaps was one of the first black storeowners in Amelia County, Virginia.

Bettie Archer Harris   Junius Archer (taken from Ancestry.com Photos

Aubrey Archer

Pearl Brown

Joseph Archer

Left to right. Mr. James Archer and Victoria R. Archer

Sylvia Archer

Below Deacon Eyser (Ike) and Joan Archer Owens

Edinboro Archer (July 1849 – 1907) was born a slave in Amelia, County, VA. His mother was a slave; Amy Archer, daughter of Kate Archer. His father was slave owner, Robert P. Archer and he was later a slave on Robert P. Archer's uncle's plantation, William Barksdale, and was priced at $700.00. By 1869, Edinboro had moved to Richmond, VA and worked as a carpenter. He later owned and ran a liquor store. He married Amanda Seay. In 1880 he moved to 1006 North Eighth Street in Richmond, which was his permanent residence until his death. Edinboro was a member of First African Baptist Church and was expelled from the church in 1880 after protesting over Rev. James Holmes and deacons. He later joined Fifth Baptist Church and was well known and loved in his community. In 1882, Edinboro was elected to the Richmond City Council's two boards; the Common Council from Jackson Ward and was also appointed to four committees of the Common Council of Richmond City from 1886 to 1888. Also, he was one of the six blacks who were admitted to the knights of labor reform caucus. Edinboro worked as a wheelwright and foreman for the Pioneer Transfer Company as well. In 1906, he worked for Evergreen Cemetery in Richmond, VA, where he served as superintendent of the cemetery. On December 3, 1907, Edinboro passed away and was buried in the Union Sycamore Cemetery in Barton Heights.

Jackson Ward in the early 1900s bottom left.   Present day Jackson Ward bottom right

Courtesy of the Valentine Museum

Pastor Tara Archer Owens is the daughter of Ms. Sylvia Archer, the granddaughter of James W. and Victoria R. Archer; and is one of the many descendants of Thacker and Virginia "Jincy" Gray Archer. She attended and graduated from the Amelia Public School System; and she united into holy matrimony on May 27, 1989 to Deacon David L. Owens, known as "Deacon Tony." They are the proud parents of three children and have been blessed with three grandchildren. Although still young, Pastor Tara Owens has been steadfast in carrying the word of God. After serving for many years as a minister, God gave Pastor Tara and her husband Deacon Tony a vision of a new ministry in the county of Amelia, and Destiny Worship Center was born. Since its inception just a few years ago, Destiny Worship Center (DWC) is standing strong as a beacon of hope for so many, including myself. Pastor Tara and Deacon Tony remain steadfast in winning souls for the Kingdom of God. In 2015, Pastor Tara Owens baptized 14 converts at one baptism. Although a new ministry, DWC is a progressive ministry that has a great Pastor that is nurturing us to be effective Christians through studying and ministering the word of God. Pastor Tara often reminds us that we are just imperfect people serving a perfect God. With her husband at her side, Destiny Worship Center is progressing daily; and because of the direction of our leader, and the prayers, labor and faithfulness of the members, the members of Destiny Worship Center are now owners of a property located in the Promise land section of Amelia, VA. We have successfully moved to our new church location. I am happy to be a part of this ministry and thank God for the labor, love and dedication of our Pastor Tara Owens and Deacon Tony Owens. To God be the glory for all the things he has done, and will do through DWC.

Richmond Common Council

This photograph was taken in 1909 at the State Capital in Richmond, VA when some of the city African American leaders met with President William Howard Taft. Edwin Archer Randolph is on the second row (Far left) The other leaders were all prominent successful men in Richmond, VA. 1st row:

The Harris family

The Harris family ancestors, can be traced to John Harris and Suckey they had a son John Harris (1824 – 1894)

John Harris (1824 – July 1894) was first married to **Julia** and later married **Fannie "Chritty" Jackson** (1852 – November 21, 1931) The daughter of Andrew Jackson (1810 – 1885) in Amelia, Virginia.

<u>Known Children of John Harris</u>

Overton Harris (1859 – 1922) was the son of John and Julia married Peggy Banks (1860 – 1942) in 1883. They had three children; 1. Violet Banks (1882 - 1882), 2. John Leslie Harris (August 20, 1889 – 1952) married Mary Harris. In 1920 John worked for Mr. George Perdue as a farm laborer. John and Mary Brown had one daughter Dora Brown. 3. Willie Harris (1893 – 1955) married Mary St. Clair Brown. (For descendants please see the Brown Family section)

John Harris (1870 – 1871) died at the age of 1.

Sep Harris (February 8, 1871 – March 30, 1940) lived on 1114 Catherine Street in Richmond, VA. He married Mary Wood on February 12, 1913 in Amelia County, VA. The couple divorced on July 22, 1921.

Rodger Harris (1877) married Bettie Robertson on August 21, 1957 in Amelia, VA.

Preston Harris (December 10, 1882 – October 1, 1958) worked as a farmer. He had one known son Edward "Eddie" Harris (deceased) who lived in the Pleasant Grove Community.

Ellen Harris (1885)

Geddes Harris (July 4, 1886 - April 22, 1957) moved to Richmond, VA and worked at the coal yard. Geddes married Rosa Bell Scott daughter of Dan and Ann Scott in Richmond, VA on October 16, 1913. In 1930, the family lived on Calhoun Street in Richmond, VA with two other family members Charlie Washington, and James Washington. Children: John Harris (1914) James Harris (1915) Isabelle Harris (1920 – 2003) Anna Harris (1923) Vernelle Harris (1926 – 1956) moved to District of Columbia. She was the mother of three children, Allen Harris, Maxine Harris, Arthur Brown. Eloise Alice Harris (1930) who married the late Mr. John Banks. For more information on Mrs. Eloise Banks family line please see the banks family section of the book.

Sarah Harris

Milton Harris

I am still researching the Harris family and will update at a later date.

The earliest Johnson slave I could trace in the Red Lodge Plantation was **Billy Johnson** (1810 – 1874) who was a farmer and was married to **Fannie Johnson** (1812). Because of the selling of slaves from one plantation to the other, it is not known how many children Billy and Fannie had. Only three have been confirmed.

Flora Johnson (1850) married George Brown (see The Brown Family section)

Archer Johnson (1853 - 1874)

Gifford Johnson (1854) moved to Richmond, VA in the 1890s

John Johnson (1836) was also a Johnson family slave on the plantation who was married to Phillis Johnson. The family connection to **Billy Johnson** is unknown. Phyllis was previously married to Joe Brown and lived in Red Lodge

John Johnson and Phillis had five children together: Jinny Johnson, Gus Johnson, Eliza Johnson (1870), Charles Johnson (May 25, 1873) married Sallie Roane on June 10, 1902 in Richmond, VA. They had one son Solomon Johnson (December 25, 1902 – 1968) was born in Richmond, VA and worked as a shoe shiner. He married Elizabeth Johnson and had a daughter, Helen Hortense Johnson Otley (December 6, 1929 – June 13, 1997). Peter Johnson (1876) who married Rebecca Ruffin Brown.

Ex-Salves Henry Johnson and Matilda Banks Johnson and Descendants

Another connection I was able to find to the Johnson family of the Lodge Plantation was the lineage of ex-slave **Henry Johnson** and **Matilda Banks** (1830) who is believed to be the sister of former slave Warner Banks. The couple had six children: Lewis, Jordan, Washington, Lucy, Charles, Baylor, and Maria Johnson. Henry appeared on the 1870 census and by 1880, Matilda was a widow living next door to her nephew Frank Banks near Red Lodge.

Children of Henry and Matilda Banks Johnson

Lewis Johnson (1842 -1892) who married Emily Anderson daughter of Queen Anderson who lived in the Lodore area of Amelia, VA on March 9, 1875 in Amelia, VA. Children of Lewis and Emily Johnson: Lin Johnson (1866), Willie Johnson (1867) Judge Johnson (1868) Millridge Johnson (1870) Josephine Johnson (1880 – 1907) was married to Ezekiel Brown. She had two daughters, Eliza Ann and Louise Johnson Wilson whom was also the daughter of Harrison Hyde; Pinkie Johnson (July 1882 – September 24, 1923) she lived in Amelia County, Virginia. Children of Pinkie Johnson: Judge Johnson (1897) moved to Philadelphia and fathered four children: 1. Florean Johnson (1920 - 2003) lived in Pennsylvania. 2. Inez Johnson (1921) 3. John E. Johnson (1924 – 1972) 4. Edward Johnson (1925) Porter Johnson (1902) Lewis Johnson (1904) Lee Johnson (1907) William Johnson (1908), Thomas Johnson (1916), Ivory Johnson (1917) and Woodbury Johnson (October 16, 1919 – February 23, 2003) who served in the United States Army and resided in Philadelphia, Pennsylvania; Ella Johnson (1882 – August 26, 1963) worked for a white widowed farmer "Plum" W.C. Purdie and lived in his home on Genito Road. She later lived for many years in the Pleasant Grove Community in Amelia, VA. Children of Ella Johnson: Emily Johnson Clements (August 16, 1906 – February 4, 1974) was the second wife of Ben Clements (1884) the son of Fredrick Clements and Mary Branch. Ben already fathered children by his late first wife Cora Sales. Emily known as Emma also had one son from a previous relationship: Junius Tyler, Jimmie Clements (1919) Paul Clements (January 1, 1923 – August 24, 1988), Alaska Clements, Ben Carter Clements, Charlie Clements, Ora Bell Clements (August 7, 1924 – December 26, 1931), Lyn Clements (1925), Samuel Clements (1926), Elizabeth Laverne Clements was born in 1927 married Moses Harding Mitchell on November 24, 1951 in Amelia, VA; Helen Clements (October 20, 1929 – March 1, 2001) lived in Philadelphia, PA; Mary Clements Jeter (February 21, 1931 – October 17, 2005) she married Deacon Charlie Jeter on March 17, 1951 in Amelia, VA. Mary was a lifelong member of Liberty Baptist Church and also supported the Flower Hill Baptist Church where her husband, Charlie Jeter was a faithful member; Rosa Clements Smith (December 12, 1935 – October 10, 1991), Sarah Clements Squires (October 17, 1937 – February 9, 2001) married William Preston Squires on December 22, 1967 in Richmond, VA; Queen Victoria Clements was born in 1939 married Robert Reed on June 27, 1959; Charlie Clements (August 29, 1944) married Pearl Barksdale on July 8, 1978 in Alexandria, VA; Catherine Ellen Clements (February 26, 1946 – April 10, 1984), and Matilda Clements.

The descendants of Ben and Emily includes grandchildren, great – grandchildren and great – great grandchildren.

Mildred Johnson (1908)

Lucy Johnson Dilworth (1912 - 1978) married Arthur Lee Dilworth the couple had several children. One known Arthur Lee Dilworth (July 12, 1928 – October 14, 2015)

Jordan Johnson (1850) married Margaret Venable daughter of Lydie Venable in Amelia, VA. She was raised by her step – father, Tilman Venable.

Children of Jordan and Margaret Venable Johnson

Annie Johnson (1871 – June 15, 1923) who married **Matt Tyler** (1867 – 1934) on October 23, 1889 in Amelia, VA.

Eddie Johnson (1879 – October 1894) John Johnson (1883) married Phoebe Bannister the daughter of Monroe and Ellen Bannister in Powhatan, VA on November 27, 1905. From this union one son was born Sylvester M. Johnson (December 13, 1912 – July 19, 1973) married Lilington Odessa Coleman (October 25, 1916 – February 14, 1989) the daughter of James Coleman and Jane Jones on December 6, 1942 in Richmond, VA. The couple lived on 317 South Granby apt.4 in Richmond, VA Sylvester worked as a construction worker in Richmond, VA. Fiby Johnson (February 1885) Maude Johnson (1889) Joseph Johnson (1892 – April 4, 1957) worked as a janitor and lived in Richmond, VA.

Washington Johnson (1858) married **Edmonia Brown** daughter of George and Emily Brown. He was the father of Flora Johnson who married Archer Jones (see Brown section). Lucy Ann Johnson (1859 – July 1889) died at the age of 30 she has no known descendants. **Sheppard Johnson** (1862) appeared as son of Henry and Matilda Johnson in the 1870 census. His descendants are unknown. **Baylor Johnson** (October 1869 – June 5, 1914) a lifelong farmer married **Alice Smith** on May 3, 1879 the daughter of Jim and Martha Smith in Amelia County, Virginia. Baylor's home was located on Genito Road across from present day Whittington farm. The home in which he lived in burned down and a new home was built before 1920. The new home which his wife Alice lived in until moving to Baltimore, MD. After Alice moved her daughter Bessie lived in the home raising her nephew Cyrus Johnson, her children, and grandchildren.

Children of Baylor and Alice S. Johnson:

Pollie Johnson (1881) Leslie Johnson (1884 – February 5, 1928) married Elnora Harris on December 5, 1905 in Powhatan, VA. Leslie later married Maria Harrison (1880 – 1975) daughter of Joe and Malinda Harrison on August 8, 1911 in Richmond, VA. In 1910 Leslie worked at a dairy barn and Maria worked as a Tobacco hand at a Tobacco Factory. The couple lived on Second Street in Richmond, VA. By 1920 the couple resided at 1204 First street in Richmond, VA. Children of Leslie and Maria: Esther Johnson (1902) Edward Johnson (1910) Edna Mae Johnson Willis (1912 – 1964) married James Willis on October 23, 1939 in Richmond, VA. James worked as an Electrician in the city of Richmond. Sylvester Alder Johnson (1916 – 1994) married Notice Elizabeth Singleton on November 24, 1951 in Richmond, VA. Sylvester worked as a guard and the couple lived on 509 Randolph Street in Richmond, VA. Sandy Lee Johnson (1923 – 1954) married Lillie Mae Randolph daughter of Peyton Randolph and Alvena Ellis on September 19,1946 in Richmond, VA. James Johnson (1885 – August 11, 1935) worked as a Jewelry Manufacture and married Mary Johnson. Lottie Johnson (1888) Grace Johnson (1890) Mary Johnson (1895) Martha Johnson Epps (1894 – November 7, 1971) was married to Edmund Epps. The couple resided in the Pleasant Grove Community in Amelia, VA. Martha was known as a great cook, and was well known in the community. Martha passed away in Glen Burnie, MD. Martha was the mother of three children, Cyrus Johnson (died in 1993) also known as Teddy who worked for the saw mill and for Wood Farm. Cyrus married Harriet Bannister and Mrs. Joanna Epps Watts Smith (March 17, 1915 – May 23, 1997) also known as Joan married James Smith of Richmond, VA on April 20, 1936 in Richmond, VA. and

Edward Sidney Johnson. Pearl Johnson (1899) David Johnson (1901 – May 25, 1916) Bessie Johnson Banks (see Warner Banks section), Alice Johnson, Daisy Johnson (1916 – July 20, 1916)

John Johnson (1836) was also a slave on the plantation who married to **Phillis Johnson** on November 26, 1868. Phyllis was previously married to Joe Brown who had three children by her previous marriage: Caroline Brown Banks (1860 – 1910) who later married Frank Banks. James Brown (1863) and Gosset Brown (1868)

 John Johnson and Phillis had five children together

Jinny Johnson (1861), **Gus Johnson** (1864), **Lizzie Johnson** (1867), **Eliza Johnson** (1870) **Charles Johnson** (1873) was married to Sallie Johnson in Amelia, VA. They had one son, Solomon Johnson (December 25, 1892 – July 30, 1968) was married to Elizabeth Johnson and they had two children: Helen Hortense Johnson (1929 – 1997) was married to Eddie Jackson Sr. (1916 – 1975) and later to William Andrew Otley. Helen had six children; Eddie Jackson Jr., Horatio Jackson, Michael Jackson, Kevin Jackson, Andre Jackson, and Colita Jackson. Alma Johnson Mariani (1931 – 1999) she had two children, Darryl Johnson, and Orlando Johnson.

Peter Johnson (1876) lived in Amelia and later married Rebecca Ruffin Brown and lived in Red Lodge off of present day Rocky Branch Rd.

Bessie Johnson and family

Home of Bessie Johnson

Martha Epps, Cyrus, Harriet Johnson, Keith and Kenneth Johnson   Cyrus Jr. and Mary Johnson

Mary, Cyrus Sr., Harriet and Cyrus Johnson Jr.   Martha Johnson Epps

Clements Family

Ben Clements and Robert Brooks

Johnson & Clements Family

Peter Clements

Isabelle Jasper Clements

Victoria Searles

Royal Clements

Susan C. Smith

William Clements

Floyd Clements

Home of Ben Clements

Lee Johnson

Mary Clements Jeter

Woodbury Johnson

Queen Clements Reed

Sonny farming

Junius Tyler

Matilda Clements

William Jr., Lynn, and Sonny Clements

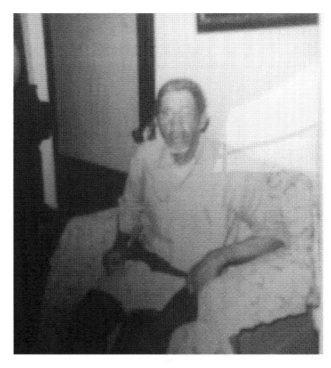
William Sonny Clements

Unknown Pics of the Johnson

Pics submitted by: Gladys Clements and Lorraine C. Patrick

Gladys, Daniel, and Sonny

Floyd Clements

Lorraine, baby Daniel and Gladys

Arthur Lee Dilworth

Venable Family

In 2012 while researching the Red Lodge plantation, I came across a story about The Lodge in a book entitled "Old Homes and Buildings in Amelia County, Virginia from the memoirs of Mrs. Kate S. Berkeley. In the story, it mentions a slave named Tilman who was the carriage driver for the Archer's. After finding William S. Archer's 1855 Inventory Account with the list of names of the slaves I saw Tillman's name and it caused me to further research him. Since that time, I have found and connected many of the families of Amelia and Powhatan to Tillman Archer who after 1870 along with his wife and children, changed his last name to Venable.

Tilman "Archer" Venable (1823) married **Lydie Archer Venable** (1840) after 1870 the family moved from The Lodge to Ruffin Lane.

Children of Tilman and Lydia Venable

Margaret Venable (1854) who daughter Annie Johnson married Matt Tyler. She is the grandmother of Frank B. Tyler Sr.

Louisa Venable (1855) married John Brown and was the mother of Ada Ruffin and also the grandmother of John Allen Ruffin and Geneva Ruffin.

Tom Venable (1869) married Caroline Taylor on August 21, 1892 in Powhatan, VA. The couple had eight children: Mary Venable (1883) Lydia Venable (1889) married Douglas Hudson (1879 – April 28, 1967); Tom Venable (1892) Kate Venable Brown (August 26, 1895 – December 15, 1922) married Henry Brown; Ella Venable (December 26, 1900 – December 26, 1919) Betty Venable married Douglas Hudson on December 15, 1920 in Powhatan, VA; From this union seven children were born; 1. Mary Hudson (1921) 2. Caroline Hudson (1924) 3. Lizzie Hudson (1926) 4. Fannie Hudson (1928) 5. Florine Hudson (1930) 6. Douglas Hudson Jr. (1932) 7. Queen Victoria Hudson (1932); Oliver Wingo Venable (1907) married Loretta Thomas; Annie Venable (1894 – 1896) Walter Venable (October 1, 1875 – October 3, 1943) married Lucy Venable on February 8, 1896 in Amelia, VA. He later married Lucy Green on February 8, 1896 in Amelia VA and resided on 1828 Parkwood Avenue in Richmond, VA. He worked as a HOD Carrier he would carry a three - sided box filled with bricks or mortar. Children of Walter Venable: Hattie Venable (1894) Walter Thomas Venable (May 6, 1896 – March 21, 1965) Gussie Lewis (September 17, 1899 – January 30, 1961) married Theodore Lewis (November 27, 1897 – February 9, 1948) on February 28, 1916 in Richmond, VA. The couple had three children, Theodore Lewis Jr. (1917) Dorothy Lewis (1918) Frank Lewis (1919)

Octavia Venable (1903 – 1951)

Page Berdelia Venable Armstrong (1904)

Samuel W. Venable (1907 – January 28, 1952) had one son Julian Venable.

Allen Venable (1910 – 1932)

Scott Family

Since I was young, I have always heard the Red Lodge residents speak of Caroline Scott place which was located near the Smith Family home on present day Rocky Branch Road. I was told that the Scott home stood for many years and several families lived at the residence after the Scott family. The eldest Ancestors I have traced of the Scott family is **Edmund** and **Polly Scott**. After Edmunds death, Polly later married **James Thrower** (1815)

Children of Polly Scott Thrower

David Scott (1851) married **Caroline Patrick** the daughter of Charles and Louisa Patrick on August 25, 1875 in Amelia, VA. David was a farmer and Caroline was the nurse and midwife of the neighborhood. The couple had seven children; Edmoline Scott (1885) Wilson Scott (1888 – 1955) Sarah Scott Calloway (1890 – 1952) Mary Scott Shields (1893 – 1940) lived in Richmond, VA lived on G24 North 28th street Richmond, VA. She is buried in the Liberty Baptist Church cemetery. Anna Scott Jasper (1900 – 1975) married Warner Jasper (1895) the couple had four children: Ben Warner Jasper (1917), David Jasper (1919), James Wilson Jasper (1919 – 1991), Mary Jasper Randolph (February 14, 1924 -June 11, 2015) married Burnis Randolph (1921 – 1987). Sarah Scott Callaway (May 10, 1905 – August 22, 1952) Amelia, Virginia. She married Robert Eldridge Callaway of Lynchburg, VA. The couple resided in Richmond, VA. They had one daughter, Blanche Callaway Jones (December 1, 1919 - June 19, 1970) who married Louis Jones son of Edwin and Lizzie Hyde Jones. Louis and Blanche lived in Richmond, VA. Blanche was baptized and joined the Sharon Baptist Church at an early age. Blanche was educated at the Richmond Public Schools System and graduated in 1936. She later furthered her education and later received her Master's degree from Virginia State College. She then started a teaching career in Spotsylvania County and later in Richmond, VA. She is buried at Mount Minnis Memorial Park in Richmond, VA.

Blanche Calloway Jones

Mary Jasper Randolph

Fisher Family

Harry Hyde Fisher (1818) and his wife **Dinah Brown** (1827) was a former slave of the Lodge. Harry was a farmer and after slavery the family moved to Powhatan, VA.

<u>Harry and Dinah Fisher's Children</u>: **Joseph P. Fisher** (1854 – 1939) born in Amelia, VA. On November 14, 1877 **Joseph** married **Jardenah Granderson** in Powhatan, VA. From this union five children were born, Martha Fisher Thomas (1879), Reverend Joshua Harry Fisher (1881 – 1979) was the pastor of Hollywood Baptist Church in Powhatan, VA. Joseph Fisher (1885 - 1979) married Blanche Turner Fisher on May 16, 1912. He later married Maggie Scruggs Fisher on January 10, 1932 in Powhatan, VA. He fathered six children: Joshua Fisher (1916) Gertrude Fisher (February 25, 1917 – December 27, 1978) Lillian Fisher (1920) Paul Fisher (December 8, 1921 – December 28, 1998) Joseph Robert Fisher (December 7, 1922 – August 15, 1999) lived in Powhatan County, VA. Blanche Fisher (1926), Fannie Fisher (December 4, 1889), Jardenia Fisher (1893 -1957) married Joseph Granderson on March 18, 1915 in Powhatan, VA. The couple had three children, 1. Garland Peyton Granderson (1915 – 1967) married Mary Elizabeth Goode (1920 – 1994) on October 25, 1941 in Richmond, VA. Thelma Granderson Robinson (1918 – 1992) married Edward Blair Robinson in Richmond, VA. Elizabeth Granderson Johnson (September 21, 1921 – August 9, 1985) married Oliver Johnson and had one daughter, Jerdenia Johnson Robinson. Berkeley Kelster Dabney Fisher (1896 – 1965) **Berkeley Fisher** (1855 – March 17, 1939) was born at Red Lodge Plantation and was later owned by William Barksdale until he was emancipated. Berkeley married December 29, 1882 to Nancy Bannister daughter of Jordon and Betsey Bannister, Cordelia Turner (1866) on December 27, 1908 in Powhatan County, Virginia. And he later married Mary Brown (1885). He had one son, James Fisher. **Edith Fisher** (1865) married Jefferson Jones (1859) son of Ro and Eliza Jones on February 24, 1881 in Powhatan, VA.

Ida Graham (1873 -1949) lived in Amelia, VA.

Name:	Edith Fisher
Gender:	Female
Marital Status:	Single
Race:	Black
Age:	16
Birth Date:	1865
Birth Place:	Amelia Co.
Marriage Date:	24 Feb 1881
Marriage Place:	Powhatan, Virginia
Father:	<u>Harry Hyde Fisher</u>
Mother:	<u>Deana Fisher</u>
Spouse:	<u>Jefferson Jones</u>
FHL Film Number:	2048470
Reference ID:	Powhatan Image 306

Rev. Joshua Fisher

The Jasper Family

Tom Jasper was a slave from the Peachy Family was most likely born in Fluvanna, VA and was related to Rev. John Jasper. It is believed through DNA analysis and other sources that Tom Jasper was the brother of Phillip Jasper (the father of John Jasper). The name of Tom Jasper's wife is unknown at this time. There is only one son that has been identified, his name was Warner Jasper.

Warner Jasper (1811 – December 1881) lived in Amelia County, Virginia where he worked for many years as a farmer. Warner was married to **Phoebe Jefferson Jasper** (1814 – December 20, 1879) who was a slave of Red Lodge and Dr. Randolph's Plantation.

Children of Warner and Phoebe Jasper: **Martha Jasper** (1833 – 1913) moved to Norfolk VA. **Cary Jasper** (1852 – 1930) married Lydia Bannister (1860 – 1930). Cary served in the Civil War and after the war ended in 1865. Children of Cary Jasper and Lydia Bannister: **James Jasper** (1874 – 1959) known to all as Mr. Jim Jasper married Emma Jane Clements (1875 – 1942). James and Emma divorced on September 1928, he married Peggie Thomas Tinsley Clements. James and Emma had seven children: 1. Freddie Jasper (October 4, 1895 - May 10, 1963) was a World War 1 veteran. He was a farmer and was married to Victoria Jones of Powhatan, VA. He loved to deer hunt and adopted two children, Eli and Audrey Jean Jasper as his own. George Jasper (1898) 2. Warner Jasper (May 22, 1899 – June 24, 1929) married Anna Scott daughter of David and Caroline Scott on July 26, 1916. They had four children Ben, James, David, and Mary Scott 3. Rosa Sue Jasper Thompson (1901 – March 14, 1958) for many years "Mrs. Sue" as she was called, worked for many years as a babysitter. She married Augustus Thompson (1894 – 1986) son of Essex and Maria Jackson Thompson. The couple had two children, Maria Thompson (1917) married Frank Clements and had one daughter, Blanche Clements and a son, James Augustus Thompson (1918 – 1962) whom was known as Essex, was married to Bettie Banks daughter of Mckinley Banks in Amelia, VA. He worked at the sawmill and also raised gardens. 4. James Jasper (1904) 5. Mary Jasper (1904 – 1921) 6. McKinley William Jasper (July 22, 1908 – July 12, 1986) was known to the Lodge community as "Snowbird." He was an avid hunter and a hard worker. He was employed for many years at Wood Farm, Crawford Manufacture, and for the Wildlife. He married Senia Robinson (July 4, 1911 – February 6, 2004). She was the daughter of Albert Robinson and Nannie Hines Brown. From this union eight children were born. John James Jasper (January 20, 1929 – December 16, 1969) McKinley Melvin Jasper (May 12, 1930 - December 29, 2012) known to all as Jake worked for the Anderson sawmill, The Vaughan's, Charlie Gryder, the Richmond Foundry and also, Richfood where he retired in the early 1990's. He was married to Martha Elizabeth Gaskins daughter of Nelson Gaskins and Rosa Lewis on July 25, 1959 in Powhatan, VA. The couple had an adopted daughter Teresa Brown and two daughters, Doris J. Jasper who married Monroe Mayo and Elaine Jasper who married Warren Raymond Howell. Walter Fred Jasper (1933 – 2016) and married Mary F. Mondrey on May 6, 1956. From their union several children were born, Walter Jasper, Joyce Ann Jasper Johnson, Wayne Jasper, Connie Jasper, and Stephen Jasper. Roosevelt Jasper (1936) married Ms. June Taylor in 1958. Children of Roosevelt and June Jasper, Vanessa Jasper is married to Jeffery Booker. Brenda Jasper Scott married to the late Alphonso Scott. Daphne Jasper is married to Javan Holman. Anita Jasper is married Henry Royal. Minister Rhonda Jasper is married to Robert "Bobby" Jones. Nannie Marie Jasper (living) married Herman Sheff; William Franklin Jasper (living) married Gayle Brown and has children, and grandchildren. Lawrence Jasper (deceased) Joe Jasper, Emma Jasper (living). 7. Nora Jasper Jones (1878 – 1981) married Preston Jones. (see the Jones Family Line**)**

Isabelle Jasper Clements (April 26, 1883 – February 21, 1924) married Peter Clements (1880 – 1935) on April 15, 1903 in Amelia, VA. Children of Peter and Isabelle Clements: Harry Clements (January 12, (1904 – September 30, 1927) Noyed Clements (1907 – December 1958) married Rachel Brown daughter of Isaac and Susie Brown of Powhatan, VA. Jerry Clements (1907- 1980) who married Caroline Jefferson on December 24, 1958 in Powhatan, VA. They had four children, Kenneth Clements (1928) Jerry Clements Jr. (1928 – 1928) Osborn Clements, John Harry Clements (April 27, 1935) married Caroline Jefferson (1938) in Powhatan, VA. Sadie French (1909 – 1985) Lillie Clements (1911) Gertrude Clements (1911 – 1975) Victoria Gwen Clements Searles (January 31, 1913 – April 27, 1984) married George Searles. Gertrude Clements Farthing (1911 – 1975), Royal Lafatal Clements (1917 – 1973) was raised by his aunt, Nora Jasper Jones. in 1940 Royal worked as a carpenter, and lived as a boarder in New Jersey and later resided on 1420 Chapin street in Washington, DC where he worked as a Clerk. He was married to Ruth Clements and had several children, Ruthann Clements Murphy, Shelia Robinson, Barbara Moore, and Harry J. Clements; Susan Virginia Lee Clements (1924 – 1994) raised by her aunt Nora (For more information please the Smith Family page) **Haskins Jasper** (October 30, 1892 - October 24, 1965) was a farmer for many years and worked for Willie Wright farm once a year. He loved to hunt until later in life he became crippled from a debilitating disease. After his health began to fail, Haskins did not give up. He would often crawl to visit his niece Rosa Sue Jasper. Recalling a story told to me years ago, Deacon Emmett Robinson had a horse pasture in between Haskins land and Rosa Thompson's house. Haskins on several occasions, would crawled his way to the gate and opened it, the problem was once he opened the gate he could not shut it which caused the horses to run out of the pasture. Emmett would often laugh telling the story how he had become tired of getting those horses back in the pasture, so he decided to make a door on the gate. The door was close to the ground which made it more accessible for Haskins to open and close. After Mr. Haskins died, he was buried on his property beside his wife Nellie Brown Jasper. His land is owned by the Epperson family and although the gravesite is now wooded, every year wild flowers covers Haskins and Nellie's grave. Haskins had one daughter, Victoria Jasper (deceased). He also had a son by another relationship, Ivory Johnson (deceased). Georgie Jasper (1893 - 1968) married John Hutchinson son of Henry and Bertha Hutchinson of Mecklenburg, VA. She moved to Essex New Jersey. They had one son, James John Hutcheson (1911 – 1966)

Phoebe Jasper Cables (1891 – February 11, 1941) moved to Richmond, VA and worked as a servant for the Cohen family who lived on Grace Street. Phoebe later moved to Gloucester, New Jersey where she worked as a servant for Mr. R. Hilliard Gage who lived on South Princeton avenue. At the time of her death, Phoebe was living in Philadelphia, Pennsylvania.

Cary Jasper Jr. (October 25, 1895 – October 11, 1958) married Rosa Brown daughter of Beverly Brown

Landon Jasper married Leona Bannister

Warner Jasper Jr. (1840)

Alice Jasper Walker married **Israel Walker** (1824) it is believed that he was named after his father Israel. Israel worked as a wheelwright repairing wooden wheels in Amelia, VA. Israel and Alice children: Caroline Walker (1852 – August 7, 1955) lived in Pennsylvania. Jessy Walker (1859) Phoebe Walker Branch (1861 – February 23, 1918) lived in Richmond, VA. She worked as a laundress and lived on Boyd Street in Richmond, VA. Nancy Walker (1862) married Armstead Scott on June 30, 1883. Emily Walker

(1865) Dinah Walker (1867) Amy Walker Anderson married Walter Anderson son of Sam and Mary Anderson on October 18, 1893 in Amelia County, VA. Amy Walker (November 26, 1894 – August 7, 1989) died during the birth of her only child, Alice Amy Anderson Lewis (1894 – 1989). Alice, married John Lewis (1885 – 1955) a successful black business man who was a large landowner of Amelia, County. Virginia. He was the son of Granderson Lewis and Lavinia Warren Lewis who lived in the Mattoax area of Amelia, VA. Alice worked for a while for the novelist Ellen Glasgow. Darlene Lewis Robinson who is the granddaughter of John and Alice Lewis, remembers her grandmother as a great cook. She also stated that her grandmother made good homemade biscuits. Alice was a lifelong member of Flower Hill Baptist Church and her husband John was a member of Liberty Baptist Church. (For the descendants of Amy Anderson Lewis please see Carrie Branch Ruffin descendants on the Brown family page.)

Peachy Jasper (1857 – 1930) married Jane Robinson (1859) the daughter of on October 30, 1879 in Amelia, VA. Peachy was a carpenter and own his personal farm.

Children of Peachy and Jane Robinson Jasper

Blair Jasper (1881 – 1938) married Ellen and had two children, Melvin Jasper and Marie Elizabeth Jasper.

Thomas Jasper (1884 – 1936) married Fannie Pride (1890 – June 22, 1918) on June 23, 1907 in Amelia, VA. He later married Ellen Miller on January 11, 1908 in Amelia, VA. Thomas and Fannie had two daughters: Caldonia Jasper Mitchell (1907 – 1959) was married to Charlie Mitchell (1908) Charles was a farmer and very hardworking. Children of Charles and Caldonia Mitchell: Christine Mitchell Ross Coleman (February 19, 1929 – October 3, 2010) she was the mother of three children, Yvonne Harris, Carolyn Ruffn, Cornelia Turner who is married to Wayne Turner. Fannie Mitchell (March 20, 1932 – November 2, 2006) married Rev. Willie James Henderson son of Willie Henderson and Rozelle Miles on December 3, 1949. He was better known as Rev James Henderson or "Pork Chop". Children of Rev. James and Fannie Mitchell: Verline Henderson (1951 – 2009) was an educator and lived in Petersburg, VA; Melinda Mckonnen, James Henderson Jr. (deceased) was married to Sharon Jefferson; Warren Henderson, and Gerry Henderson; Jennie Mable Mitchell Henderson (March 5, 1935 – Jan 1992) married Deacon Fred Henderson (February 17, 1930 – August 15, 2015). Children of Deacon Fred and Mable Mitchell Henderson: Evang. Delois Henderson, Joyce Henderson Morgan, Fred Henderson who is married to Grace Butler Henderson, Viola Henderson, Rex Henderson, Lonnie Henderson married Charlotte Hill; Charles Joseph Mitchell (March 12, 1937 – November 22, 1999) who was formerly married to Virginia Ruffin. From this union three children were born, Charles Joseph Mitchell Jr, Charlotte Mitchell and Brad Mitchell; Catherine Dorothy Mitchell Nash (August 26, 1940 – June 6, 2003) was known to all as "Dottie" married Wardell Nash Sr. son of Ernest Nash and Annie Brown on November 20, 1960 in Amelia, VA. Children of Waddell and Dottie Nash: Sharon N. Edwards who married Thomas Edwards, Corrine N. Owens who married John Anthony Owens; Wardell Nash Jr. and Steven Nash who is married to Melita Nash; Courtney Laura Jasper Smith (1914 – 2004) married Willie Smith Sr. (1937 - 1996) and had two known children, Willie Smith Jr. (1937 - 1996) and Regina Smith (1938) Laura Jasper Clayborn (1894) lived in Bronx, NY. James Jasper (1894) Florence Jasper Baptist (July 26, 1894 – April 7, 1975) married James Baptist. Bolding Branch Jasper (1899 – December 5, 1963) married Ruth Japer who lived on 301 Grayland Avenue in Richmond, VA. Dorothy Jasper Tyler (1904 – 1988) was a school teacher for many years at the Promise Land School and Russell Grove High School. She was married to Joseph Moody Tyler in Amelia County, Virginia. She was a faithful member of Pleasant Grove Baptist Church.

Jenny Mabel Mitchell

Fred Henderson Sr.

Christine Coleman

Carolyn Mitchell Ruffin

Fannie Henderson

Dorothy Jasper Tyler

Min. Lonnie Henderson

Verline Henderson

Georgie Jasper Hutchinson

Charles Mitchell Jr., Fannie Henderson, Christine Coleman, Catherine Dottie Nash, and Alvah Mitchell

Charles Mitchell and James Henderson

PENSIONERS now on the ROLL are NOT required to make new application, but must file annual certificate.

This Application must be filed with the Clerk of the Corporation Court of Your City or Circuit Court of Your County

(No application will be entertained not on the printed form.)

FORM No. 6

APPLICATION of a person who served the Confederate States in the war between the States as body servant of a soldier in service, cook, hostler, teamster, Confederate guard, or who buried the Confederate dead, worked on breastworks, in railroad shops, blacksmith shops, in Confederate hospitals, under the direction of the Confederate Government, by act approved March 14, 1921, as amended March 30, 1926.

I, Cary Jasper, do hereby apply for a pension under the provisions of the Act of the General Assembly of Virginia, approved March 14, 1924, as amended by act approved March 25, 1926, relating to Confederate pensions.

I do solemnly swear that I am a citizen of the State of Virginia, and that I have been an actual resident of the said State for two years next preceding the date of this application, and that I served the Confederate States Government in the War between the States as __laborer__ and that I am now disabled and from the effects of such disability, I am incapacitated from following any occupation for a livelihood; and that during the said war I was loyal and true to the Confederacy and duties assigned me, and by reason of such service and disability, I am now entitled to receive the pension under the provisions of said act. And I further swear that my income from any source of employment, or any other source does not exceed four hundred dollars ($400.00) per annum. I do further swear that I do not receive a pension from this or any other State, or from the United States. I do solemnly swear that the answers given to the questions which I am required to answer in this application are true to the best of my knowledge and belief.

ALL QUESTIONS MUST BE ANSWERED FULLY

1. What is your name? **Cary Jasper**
2. What is your age? **About 90** years
3. Where were you born? **At Clay Hill, Amelia County Virginia**
4. How long have you resided in Virginia? **All my life**
5. How long have you resided in the City or County of your present residence? **All my life.**
6. In what branch of the service were you employed? **Laborer on breastworks and trenches**
7. What service did you render? **Laborer on breastworks and trenches**
8. Under whose order or by whose request did you render the service above explained? **George Thraves**

9. Who was your master at the time of entering upon duties in the war between the States? **William R. Barksdale**
10. If he or any one of his family is living, give name and address. **Mrs. J.C. Jefferson (Grand Daughter) Amelia, Va. Mrs. Nannie Bolling (Grand-daughter) Alexandria, Va.**
11. When did you begin such service? **1863**
12. Where did you begin such service? **Chickahominy Swamp**
13. When and why did you leave the service? **At end of war. Last worked at bridge at Mattoax, Va. on Appomattox River.**
14. Where do you reside? If in a city, give street address.
    Postoffice **Mattoax**
    County of **Amelia** Virginia
15. What is your occupation for earning a livelihood? **Have been a farmer but am unable to work now.**
16. What is your annual income from all sources? $ **nothing except what my children may give me.**

A signature made by X mark is not valid unless attested by a witness.

WITNESS _____

_____
Signature of Applicant.

I, **Jos. K. Irving** a **commissioner in Chancery** in and for the **Circuit Court** of **Amelia County**, in the State of Virginia, do certify that the applicant whose name is signed to the foregoing application, personally appeared before me in my **County** aforesaid, having the aforesaid application read to him and fully explained, as well as the statements and answers therein made, the said applicant made oath before me that the said statements and answers are true.

Given under my hand this **3rd** day of **June**, 1929.

_____
Commissioner in Chancery
Signature of Officer.

McKinley Jasper and his wife: Senia Robinson Jasper   Roosevelt Jasper

Walter (Mickey) Fred Jasper   Walter and Mary Jasper and family

Mckinley Jasper   Anita, Rhonda, Daphne, Brenda and Vanessa   Mrs. June Jasper

Family and history of Rev. John Jasper

Over 20 years ago, my aunt Dr. Sandra Seay who is and longtime educator, noticed my appreciation for African American history and gave me a book of the sermon by Rev. John Jasper entitled: "De Sun do Move." I vividly remembering showing McKinley "Jake" Jasper the book and he said to me that he was told he was related to Rev. Jasper. From an autobiography written by Edwin Archer Randolph and many other documents, I have pieced together this family relationship. It appears that Tom Jasper the ancestor of the present day Amelia Jasper Family is the brother of Rev. John Jasper father, Phillip Jasper. As said earlier, The Peachy Family owned the Jasper family who later were sold, willed or given to their relatives and friends including the Bannister, The Tabb's who owned the Forest Plantation, and Archer's The Lodge Plantation among others. The Peachy Family were huge land owners owning plantations in Fluvanna, James City, Amelia County, and Williamsburg, VA Some of the names of the plantations: Tazewell Hall, Sands Quarters, and Old Spring Lot.

Slave Phillip Jasper (1762 – 1812) was born in Fluvanna County, VA and married Tina Hammond on June 12, 1780. He is believed to be the brother of Tom Jasper. The couple had 24 children and the youngest child, later became known throughout the United States. Tina started out as a farm hand in Fluvanna but later was sent to some of the Peachy family in Williamsburg where she worked the land but her primary duty was making clothes for the slaves on the plantation. Tina later was sent to Amelia, VA where she spent her last years working in the Peachy house. According to Edwin Archer Randolph's book, Tina would often visit family on neighboring plantations with the permission of the Peachy's family. Out of the 24 children Tina had there is only 1 that I was able to research, the great Reverend John Jasper.

Reverend John Jasper (July 4, 1812 – March 30, 1901) whose first occupation as a child was to be a cart boy. His main task was to stand before the oxen while cart is being loaded and unloaded. The other position the cart boy had to help the driver manage the oxen which pulled the ox cart. As he grew older, John was sent to live in the Peachy home. His duties were: Being a waiter during meals, and yard work. He later was hired out by Mr. McHenry for a year to work in Richmond, Va. The following year, he was hired out to Dr. Woolridge in the Coal mines of Midlothian and Chesterfield, VA. He accepted Christ as his personal Savior while walking around Capital Square on July 4, 1839. He later answered God call for his life to carry the Gospel of Jesus Christ at the age of twenty-seven. In 1842 he began his ministry at the First African Baptist Church. Rev. Jasper was an awesome preacher who could deliver a sermon that lifted the souls of blacks and whites during and after Slavery. While a slave Jasper preached many slave funerals in just about every city and county throughout Virginia. Once while he was preaching, a group of angry white men stopped Jasper saying that it wasn't right to have a colored preaching the Gospel. A young white boy defended Jasper and proclaimed to the men that Jasper was preaching the truth.

Not one day did Rev. John Jasper spend in a classroom, yet while being led by the Holy Spirit he caught the attention of many later becoming one of the most influential black leaders of his time. Using what little he learned to preach the word of God. While a slave, John was allowed to occasionally preach to Freedmen at the

First African Baptist Church. Carrying the word of God for Jasper meant carrying his own cross. Rev. John Jasper was sent to Petersburg to carry donations given by the colored Baptist Churches to the Foreign Missionary Board all proceeds were sent to Africa. During the war, Rev. John Jasper preached to the wounded Confederate soldiers on Chimborazo Hill in Richmond, VA. He also preached at the Mills on the James River. During hard times Rev. Jasper cleaned bricks for a living and also learned how to make lent. Rev. Jasper organized the First Colored Church of Weldon, North Carolina. He was later called to pastor the flock but because of all of his church duties in Richmond, VA he declined the offer.

After being a guest speaker in Petersburg, VA, Rev. Jasper became founding pastor of Sixth Mount Zion Baptist Church in Richmond, VA. The first service was held, September 1867 starting with nine members in a former horse stable. One of his most famous sermons that he preached around the United States was "The sun Do move." A profound sermon with scripture backing to back his own theory of the rotation of the sun and the power of God. Many were right to believe that the sun did not move however all that heard this sermonic lecture were captivated not just by his sermonic delivery but also by his personality. He led many to Christ and according to The Jackson Michigan newspaper The Jackson

Citizen, he once Baptized 300 candidates in two hours, or one every twenty- three seconds. John preached sermons that beckoned and called many sinners to Christ. Although he was unlearned, his faith and daily walk with God allowed his ministry to expanded. He made many lectures in Baltimore, MD, out of all the sermons he preached there is one that is best remembered "The Sun Do Move" which he eventually preached across the globe. John Jasper was married three times his first marriage was to Elvy Weaden in Williamsburg, VA. The marriage only lasted for one day, he was sent to Richmond, VA the night they were married. His second marriage was to Candus Jordan which ended in divorce. His third marriage was to Mary Ann Cole (pictured bottom left) in 1863 and remained married until her death August 6, 1874. Children of Rev. Jasper: Shedrick Jasper (1844 – 1902) served in the Civil War and later married Juda Randolph (1847) in 1875; Martha Ann Kenney (1895) married Willie Fox on March 9, 1914 in Richmond, VA; Maggie Jasper (1879), Green Acres Jasper (1880), John Jasper (1883 – 1934), Bettie Jasper (1885), Daisy Jasper (1887 – 1920) moved to Chicago, Ill. Abraham Jasper (1848) Irene Jones (1861 – 1930) Mary Elizabeth Jasper Glover (1875) Martha Jasper

In later years while not preaching John spent many days fishing it is documented that he caught fish. On news of his death traveled nationwide in every newspaper in the United States. He was known to all as a great leader and preacher by all who heard him, Rev. John Jasper a man who preached his way out of the shackles of Slavery. He led people into the dawning of a New Day freedom. On March 30, 1901 his last words were "I have finished my work." I am standing at the brink of the river, and waiting for my orders from above." After his death, tributes were made all across the world of a man who proved his loyalty to God and leadership to mankind while he was here.

This document is the birth records from Rev. Jasper Family bible

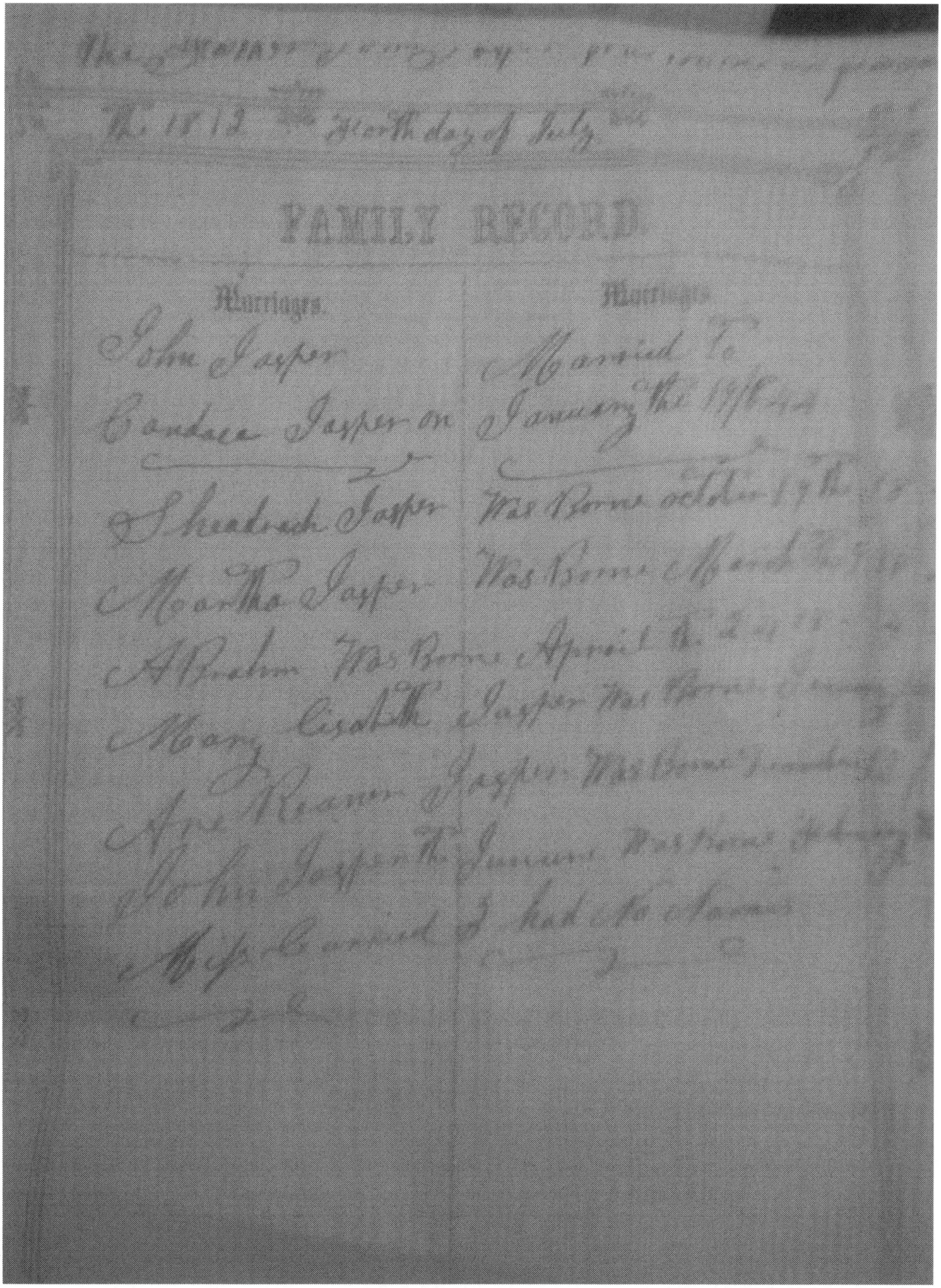

the 1873 the 4th day of July

FAMILY RECORD

Marriages. | **Marriages.**

John Jasper — Married To
Candace Jasper on January the 19th

Shedrech Jasper — Was Borne October 17th
Martha Jasper — Was Borne March
Abraham Was Borne April
Mary Elisabeth Jasper Was Borne January
Ann Eleanor Jasper Was Borne
John Jasper the Junior Was Borne
Wife Leaured & had no Children

217

The Sixth Mount Zion Baptist Church was founded by Rev. Jasper in 1867. The church was organized on September 1867 two years after the ending of the Civil War. Rev. Jasper and ten church members held church services in an abandoned Confederate horse stable near the James River. The church membership quickly began to grow. In 1869, the church moved its location to Duval Street to a small church which was a former Presbyterian Church. The church held approximately 200 – 250 people. It was in this small church that the "Sun Do Move" was first introduced many came from far and near to hear what become one of the most celebrated sermons of that time. In 1887, with the increasing of membership plans for a new church building was came into action and a new church building was built. After several years of constructing the new church. The first service was held in the new church in 1890. After Rev. Jasper's death in 1901, Rev. Randolph Peyton suceded him as the pastor of Sixth Mount Zion Baptist Church. Reverend Peyton was noted as a dynamic speaker and a strategic planner. Rev. Peyton organized organizations in the church. He also organized the Sick and Poor Society and the Negro Baptist Old Folks home. Rev. Peyton is highly noted for baptizing 500 baptism candidates in a month. During this time. there were 2 churches that were birthed out of Sixth Mount Zion Baptist Church: Trinity Baptist Church and Greater Mt. Moriah Baptist Church. In 1912 Rev. Peyton resigned as pastor and 1914 he was asked and agreed to return to lead the great congregation again. He resumed his pastorate position until officially resigning in 1922. On April 5, 1924, Rev. Augustus Walter Brown (1885 - 1967) who was originally from Anderson South Carolina was installed to be the third pastor of the church. In 1925 started a renovation process much of the original portions of the church during the leadership of Rev. Jasper was restored and the church was expanded and the black architect Charles Russell and a black contractor I. Lincoln Bailey. Rev. Brown devoted his life to his church and mission work serving for over 20 years on the Lott Carey Foreign Mission Convention. Rev. Brown preached in several countries

and all over the United States. Rev. Brown founded an annual day to honor the memory of Rev. John Jasper founded the John Jasper Memorial Museum. In the 1950s the Richmond – Petersbug Turnpike Authority Rev. Brown advocacy preserved the Sixth Mount Zion Church building from being demolished or relocated during the time U.S Highway I – 95 was constructed. In 1956 hundreds of homes were destroyed but because of the preserverance of Rev. Brown and others, the highway was built around the church building. Rev. Brown served until his death. The fourth pastor of Sixth Mount Zion was Rev. Barry Hopkins who started his pastorate in 1968 through his leadership a fellowship hall was renovated and renamed the Rev. A.W. Brown Memorial Hall. In 1970 Rev. Hopkins ended his tenure. On March 13, 1972, Rev. Isadore Mims a South Carolina native was installed to lead as the fifth pastor of the church. Rev. Mims resigned in 1991. In 1993 Rev. John Johnson Jr. a Richmond Native became the sixth pastor to lead Sixth Mount Zion Baptist Church. During his pastorate the church birthed out the Gilpin – Jackson Family Life Skills Center which had youth and adult training and childcare as well as adult daycare. Rev. Johnson resigned in 2003 and Rev. Tyrone Nelson a Richmond Native answered the call of God to lead this great historical congregation. Rev. Nelson is a well recognized leader in his own right who has taken the church to another level reaching a younger generation while preserving its legacy. Not only is he the leader of the church, but also a significant city leader as well. Rev. Nelson also served on several boards as well, such as Virginia Commonwealth Univerity Board of Visitors, Baptist General Convention of Virginia, and Richmond Metroplolitan transportation Authority just to name a few. He and the members of Sixth Mount Zion Baptist Church continues under the God's divine power to keep this great church historical yet progressive and effective for such a time as this. May God Always Bless Sixth Mount Zion Baptist Church.

Sixth Mount Zion Baptist Church and the John Jasper Museum

On May 19, 2016, I visited the Sixth Mount Zion Baptist Church on Duval Street in Richmond, VA. There was several us given a tour by the church historian Mr. Benjamin C. Ross (pictured with assistant) who guided us through time of the church history and Legacy. Mr. Ross shared with us not only the history of its founder, Rev. John Jasper but also the history of the church. Mr. Ross had detailed information of all of the Sixth Mount Zion Church past pastors and also the present, Rev. Nelson.

Mr. Ross and his assistant Guided us from the front door the sanctuary starting on the founding of the church. In the basement the church has a room dedicated to the memory and legacy of Rev. John Jasper called the Rev. John Jasper Museum. The room is filled with the pictures and other memorabilia such as his podium, chair, tambourines, and many other items. Mr. Ross also gave me a copy of Rev. Jasper personal bible family births and marriage record. Thank you Mr. Ross and the Sixth Street Baptist Church for your continued efforts to preserve the history of African American History with keeping the legacy of Rev. Jasper and the Sixth Mount Zion Baptist Church history alive for future generations.

Mr. Ross

The podium of Rev. John Jasper

Tourist who visited the Museum

The Hines Family

The **Reverend Isaiah Henry Hines** who is also known as slave name John or Jack Hines was a slave at the Wigwam Plantation which was owned by Gov. William B. Giles and later Samuel Jones. He was later hired out by the Cocke family and for a period of time, he was owned by Richard T. Archer in Mississippi. He was married to Elizabeth Brown was said to have Native American ancestry. After her death, He married Rosa. In 1870 he was still living in the neighborhood of the Big House presumably in a cabin. In 1880 Isaiah and his family were living in the Mattoax area off of present day Mattoax road in Amelia, VA. He served as pastor of the Liberty Baptist Church in Amelia, VA. Isaiah later moved to Richmond, VA and resided at 1220 N 7th street in 1904 and he worked as a Butler. Around 1914 he became a full time pastor and in the 1920's John lived at 514 South Harrison Street in Richmond, VA. During his tenure Rev. Hines was responsible for building second. He led the church and its membership increased to over 200 members.

Children of Isaiah H. Hines and Elizabeth: **Jennie Charlotte Hines** (1863 – 1928) also known as Jennie Mosely on her marriage license however according to her death certificate signed by her daughter Betty Moody and oral historical accounts, it is confirmed that she was the eldest child born to Isaiah "Jack" and Elizabeth married Samson Smith son of ex - slaves Major and Katie Smith who lived in Mattoax, Virginia. From this union child were born, Paul Smith (1883), Betty Smith Tyler Moody (1883) who was married to Robert Tyler and lived in Red Lodge. After Robert Tyler's death, Betty later married Charlie Moody who owned and operated a sawmill in the Red Lodge; George Smith (1893 – 1960) Thomas Smith (1895 – 1963) Beverly Smith (1896 – 1955), Mary Smith Tyler (December 1897 – February 17, 1972), Samuel Smith (1898 – 1965) who married Elnora Perkins (1912 – 2001) of Buckingham, VA and had several children, Lizzie Smith, Katie Smith Cleveland formerly married to the late Roy Edward Cleveland from this union, several children wer born; Mary Jane Smith Banks (August 4, 1937 – October 21, 2012) married the late Mike Banks Jr. on October 6, 1957; Annie Smith Mondrey (January 17, 1940 – March 27, 2002) was married to Deacon William James Mondrey on October 19, 1958. From this union several children were born; Virgie Smith was formerly married to the late Roosevelt Banks. Samuel Smith (February 13, 1946 – February 20, 1946); Betty Smith.

Elizabeth Burwell (1899 – 1919)

Nannie Hines (1865 – October 24, 1924) was raised in Mattoax, VA and later stayed briefly in New York. She later returned to Mattox Rd. Amelia, VA and also stayed for short time in the Eastern Shore Area. According to oral history, Nannie met Walter Brown of New York and later Albert Robinson. Both men were said to be the father of her children. Nannie and her family, moved to the Eastern Shore area on a Island near Chincoteague VA which is in Accomack County, VA. They moved there to work as potato and strawberry pickers. Nannie and her daughters returned later to Amelia, VA however, her sons stayed and lived in the Hampton area. Children of Nannie Brown: Charles Brown (1893) lived in Amelia and later eastern shore. George Brown who changed his name to Reed Brown. Edward Lee Brown (July 8, 1894 – October 12, 1970) served in World War 1. He lived in Hampton, VA and after he retired, he returned to Amelia County, VA and lived behind

Liberty Baptist Church. Lawrence Brown (1898) worked at Shipyard. Marie Brown Hill (1899 – 1988) was married to Edwin Hezekiah Hill and had two sons; William Hill and Edwin Lawrence "Snookum" Hill. According to Stephen Brown, Mrs. Marie begin her early years as a babysitter on Sundays. She was paid one quarter per Sunday for work. Jane Robinson Gray (1903 – 1991) children were Ernest Gray, Dorothy Gray who married Albert Archer. Barbara Ann Gray, Ida Lou Gray, Robert Gray, Albert Gray, Charles Gray Jr. and Mary Alice Gray.

Nolie May Brown (1909 – 2006) later married Augustus Thompson (1894 – 1986) son of Essex and Maria Jackson on November 3, 1958 in Amelia County, VA. Mr. Gus as he was called, was a hard worker, he worked for the Boyd farm which later became the Crawford farm. He also worked for the Saunders family and also at the saw mill. Earlier in his lifetime he had lost his arm but that did not stop him. He raised livestock, had gardens, a corn field and did almost anything with one arm that a person could do with two. Mrs. Nolie worked for the West family, The Jones family, The Epperson family. Mrs. Nolie had a great sense of humor and years ago she told me stories of many of the ancestors in this book. She was a woman full of wisdom and definitely was one who spoke her mind. She was the mother of four children, Annie Mae Brown who married William Wade the couple has two children; Thomas Brown served in the United States Army and in the United States Air Force. He is a great researcher and speaker, and has been faithful in giving annual lectures of African American History. Thomas is a scholar in his own right and has been a great resource to this project. He is married to Phyllis Wilkinson Eggleston Brown the granddaughter of Rev. Isaiah Wilkinson the former pastor of Liberty Baptist Church. Thomas has four children and grandchildren. Calvin Brown (1938 – 1987) served in the United States Army for 21 years. He served in the Vietnam War and did two tours. He was wounded in Vietnam and received a purple heart. Stephen Brown, who has also been an asset to this project. He served in the United States Army 1960 – 1963. He was married to the late Audrey Clarke of Powhatan, VA; Senia Robinson Jasper (1911 – 2004) married McKinley Jasper (see Jasper family section). While in the process of linking the Hines/ Brown genealogy Mr. Stephen "Dale" Brown confirm these findings by telling me stories that his mother Mrs. Nolie and others told him many years ago.

John Hines (1872 – September 8, 1912) worked as a laborer at a Tannery and lived in Midlothian, VA until his death.

Rev. Isaiah Henry Hines (December 16, 1873 – June 7, 1961) served as pastor of St. Paul Baptist Church in Richmond, VA. He also served as the pastor of 31st street Baptist Church for thirty-five years. He was revered as a dynamic preacher whose leadership caused his church to function through the depression, World War II, The Korean War, and through the 1950s. His vision and plans to expand the church was made a reality and before his death, the church was debt free. According to newspaper articles, many came from far and near to attend the funeral of Rev. Isaiah Hines Jr.

All of the Descendants of Isaiah Hines are too numerous to mention.

Reverend Isaiah Hines

Nolie B. Thompson

Senia Jasper

Nolie Thompson

McKinley Jake Jasper and his mother Senia Jasper

Pictured Left: The Birthday Celebration for Mrs. Nolie and Mrs. Senia.

McKinley Jasper

Stephen and Audrey Brown

Roosevelt Jasper

Stephen "Dale" Brown

Walter F. Jasper

Thomas and Phyllis Brown

Dale, Annie, and friend

Mary Jane Smith Banks

Annie S. Mondrey

Gary Family

George Gary born in 1820 a slave at the Lodge and was one of the many who were sold or sent to Archers Plantation in Sunshine County, Leflore, Mississippi. After the ending of slavery, he walked back to Amelia, VA where he lived the remainder of his life. In the 1870's and 1880's George lived in the Lodge and was a neighbor to Robert and Jennie Hyde and family. The Gary family later lived in the Pleasant Gove Area of Amelia County, Virginia. It is believed that the Gary surname may have originally been called Gray.

George and his wife **Mary Anne Gary** (1840) had several children: Anne Texana Gary (1869) Fleming Gary (1874) Rebecca Gary (1877) Louisiana Gary (1871) George Gary (1873) who lived in the Pleasant Grove Community. Mary Gary (1879 – 1879) I was not able to find the Gary family descendants at this time.

The Jackson Family

Andrew Jackson (1810 – June 23 1885) was a slave of the Lodge and a lifelong farmer. He was the husband of **Margy Jackson** It is not clear how many children they had but one has been confirmed. **Fannie Critty Jackson Harris** the wife of John Harris. It is also certain that the Jacksons of Red Lodge and the Jackson's of Lodore are related.

Moses Jackson (1825 – 1875) possibly brother of Andrew Jackson was born a slave at the Lodge. He was married to Jinny Jackson (1825) the couple had a son Jacob Jackson (1847 – 1887) who married Nancy Jackson and from this union four children were born: 1. Willie Jackson (1863) 2. Richard Jackson (1867-1932) 3. Mary Eliza Jackson Woodson (1871 – 1948) who married Archer Anderson (1870) son of Creed and Sarah Anderson on September 13, 1892 in Amelia, Virginia. Later she married Charlie Woodson (1854) in Amelia, VA. Children of Mary E. Woodson: Florence Anderson Cook (1895) Nancy Ruffin (1898 -1968) married Phillip Hardaway Ruffin (1891 – 1976) son of Edwin Ruffin and Josephine Hardaway on August 2, 1913 in Amelia, VA. They lived on 427 South Harrison Street Richmond, VA. Nancy and her husband had seven children, Mary Ruffin (1914), Edward Ruffin (1917), Phillip Hardaway Ruffin Jr. (1918 – 1947), Lucille Ruffin (1918), Sarah Eva Ruffin Wilson (1922 – May 22, 2004), Mary E. Anderson (March 5, 1900 – March 13, 1962), Robert Anderson (1900 – 1972) who married Florean Harris and from this union, two children were born: Arnette Anderson and Wilnette Anderson; Mary Anderson (October 26, 1909 – 1978) and Lillian Woodson White (1911 – 1981). 4. Irving Jackson (1872)

Pictured left: Lillian Anderson White

Tyler Family

The earliest ancestors of the Tyler family Ben and Nancy Tyler. Wilson Tyler (1842) a lifelong farmer was twice married. According to his marriage license Wilson was born in Nottoway, VA. There are other accounts that mention Wilson was born in Powhatan, VA. According to several documented accounts, he was raised in Powhatan, VA. The Tyler family of Amelia are connected to the Tyler's in Powhatan, VA as well as Goochland. It is assumed that his father Ben Tyler was born in Goochland, VA. Wilson Tyler's first marriage was to Amanda Cox (1850 – 1886) whose surname was also Redd and Wilson. She was the daughter of James and Lily Cox of Amelia, VA. After Amanda's death, he later married Mary Vaughan (1868) on April 3, 1889 in Powhatan, VA. On February 10, 2016, I found a 1908 Chancery suit which is located in the Virginia Chancery Records index number 1908 – 0208. These are documents are at the Library of Virginia. According to Virginia Chancery Records, my great - great grandfather Robert Hyde testified that knew Wilson Tyler his entire life. It is believed they met in Nottoway, VA and was possibly on the same plantation and sold to Powhatan, VA. On some of his children records it is documented that he was born in Powhatan however according to his marriage license he was born in Nottoway. Like the Hyde family the Tyler's were sold or sent from Nottoway and Powhatan, VA

A brief part of the Chancery as proof of Robert Hyde's testmony

Children of Wilson and Amanda Tyler

Louisa Tyler Jackson (1864 – April 13, 1926) was married to James Everett Jackson a native of Jackson, Ohio on August 18, 1900 in Amelia, VA. The couple moved to Canal Street Richmond, VA where they resided until their death.

Matt Tyler (1867 -1934) was a farmer, store owner and to my knowledge was one of the first morticians in the Tyler family. He built a two story frame home in the late 1890s, A store was later built behind the house. His first marriage was to Jane Baugh (1857 – 1887) they had a daughter Eliza Belle Tyler White. Matt, later married Annie Johnson daughter of Jordan Johnson. The couple had eight children: Mary Tyler (1892 – 1952) married Watsey Harris (1890 – 1958) on April 15, 1914 the couple had five children: 1. Herman Harris (February 2, 1915 – June 10, 1940) worked at a saw mill. 2. Elaine Juanita Harris Schmidt (December 1917 – May 1972) married Judge Harvey Schmidt on August 17, 1940 in Amelia, VA. Harvey and Elaine resided in Philadelphia, Pennsylvania where Judge Harvey Schmidt was a leading African American citizen of Amelia, VA. In 1998, he was inducted into Barrister's Association Philadelphia Hall of Fame. The couple had two daughters Barbara Schmidt Vance and Mary Schmidt Campbell and a son Harvey Smith. They also have grandchildren and great – grandchildren. 3. Gladys Lillian Harris Nutt (September 20, 1920 – 1994) resided in Philadelphia, Pennsylvania. 4. Annie Constance Harris Wormely (1923 – 1998) resided in Philadelphia, Pennsylvania. 5. Watsey Egbert Harris (May 13, 1930 – April 9, 1984) lived in Amelia, VA and was married to Ethel Booker. The couple had one daughter, Donna Lisa Harris. Matt Tyler Jr. (November 18, 1894 – November 25, 1963) served in World War 1. He married Bernice Eggleston (April 13, 1898 – October 21, 1971) the daughter of Cary Eggleston and Nellie Gray Eggleston in Amelia, VA. They raised one son Rev. Frank Tyler (July 26, 1926 - January 15, 2006) who after graduating High school enlisted in the United States Army on May 20, 1946. On October 24, 1953 Frank married Rev. Alice Scott in Mattoax, VA. Rev. H.W. McNair officiated the marriage ceremony. Frank served as faithful deacon and formerly served as pastor of two churches. Today, Rev. Alice Tyler remains a pillar in her church and community and serves as a minister at the High Rock Baptist Church under the leadership of Rev. Bernard Hill. One of her favorite scriptures is Romans Ch.1 verse 6. Rev. Frank and Alice had three children: Glenn Tyler (deceased) twice married, his first wife was Angela Smith and later he married Irene Taylor. He had children and grandchildren; Keith Tyler who married Carrie Trent and Valerie Tyler Foster who married Howard Pegram (deceased) and later Steven Foster. Rev. Frank and Alice has grandchildren and great – grandchildren.

William Tyler (July 1896 – February 17, 1972) "he was known as Bill" married Mary Smith (1897) daughter of Samson and Jenny B. Smith of Amelia, VA. While in Amelia, VA William, worked on his father's farm. After the passing of his wife Mary, William a widower married Fannie Tyler and by 1930 was living in Richmond, Virginia on 444 Parkwood Avenue. During this time, William worked as a truck driver for an envelope company. He later worked as a shipping clerk. He moved to 226 Temple Street and at the time of his passing, William lived at 2386 West Bethel Street in Richmond, VA. William was the father of two children, 1. Helen Sue Tyler (1927) 2. Junius Tyler son of Emily Johnson Clements who married Nellie Tyler and resided White Plains, New York.

Edward Tyler (March 12, 1898 – September 2, 1970) known as Bubba resided in the Red Lodge Community. He was a farmer and married Alice Pitchford (November 1, 1901 – November 6, 1948). She was a business lady and was a close friend of Maggie Walker.

Children of Edward and Alice Tyler: William Matthew Tyler (June 27, 1925 – June 15, 1979) served in the United States Navy from September 25, 1943 until May 3, 1946. William married Mary Elizabeth Robinson daughter of Leon and Lucy Helen Archer Robinson on January 18, 1947 in Amelia County, Virginia. For a time, William owned a store and was well loved by the community. The couple had one daughter Chermine Tyler Mondrey Booker who had two children, one deceased, Jerry Mondrey. She also has grandchildren, and great- grandchildren. Alice R. Tyler who married Theodore Winfred Mabry on June 9, 1959. Alice is a retired school teacher who taught for many years at Russell Grove High School.

Florence Tyler Thompson (1901 – 1983) married Richard "Dick" Thompson (1899) of the Pleasant Grove Baptist Church Community in Amelia, VA. From this union three children were born. Lula Thompson (December 4, 1920 – June 29, 1994). Frances Gay (1923 – 2013) married Emory Eggleston was the mother of Brenda Francine Eggleston Chappell Banks (1947 – 2001) and later Kenneth Gay who died January 2002. In 1959 she received her Cosmetology certificate and opened Frances Beauty Shop. She worked hard in the city of Richmond as a part of Jackson Ward beautification committee and was one of the pioneers of the Second Street Festival. She was a very active member of Second Baptist Church for many years. Westmoreland Gordon Thompson Sr. (January 9, 1926 – January 8, 1998) enlisted into Camp Lee on May 24, 1944. He married Pearl Booker daughter of Levi Booker and Lillian Anderson on October 14, 1944 in Amelia County, VA. Westmoreland and Pearl Thompson children, Barbara Ann Thompson Eggleston married William Eggleston, Dorsenia Thompson, Westmoreland Thompson Jr (1951 – 2016) married Rosa Gordon and Richard Thompson. He has grandchildren and great – grandchildren.

Theodore Teddy Tyler (1901 – May 31, 1959) enlisted into the military on August 28, 1942. Teddy married Lydia Clements. The couple lived in Amelia, VA. He had an adopted son Roscoe Tyler (1934 – 2005) who married Annie Harris and had two children, Pamela Tyler who has one daughter and Roscoe Tyler Jr. who married Tammy Johnson and has one child; Joseph Moody Tyler (1904 – 1998) known to all as "Moody". married Dorothy Jasper the daughter of Peachy Jasper.

Frank B Tyler (1905 – 1971) married Lucy Harris Tyler. He was employed at Wood Farm later becoming a former operating a general store, baseball team, was a farmer and also, was the director of the Frank B. Tyler Funeral Home for more than 30 years. He was an active member of Pleasant Grove Baptist Church where he served faithfully as chairman of the Trustee board for many years. He was married to Lucy Harris Tyler (September 12, 1911 – March 25, 1998) who was an educator at the Russell Grove School in Amelia, VA. She served as a pianist for Pleasant Grove Baptist Church for 55 years.

The couple had two children Irma Estelle Tyler who married Floyd Henderson on June 21, 1959 in Amelia, VA the couple has two children and Frank Tyler Jr. who is the father of two children.

Eliza Tyler White of Brooklyn, New York

Matt third wife Eliza Jane Thompson of Westmoreland, VA was the daughter of George W. and Millie Jones Thompson daughter of Rev. Preston Jones and Nancy Brown formerly of Amelia, VA. They had no children.

Rosa Tyler (1869 – 1887) died at the age of 18.

Alfred Tyler (1876) married Ada Tyler (1886 – 1936) they had five children, William Tyler (1904), Edmonia Tyler Hughes, Gertrude Tyler Thompson, Ruth Tyler Jones, Carrie Tyler Jones

Wilson Tyler Jr, (November 1874 - March 2, 1936) was a farmer. He married Julia Scott Tyler (1878 – 1936) and had six children: 1. Herod Tyler (1894) Henry Tyler (1896 – June 7, 1963) lived in Red Lodge. 3. Jackson Tyler (1900 – 1968) better known as "blind man Jack". Although he was blind, he would walk around Red Lodge and could cook for himself. 4. Rosa Etta Tyler Banks (1902 – May 20, 1955) was married to Iredell Banks and lived in the Pleasant Grove Community of Amelia, VA. 5. Gertrude Thompson (1908 – 1964) married Eugene Thompson Sr. The couple moved to Yonkers New York. In the 1930's they lived on 29 Fegan Street in Yonkers. By the 1940's the couple lived on School Street in Yonkers. From this union six children were born: William Thompson (1928), Frank Thompson (1930), Eugene Thompson Jr, (1930 – 1989), Theodore Thompson (1933), George Thompson (1935 – 1997) and Arnetta Thompson.

Alfred Tyler (1876 – November 9, 1939) was married to Ada Jones and moved to Chesterfield, VA. They had five children: William Tyler (1904) married Esther Jones on January 22, 1943 in Richmond, VA. Edmonia Tyler (January 9, 1908 – December 1986) married Andrew Hughes and lived on 901 Norton St. in Richmond, VA. They had one daughter Marie Hughes (1940) who married Earnest White (1940); Gertrude Tyler (1909 – 1916), Ruth Tyler (1909 – 1958) worked in Richmond, VA as a servant for Harvie Goodin on Belle One Avenue. Carrie Tyler Jones (May 2, 1910 – July 25, 1988)

Robert Tyler (1878 – 1914) was married to Bettie Smith. He is buried in the Miles/ Baugh/Perkins cemetery which is located off of Rocky Branch Rd. in Red Lodge. The couple had three children, Jennie Tyler Claiborne (August 10, 1905 – April 13, 1986) married James Claiborne on August 23, 1952 in Amelia, VA. Amanda Tyler (May 10, 1908 – June 29, 1989) married William Henry Walker on October 14, 1971 in Jetersville, VA; James Buster Tyler (October 10, 1910 - January 26, 1970) was a farmer and lived on present day Rocky Branch road near the old baseball field in Red lodge. Ella Tyler (1882) married Macon Pegram on October 11, 1903 in Amelia, VA.

Nancy Tyler Malone (1880 – 1942) was married to George Malone (1872) son of Amanda Brown of Amelia, VA. From this union Eleven children were born: 1. Nettie Malone (1902) 2. Estelle Malone (1904) 3. Irene Malone (1905) 4. Ruth Malone Booker (November 9, 1906 – January 2, 1948) married to Bennie Booker in 1928 in Philadelphia, PA and lived on 2451 W Cumberland Street Philadelphia, PA. 5. Irene Malone (1907) was living in Philadelphia, PA in 1940 6. Annie Malone (1909) 7. George Malone Jr. (April 11, 1912) by 1940 he was living in Philadelphia, PA. 8. Macon Malone (1914) moved to Philadelphia, PA. 9. Wesley Malone (1916 – 2001) 10. Nancy Dickerson El (1919 – 1985) 11. Thomas Malone (1920 – 1936) 12. Wilson Malone (November 4, 1922 - February 17, 1923).

Ella Tyler Pegram (1882) married Macon Pegram (1878) Children of Ella Tyler Pegram: Silvia Pegram (1903) Virginia Pegram (1903) Ceo Pegram (1904) Henry Pegram (1906) Warren Hardina Pegram (1909 – November 18, 1946) married Virgie Annie Pegram (July 3, 1910) Vernelle Pegram (1913) married Isaiah Mcghee son of William Mcghee and Rosa Bland on August 21, 1943 in Amelia, VA. She later married Eli Braxton in Amelia County, Virginia on May 15, 1948. Sarah Pegram (May 25, 1915 - December 13, 1988) married James Faulkner on June 3, 1944; Arthur Pegram (1917)

Norman Tyler (1890) moved to Arundel, Maryland.

Edith Tyler (1892)

Lonnie Tyler (1895)

The descendants of Wilson Tyler are too numerous name.

Mrs. Lucy H. Tyler

Frank Tyler Sr. and Frank Tyler Jr. With their cows at the Amelia County Fair. (picture taken from the Amelia Bulletin Monitor Book)

Mrs. Ethel Harris and Donna Lisa Harris

Frank Tyler Jr.

William Tyler and Mary Tyler and their daughter Chermine Tyler Mondrey Booker

Memories

Amenta Ruffin Johnson, Jerry Mondrey, Darlene Robinson and Iollette Mondrey

The Hicks Family

According to shared information and documentation of the Hicks family, I have learned of the success and the legacy of this great family. In a brief interview with the Hicks Family historian Ms. Sylvia Hicks a few years ago, I still can recall her sharing with me how that her family came from Dinwiddie, VA. She also gives a great account of her family history in the book compiled by Dr. Henry J. Featherston: Our Stories Our Struggles: A History of American Americans in Amelia County, Virginia Volume II. The Hicks family were not a part of the Red Lodge Plantation they moved to Amelia County, VA around 1937. The Hicks family roots run deep in Brunswick and Dinwiddie County, Virginia.

Elijah David Hicks (January 12, 1891 - June 13, 1969) the son of farmer Hartwell and Sallie Hicks was born in Brunswick County, Virginia. According to Dr. Featherston's book Sylvia Hicks mentioned that

Elijah worked for the Telephone Company and they sent him to Dinwiddie County, Virginia. While living in Dinwiddie, Elijah met and married Perline Lacy (March 4, 1891 - November 9, 1948) daughter of James Lacy and Millie Wyatt on December 27, 1911. From this union seven children were born. According to Ms. Sylvia Hicks documentation, Elijah's step-brother James Sydnor had purchased farm in the Red Lodge Community of Amelia, VA. It is said that he envisioned Elijah and his boys farming the land for him. After hard work, sacrifice and dedication the Hicks family became owners of the farm and to this day, the Hicks family still maintain the ownership of the family farm. It has been proven that Mr. Hicks was not only a farmer, but he was also a strategic thinker. At the time of his death, Elijah Hicks 78 years old. The Children of Elijah and Perline Lacy Hicks: Azzie Mae Hicks Jones (1912 – 1982) Henry Hicks (July 2,1915 – February 15, 1972) was married to Alfreda; Deacon Arthur Lee Hicks (May 5, 1917 – June 12, 2003) who married Rosa Jones daughter of Edwin Jones and Lizzie Hyde Jones on November 24, 1940. Arthur was a faithful member of Liberty Baptist Church. Deacon Roger Hicks (1919 – 1988) married Lillian Harris the daughter of Joseph Harris of Amelia County, Virginia on March 7, 1949. Roger who was a U.S Army Veteran and was a farmer. He also worked for any years as a school bus driver and was a faithful member and Deacon of Liberty Baptist Church. James Howard Hicks (March 4, 1923 – April 8, 1984) married Dorothy Polite on March 27, 1949; Ethel Sylvia Hicks Robinson (August 9, 1924 - January 4, 1990) who married Deacon Emmett Robinson son of Emmett Robinson Sr. and Rosa Hyde Robinson on November 27, 1939; Calvin Hicks who married Cora Mitchell daughter of Willie Mitchell Sr. and Roena Taylor on June 26, 1949.

The descendants of the Hicks family are many and they have done an awesome job in persevering their family legacy.

Ethel Robinson and Elijah Hicks

Azzie Mae Jones

Roger Hicks

Rosa and Deacon Arthur Hicks

The Red Lodge Connections   **The Lewis Family**

While researching the Red Lodge Plantation and the Tabb family, Darlene Lewis Robinson one of the Lewis family's historians kept telling me that I was going to find out where the Lewis originated from. It has been said that the Lewis came from Charlotte County, Virginia. Countless efforts were made to find any document of Darlene's ancestor Granderson Lewis and his parents, but nothing showed up. It was not until March 20, 2016 I found a Chancery with the Lewis names as slaves of the Tabb family and later owned by Governor Giles who was married into the Tabb family. After these findings, I was able to meet some of the Lewis family members that I did not know at the repast of their cousin Jackie Holmes. Darlene Lewis Robinson and Diane Todd are awesome researchers of the Lewis family and have went great lengths to preserve their family history.

(Left to right) Rev. Nathaniel Lewis, Charlene Lewis Yates, Eric Lewis, Clarence Lewis Jr., Darlene Lewis Robinson, Diane Todd, Christian Robinson, Faye Lewis. Back Row: Gregory Lewis, (me) Emanuel Hyde III, (my father) Rev. Emanuel Hyde Jr, and Samuel "Bubba" Lewis

The first Lewis ancestor I was able to find was a slave named Granderson who is believed to be the father of John Lewis. There is very limited information on Granderson, but his name is found in a chancery along with John Lewis and Betsey Davis Lewis who were both slaves of Frances Tabb at Clay Hill Plantation, and later Dr. Bathurst Randolph. (see slave list on page 26) According to the Virginia Chancery Records Granderson was hired out to Mary Cocke Archer. After her death, her heir Amelia's native Richard Thompson Archer who moved to the Anchuca Plantation in Port Gibson, Mississippi claiming Granderson and several other slaves as his own. After a Chancery battle was resolved, they later returned to Amelia, VA and was owned by Samuel Jones. Before the ending of slavery, the Lewis family was sold to the Harrison family and relocated to the Mattoax area.

John Lewis (1800) and **Betsey Davis** (1815) There are five known children of John and Betsey: Granderson, William Peyton, Anna (also called Hannah), Harriet and Tabb Lewis. After the ending of slavery, John negotiated a payment deal to Lewis Harvie to own his own land in the Mattoax Community on Rt. 604. He became one of the few Black landowners in the Mattoax Community.

1. **Granderson Lewis** (1855 – 1909) married **Lavenia Virginia Warren** (1859 – 1947) who was from Goochland, VA. Granderson and Lavenia lived on his father's farm.

Children of Granderson and Lavenia Lewis

John Edward Lewis (June 21, 1885 – December 22, 1955) was born in Amelia, County, VA. He married Alice Amy Anderson the daughter of Walter Anderson and Amy Walker Anderson on April 3, 1918 in Amelia, VA. John was a successful businessman who started his employment working on Stigler farm and became foreman supervising the farm and its operation. John Lewis grew up and lived in the Mattoax area of Amelia, VA on the family's farm that was originally owned by his grandparents. Johnny as he was called, was the first black man to own a car in his community and possibly in the county. Johnny was always dressed and arrived to the occasion. He was also creative by taking his pulp wood truck and making it into a bus. It has been said that he charged his passengers $3 a month for services. He was a farmer, and worked as a mortician. He also purchased and sold a lot of land. Eric Lewis, recalled his dad Clarence Lewis telling him that before the county roads were paved Johnny would drive to Richmond to deliver his vegetables. It is said that Johnny and his family, was the first blacks to have electricity and phones in the Giles District. Many years after Johnny's death, Alice remained on the homestead and later moved to Richmond, VA to live with her daughter, Mamie where she remained until her death. The children of Johnny Lewis and Alice: Amy Beatrice Clements (1919 – 1961) married Floyd Clements and resided in Baltimore, MD. She had four children, George Lewis (died July 2007), Diane L. Davis, Linda Hursey, and Nancy Clements. William E Lewis (1920 – 1962) Served in World War II and was a member of Liberty Baptist Church. He was a great mechanic and worked for the Washington, D.C government for over 30 yrs. Walter Granderson Lewis (1923 – 2001) served in World War II. He met and married Rita Lee and the couple had four children, Walter Reginald Lewis (1923 - 1989) he fathered four children, Larry Lewis (died February 2011), Reginald Lewis (died in 1989), Regina L. Barrett, Tina L. Robenson. (Walter and Mamie was Twins) Carrie "Mamie" Lewis (1923 – 2013) was a nurse for many years. Mamie was married to Jerry Seaton and had one daughter, Jacqueline Beverly Seaton Holmes died in 2016 she had a son, Comus Holmes who died in 2008. Clarence Lewis (1925 - 2012) married Mary Ella Mason on August 29, 1953 in Amelia, VA. He was employed with V.Y Scott funeral home. Children of Clarence and Mary Lewis: Clarence Jr. who is married to Gail Lewis. Sheila Lewis, Eric Ryan Lewis. Alice Virginia Lewis (1928 – 2003) attended Freeman University later called Howard University Nursing School.

She was a registered nurse and had one son Maurice "Mickey" Lewis (died July 2007) Samuel Joseph Lewis (1933 – 2011) served during the Korean War and was stationed in Missouri. For many years, Sam worked for Standard Paper Company in Richmond, VA. In June 1972 Hurricane Agnes flooded the Richmond Area and caused the Standard Paper Company to relocated to another state. Sam married Eleanor Ruffin. (For the children of Sam and Eleanor Ruffin Lewis see Brown Family section)

John Henry Lewis (1927 – 1929) died as an infant.

Mamie Lewis Quinichette Thompson was married to Victor Quinichette on June 25, 1919 in Danville, VA. (Jan 1, 1889 – 1991) She lived in Washington, DC. Mamie had one son, Victor Lewis Quinichette (Deceased). He served in United States Navy where he played in the band. He worked for the Postal Service and was married to Iva.

Joseph Peyton Lewis (January 28, 1891 - November 22, 1971) was married to Violet Lewis.

Henry Lewis (1896 – 1920) Susan "Susie" Lewis Todd (December 17, 1897 – January 14, 1986) She worked as a Seamstress. She was married to Whitfield Todd Sr. and had two children, Whitfield Jr. and Delphia. Whitfield Todd Jr. had two children, Diane Todd and Gordon Todd; Delphia Todd Harris had two children, Breck Harris and Leighman Harris

Rosa Lewis Martin (February 8, 1900 – February 18, 1979) was a school teacher

2.**Anna Lewis Creamer Morton** (1859 – November 3, 1914) lived in Richmond, VA. She married Henry Creamer and had one child, Fannie Creamer (1887 -1957) who married Willie Crenshaw in 1907. Anna later married Mr. Morton

3. **Tabb Lewis** (1862)

3. **Peyton Lewis** (1863 - 1930) was married to Frances Baker Coleman and later married Josephine Lewis. He lived in Richmond, VA.

4. **Harriet Lewis** No information found

Lavinia Warren Lewis

Lavinia and son Joseph Peyton Lewis

Mamie Q. Thompson

John Lewis

Alice Amy Anderson Lewis

Rosa Martin

Alice, John and Walter

Clarence Lewis

Susie Todd

Sam Lewis

Walter G. Lewis

Amy Lewis Clements

William Lewis

Mamie Lewis

George Lewis

Jacqueline Seaton Holmes

Walter, Alice, Sam and Eleanor R. Lewis

Mamie and Jerry Seaton

Jacqueline S. Holmes

Amy Beatrice Clements

Walter and children

Sam and Gloria

Mamie and daughter Jackie

Walter Lewis

Alice Lewis Balton

Jerry Seaton

Bannister Family

I was able to trace the Bannister Family line to Jordan Bannister of Amelia County, Virginia. Jordan was a slave of Frances Peyton Tabb and was believed to work on the Clay Hill and Forest Plantations owned by the Tabb Family. Seignora Tabb Bannister was the owner of the Bannister slaves. They were later formerly slaves of Dr. Barthurst Randolph in Amelia County, Virginia.

Jordan Bannister (1808 – January 1888) married **Lucy Smith** had one son Monroe and later **Rosena Bannister** also **Betsy Banks Bannister** (1818 – 1890)

Children of Jordan Bannister

Monroe Bannister (December 14, 1845 – March 19, 1915) married **Ella Hobson** daughter of and the couple remained on the Former Forest Plantation living next door to the Tabb family and worked as a sharecropper and laborer until he moved to Powhatan, VA in the 1880s. Monroe, later married **Harriet Green** and his third wife was **Molly Walker**. **Pheobe Bannister** (1849 - 1914) married William Harris in 1878. **Joseph Bannister Sr.** (1850 – 1917) married **Jane Hobson**. From this union, several children were born: Julia Bannister (1868 – June 1890), Albert Bannister (1870) who married Carrie Belle Walker; and Cincinnatus Bannister (1873). On March 25, 1891 Joseph married his second wife **Peggy Epps** in Amelia, VA. He later married his third wife **Martha Brown** on February 19, 1903. From this union several children were born for more information on Joseph Bannister Sr. (please see the Brown Family section) **Lydia Bannister** (1860 – September 1, 1930) married **Cary Jasper**. **Rosa Bannister** (1872) married Harvey Green on April 20, 1892 in Amelia, VA. They had four children: Clarence Green (1893 – 1926) Edinburgh Green (1895) Mamie Green (1898) Adelaide Green (1900) **Harriet Bannister** (November 24, 1874) **John Bannister** (March 1880) **Jordan Alexander Bannister** (January 1, 1883 – 1961) married Martha Hobbs later moved to New Jersey. Children of Jordan and Martha Hobbs: Joseph Bannister (1912 – 1991) Elizabeth Harriet Bannister (July 30, 1914 – May 1996), Malcom Bannister (1917 - 1951)

Robert M. Bannister (1918 – 1960) lived in New Jersey and was married to enlisted in the United States Army on July 24, 1942 at Fort Jay Governors Island in New York City. Robert later worked as a truck driver. Rosie Bannister (1926) she is pictured right; Edward Bannister (1927 – 2009), James Bannister (1929) and Lillian Bannister (1930).

Yelverton Bannister (April 1885) he was only two days old when he died.

Phoebe Bannister Johnson (1887) married John Johnson (1883) the couple had one son, Sylvester M. Johnson (December 13, 1912 – July 19, 1973) lived in Richmond, VA and married Lilington Odesa Johnson (1916 – 1989)

Henry Bannister

Rosa Bannister Reed (April 1908 – October 22, 1932)

Monroe Bannister Jr. married Mollie Porter. They had one daughter, Mahalia Bannister (August 21, 1914 - March 22, 1915)

The Dixon Family

Rosa Dixon Bowser (1855 - 1931) the daughter of Henry Dixon and Augusta Hawkins was a slave of the Tabb family at the Clay Hill Plantation. After the civil war her family moved to Richmond, VA. Her father Henry who was a skillful carpenter and her mother was a domestic worker. The family were faithful members of the First African Baptist Church in Richmond, VA. She attended the Freedmen Bureau School where she proven to be a bright and advance student that caught the attention of Superintendent Raza M. Manly at the school and was selected to for a teachers training position at the Richmond Normal School for blacks. Rosa was a part of the first graduating class of the Richmond Colored Normal School and graduated from the Freedmen School in 1872 - 1873. After graduating, Rosa extended her education for another year and studied Greek, Latin, Music, and teaching. She married James Bowser (1861 – April 25, 1881) in 1879 who was also a teacher and postal worker. From this union one son, Oswald Barrington Herndon Bowser was born. For a time, she taught music at her home and was a Sunday school teacher at the First African Baptist Church in Richmond, VA. She began her teaching career in Rev. Rosa became one of the first colored teachers to teach in the classrooms in Richmond, VA. She began her teaching career at the Navy Hill school in 1883. Rosa later served as Superintendent and at the Bakers school in Richmond, VA. In 1896 she served as principal teacher as well as night classes for men. Rosa also taught classes in social skills at the Young Men's Christian Association in Jackson Ward. Her achievements are many in fact too numerous to name however, Rosa Dixon Bowser formed many of organizations that empowered and educated blacks in Richmond, VA. She was a part of groups that supported women suffrages, the welfare of children and fought diligently against lynching and racial hatred. She worked alongside her fellow church member Maggie Walker, Mrs. Mary Church Terrell and many others for the rights of African Americans. Rosa's teaching

career came to a close in 1923, after her retirement she continued being a Sunday school teacher at her church until her health failed. She enjoyed the remainder of her life reaping the rewards of her labor. In 1925 the first branch of the Richmond Public Library for African Americans in her honor. Rosa lived on 513 North Adams Street in Richmond, VA. On February 7, 1931 at 1:45 am Rosa who had been battling diabetes passed away at her home. Her funeral was held on February 10, 1931 at 3pm at First African Baptist Church in Richmond, VA.

In the 1965 a school was named after her which stayed open until 1975. Rosa Dixon Bowser

Oswald Barrington Herndon Bowser (August 10, 1880 – July 6, 1935) the son of James and Rosa Dixon Bowser in Richmond, VA. He was raised in Richmond, VA and attended Richmond High and Richmond Normal School. He later attended Howard University in Washington D.C where he received his M.D degree. In 1901 Oswald began his practice in Medicine, and spent many years in the medical field. He was highly active in Richmond, VA as a doctor, leader, and faithful member of First African Baptist Church. During his lifetime, he was an active mason and was a member of a club called the odd fellow. He was a member of the NAACP. Dr. Bowser also was featured in a book entitled: The history of the American Negro Vol. 5.

Oswald was twice married, His first wife was Lena Logan Jasper (1881 – 1906) the daughter of James and Maria Jasper. She was a school teacher in the Richmond Area. From this union one son was born, James Oswald Bowser After Lena's death, Oswald married Alice Smith (March 29, 1885 – June 29, 1952) a teacher. From this union two children were born: James Bowser (1909) and Dr. Barrington H. Bowser Sr. (1921 – 1993) was the first black pediatrician in Richmond, Virginia. He married Mceva Roach (1923 – February 10, 2015) on April 12, 1952 in Richmond, VA. Mceva was born in Elizabeth City, North Carolina. She attended and graduated from Elizabeth City State University where she received a B.S. degree in elementary education. She began her teaching career in Sussex and Louisa counties and later was employed for many years with the Richmond Public School System and also served on the Richmond School Board from (1994 – 1998) From this union two children were born, Angela Bowser and Dr. Barrington Bowser Jr. (internist of VA)

Pictured: Dr. Oswald Barrington H. Bowser and Alice Smith Bowser

Dr. Barrington Bowser Sr.

Mceva Bowser

Dr. Barrington Bowser Jr.

The Banks / Mondrey

The Banks family of the Pleasant Grove Community are also descendants of slaves who were owned by The Tabb, Randolph and Wiliam Barksdale Family.

James "Jim" Banks (1813) married **Judith Mouley** (1823 – 1888) and later **Betsy Bannister** (1818 – 1890)

Children of James Banks

Jane Banks (1847 – July 1882) **Charles Banks** (1850 – 1932) **Holcomb Banks** (1852 – 1932) married Joycie Carter Robinson on August 11, 1876 in Amelia, VA. From this union ten children were born: 1. Nancy Banks (1877 – April 6, 1924) married John Mondrey (1872 – 1924) on January 30, 1896 in Amelia, VA. Children of Nancy Banks Mondrey: Ulysses Adolphus (1899 – 1970) married Martha. Martha Mondrey (1904 – 1966) Jesse Mondrey (1905 - 1978) The couple had several children. John Mondrey (1907 – 1992) Joseph Hobard Mondrey (1910 – 1977) William Holcomb Mondrey (1912 – 1993) married Annie Gilliam. He was known to many as "Stiff" and was considered the "Mr. Fix" it of the community. If you ever had the opportunity to have a conversation with Mr. Mondrey in his later years, in every conversation he would give you words of wisdom. In any conversation, he would often answer a question by saying "Well my friend" and then he would tell you just what he wanted you to know. Ive heard that my grandfather and Stiff was good friends and they often would hang out together. I was also told that my grandmother and Mrs. Annie Mondrey were very close as well. Mr. Stiff was welll Known and respected by the community. Children of William and Annie Mondrey: William Mondrey Jr. who was married to Deaconess Annie Smith Mondrey. After Annie's death, he later married Deaconess Lois Thompkins. Mary M. Jasper who married to the late Walter Jasper on has been an asset to this project. Louise M. Harris who was married to the late Charlie Harris; Martha M. Smith who was formerley married to Junius Smith, Rev. Nancy M. Clarke who is married to Deacon William Lee Clarke of Powhatan, VA; Estelle M. Banks Tillman formeley married to James Banks and Rev. Tillman; Augusta M. Thornton who married David Thornton of Powhatan, VA. Thomas Mondrey who married Chermine Tyler Mondrey Booke; Paul Mondrey, Victor Mondrey, Andrew Mondrey, Maxine Mondrey, Audrey Mondrey, Marilyn Mondrey who is married to Deacon Garland Hicks; William and Mrs. Annie also had a baby named Sarah who died as an infant. Mrs. Annie Mondrey continues to be the Matriach of her family and a pillar in the Pleasant Grove Community. Marion Mondrey (1915 – 1951) Alvin Mondrey (1918 – 1944) and Lewis Mondrey (1922 – 1979) 2. Jordan Banks (January 6, 1883 – November 1, 1962) 3. Fannie Banks Clay (1884 - 1962) 4. Eliza Banks (1884) 5. Augusta Barksdale Banks (1886 – 1982) 5. Holcomb Peyton Banks (1891 – June 2, 1963) 7. James Alfred Banks (1891 - 1963) 8. Iredell Sherman Banks (1895 – 1978) 9. Inez Banks (1895 – 1939) 10. Willie Banks (1900 – 1948) The lineage of Holcomb and Joycie Banks are too numerous to name. **Edward Banks** (1858) **Fannie Banks** (1859) **Peyton Banks** (1860 – 1937). The step – daughter of James Banks, **Nancy Bannister** (1862) married **Berkely Fisher** in 1882.

Pictures of Holcomb Banks and also, Iredell (grandson of Holcomb Banks) and Rosa Banks are courtesy of Ms. Ayisha Johnson a researcher and family historian of the Banks family.

Holcomb Banks

Iredell Banks and Rosa Tyler

William Mondrey

From the beginning of my research, to this present moment, Mrs. Evelyn Harris has been very helpful by sharing her wisdom and history of the families of this book. At the age of 89, Mrs. Evelyn has a great memory that extends back to the days of her youth. She remembers many of the families of the community. She is a wealth of knowledge many of these stories during my research was confirmations of some of people that lived in Amelia before her time that her mother Mrs. Emma Wilson (pictured left) shared with her. Im thankful for Mrs. Evelyn Harris who has been like family to all of the Hyde family.

Mrs. Emma Graham Wilson (1887 – 1985) was born to Walter and Emma Graham. She was born in Charlotte County, Virginia. After the death of her mother, Emma was raised by Ms. Anna Robinson. Emma later worked for the Mayo family and moved to Amelia, Virginia and later Richmond, VA. In 1910 Emma lived on West Franklin Street. She married Jefferson (Jeff) Wilson son of Rev. Jeff Wilson and Margaret Goodman Wilson of Amelia, VA on December 27, 1910. Jeff's father, Rev. Jeff Wilson who was born in Halofax, Va moved to Amelia, VA. It has been reported that he married many of people in the Mattoax and Red Lodge Community. Jeff's mother Margaret was the daughter of John and Frances Langhorne Goodman. According to the 1920 United States Census, Jeff and Emma resided in Amelia, VA and returned to Richmond a few years later. In 1930 they lived on 444 Parkwood Avenue in Richmond, VA later returning to Amelia, VA where she remained until her death. She was a great cook and worked for several families including a family in Maryland. Mrs. Evelyn recalled her mother recollections of close friends such as my great – grandmother Fannie Kyle Hyde, who would often walk from Red Lodge to visit her and others who lived in the Mattoax neighborhood. Mrs. Emma, had a special love for the younger people of the neighborhood. She spent a lot of time with my grandparents Emanuel and Alice Hyde. Mrs. Emma was well loved by her family and well respected by her community. This project would be ineffective without the wisdom and knowledge she poured into her daughter Mrs. Evelyn Harris who took the time to share it with me.

Children of Jeff and Emma

Graham "Buster" Wilson (1911 – 1979) twice married, his first wife was Kate and he later married Althea McCray on December 28, 1942. Graham Wilson Jr, Germane Harris, Anthony Wilson, Grace Jean Wilson, and Johnathan Wilson. He enlisted into the U.S Navy on July 23, 1943 and was discharged October 16, 1945. Margaret Wilson Harris (1913 – 2006), Aaron Wilson (1915 – 1999), Anna Carter (1918 – 2001) married Norman Carter on April 16, 1944. Elizabeth Amelia Wilson Hawthorne (living) married the late Charles Hawthorne in 1954. Frank Wilson (1923 – 1990) married Sallie Farrar in 1948 and Evelyn L. Wilson Harris is an active member of her home church Liberty Baptist Church. Mrs. Evelyn married Joel Harris on December 4, 1948 in Amelia, VA. From this union Alice Harris, Viola Harris Booker, Donna Lee

Harris, Samuel Harris and Franklin Ray Harris (1960 – 2000) Mrs. Evelyn is blessed with children, grandchildren, and great – grandchildren.

Pictured on previous page is a picture of Mrs. Emma that local white photographer Nellie Jones produced in the early 1900s. Mrs. Nettie Jones painted many pictures of African Americans in the Mattoax area where she lived. The descendants of Jeff and Emma are to numerous to name.

Mrs. Evelyn Harris

Rev. Jeff Wilson

Margaret Goodman Wilson

Below: Jefferson Wilson (husband of Emma G. Wilson)

I would like to mention the Tabb Family Chesterfield were apart of the Tabb's Plantation in Chesterfield, VA. There ancestor was Fredrick Tabb who married Matilda Farmer. Evangelist Rachelle Tabb is one of the many descendants

Acknowledgements

There are many other families from Red Lodge and its neighboring plantations whose ancestors are not mentioned in this book. There are countless untold stories of heroic acts that has never or perhaps will ever be read in a book. However, I gave the best of what I could, I hope whoever reads this will say that I did my best. I wish to include pictures of everyone listed in the book but it was impossible at this time.

In the 1990s, Sylvia Hicks, Leslie Banks and others formed a Red Lodge Reunion Committee. The committee worked together to have the Red Lodge Reunion. It was there, Ms. Sylvia Hicks presented the hstory of the land and the slave owner. However at that time many of the slave descendant connections were not fully researched. I hope this book answered many questions. All photos other than famous public domain were used by permission some were retrieved by facebook, ancestry.com public member trees and many were given by the families who are represented in this book.

Special Thanks: First I give all praise to God for its in Him we live, we move and we have our being. Without God I can do nothing! In all I say and do I give all the Glory to God. This has been a journey that has not been easy, but certainly worth it. My parents, Elder Emanuel and Betty Hyde Jr. who has taught me to preservere thank you for for always being an giving your best. You both both have been in my corner since day 1. I appreciate you both. To my sisters: Dargenaba Anderson and Marshae Minter an my niece thanks for your support. To all of my aunts and uncles especially my aunt, Dr. Sandra Seay. To My Pastor Tara Owens and her husband Deacon Tony Owens thank you both for being Godly examples and the great Leaders you both are. Thanks for pushing me to be my best self and encouraging me along the way. To Janice Gentry , Darlene Lewis - Robinson, and Christian Robinson thanks for all the sacrifices you made to help this project be a success. Juanita Booker Coleman, Lakisha Johnson, Frank Archer, Marilyn Wilson and all the staff at Ameia County Courthouse. My church family Destiny Worship Center, Deacon and Mrs. Isaac Johnson, Dr. Henry Featherston, Mr. and Mrs. Thomas Brown, Irene Tyler, Dr. James Taylor, Carolyn Ruffin, Terri Ruffin, Lauren Whittington, Sylvia Gray, Christopher Harris, Sarah Louise Banks and family, Della Montague, Howard Hyde Jr., Stephen Brown, Evelyn W. Harris, Fannie H. Baylor, Frank Archer, Mary Banks Johnson, Selissa Brown, Doris Booker, Sylvia Archer, Joan Owens, Sylvia Archer, Annie Mondrey, Georgia Banks, Eloise Harris, Reginald Hyde, Catherine Hyde Booker, Thomas Hicks, Sarah Banks, Kathleen Hadfield, Amy Bannister, Charles Mitchell Jr., Lateefah Person, Alvin Ruffin, Reginald Hyde, Alberta Person, Monica Jackson, Andrea Ross, Sherry Banks, Carolyn Ruffin, Monica Jackson, Stephen Brown, Reginald "Dale" Hyde, Blanche (Rosa) Hyde Jefferson, Donnita Davis, Anna Hyde Bowers, Ethel Morris, Allen Ruffin, Joseph Ruffin, Mary Jasper, Mary Beth Trent, Annie Mondrey, Alberta Person, The Clements Family, Eloise Banks, Doris Booker, Bethel Martin, Benjamin Ross, Sixth Mount Zion Baptist Church, Shiridine Harris, Kirk Jones, Georgia Banks, Edwin Wilson, Helen Phillips, Garland Ervin, Essex Finney and the Finney Family, Dallas and Helen Bannister and Family, Sylvia Hicks, Helen Bannister, Archer Jones Jr, Michael Jones, Clara Jones Squire, Kirk Jones, Rev. Leon Smith, Elrean Harris, Lloyd Fleury,

Margett Owens, Ayisha Johnson, Mrs. Gladys Clements, Lorraine Patrick, Daphne Jasper Holman, Della Montaque, Elder and Mrs. Edward Walls, Pauline Walls Mays, Rosalind W. Nelson, Anita Jasper Royal, Terri Ruffin, Fannie Carey, Travis Ruffin, Javon Holman, Frank Tyler Jr. Anita Jasper Royal, Frank Tyler, Harold Jones, Karen B. Carter, Veronica Jones, Gloria Banks Williams, Lelia Banks and all of those who I did not mention who took the time out for phone and in person interviews.

Special thanks to the first historian of the Hyde Family Uncle Howard B. Hyde Jr. Thanks for the opportunity you gave me it was a seed sown. And also thanks for all the encouragement.

To my cousin Shannon Henderson thanks for your wisdom, support and love. You have proven to be a great author, and motivational speaker. Carolyn Baker Carroll (Aunt Carolyn) thanks for being committed to what you do and thanks for give me the opportunity to help you and the encouragement to work on the rediscovery of the Red Lodge Plantation.

*To Minister Amber Davidson thanks for encouraging me, praying for me and pushing me through this project. You are an added blessing to my life and you inspire me to be greater. God has a great plan for you keep declaring His word and expecting Him to the Great things He promised You. Greater is Coming! I Love You.

Research Resources

The Library of Virginia, Amelia Courthouse, Amelia Historical Society, Virginia Chancery documents, Unknown No Longer, Family Search.org, Ancestry DNA, Gedmatch, Genealogybank.com, Virginia Black History Muesum, The Virginia Historical Society, Newspapers.com, Thomas Jefferson Monticello, Sylvia Gray and the Amelia County Historical Societety, Liberty Baptist Church Commemorative Book – written by: Sylvia Hicks. The Historicial Notes of Amelia County, Virginia written by: Mrs. Kathleen Hadfield. Benjamin Ross and the Sixth Mount Zion Church John Jasper Museum, Our Stories Our Struggles: A history of African Americans in Amelia County, Virginia Vol. 1 and 2 Compiled By: Dr. Henry Featherston, and Old buildings and Homes in Amelia County Virginia by Mary Armstrong.

Cover design by: Mary Beth Trent Early Editor Assitance: Christian Robinson, Darlene Robinson

Final Editing Assistance and Formatting Assistance: Janice Gentry.

This book is dedicated to the Memory of Deacon Floyd Bates, Deacon Emmett Robinson, Mrs. Mary Wallace, Mckinley Jasper, Mr and Mrs. Mike Banks, Nolie Thompson, Geneva "Jenny" Ruffin, Geneva Banks, Westmoreland Thompson, Mrs. Senia Jasper and Mr.and Mrs. Howard B. Hyde Sr. and all the great men and women from the Red Lodge Community that has gone on before us. Most of the stories they shared with me years ago, I never will forget. Many of the stories are documented in this book. May they Never Be Forgotten.

This book is also done in the memory of SSgt. Juanita Giles Baker, USAF (retired) who was a great inspiration to me and I am thankful for the connection so many years ago.

To all the descendants who reads this book, remember the suffering, faith, and truimphs of our ancestors. We are because they were, let us continue to share the family histories from generation to generation.

Author Contact Info: Emanuel Hyde III (804) 489 – 7052 email: scoop3132@gmail.com

Made in the USA
Middletown, DE
09 June 2022